All Doors Opened

An Autobiography

All Doors Opened
An Autobiography

by

Inder Sharma

Curated by

Harbhajan Butalia & Meera Dua

Edited by

Padma Rao Sundarji

ALLIED PUBLISHERS PVT. LTD.

NEW DELHI ◆ MUMBAI ◆ KOLKATA ◆ CHENNAI ◆ NAGPUR
AHMEDABAD ◆ BANGALORE ◆ HYDERABAD ◆ LUCKNOW

ALLIED PUBLISHERS PRIVATE LIMITED

Website: www.alliedpublishers.com

© 2018, Inder Sharma

Second Impression: 2018

ISBN: 978-93-87997-14-1

Published by Sunil Sachdev and printed by Ravi Sachdev at Allied Publishers Pvt. Ltd., Printing Division, A-104 Mayapuri Phase II, New Delhi–110 064.

Foreword

Inder Sharma devoted his professional life to introducing India to the rest of the world. The many thousands—perhaps hundreds of thousands—of people who visited us as tourists under the guidance of the various companies and organizations with which he was associated, were given carefully-crafted experiences that enabled them to gain an understanding of Indian culture, history and life. They gained the confidence that they were in the capable hands of true professionals. In this way, he was India's Ambassador-at-Large to the world.

With this book, Inder has gone several steps further. He has given us—both Indians and others—a panoramic introduction to diverse aspects of Indian life: childhood in a very traditional Indian family, growing up as a student at Delhi University, settling down to a not-very-glamorous job at an entry level, and then using that as a springboard for unimaginable success. The great strengths of the classic Indian joint family become apparent, as one reads of how all family members are supported and how to triumph over inconveniences like hand-me-down clothes, a lack of money and of other material possessions.

In the same way, the parts of the book dealing with the writer's college days and immediate aftermath give readers an interesting (and for some of us, nostalgic) look at Kolkata (then Calcutta) life in the 1950s. He describes the passion for political involvement of those years, with discreet, playful touches of romance embellishing the sidelines.

The roads that led from the village to the world, from a monthly salary of Rupees 150 to prosperity for the whole family, and from a carefree youth to a thoughtful spokesperson for an entire industry, are all charted with insight and humour. And the fact that all these roads were successfully traversed without any of the contemporary aids of the internet, smart phones, and instantaneous communication will be an eye-opener for the younger generation.

Inder and I shared the belief—not very widely acknowledged at the beginnings of our careers—that tourism was an extremely important industry, in terms of the potential for income and employment, as well as a crucial element of "soft power" in the world. When we first met, the relationship between the tourism industry and the concerned ministries and government agencies was, with a few notable exceptions, frosty, if not actually adversarial. As we advanced to more senior positions, Inder and I committed ourselves to changing this, and I think I can safely say that our joint efforts ushered in a new synergistic partnership between all parties involved.

I first came in contact with Inder in the early seventies at a conference in Shimla. And I must confess that our relationship did not start on a very positive note. Both of us were involved in tourism, but with different priorities. I was trying to put Haryana on the map through domestic tourism, and he was operating on the larger canvas. He agreed with the prevalent emphasis of the times on increasing the number of foreign tourists to India and thus earning more foreign exchange. I felt that equal emphasis needed to be placed on domestic tourism and on improving the infrastructure for that, to provide a solid basis for long-term integrated development of tourism in the country. Being young and quite ardent about our respective views, we clashed, with neither willing to give ground. In later years, it was characteristic of his generosity that he publicly acknowledged coming around to my view and that the domestic sector had to be given equal, if not greater importance. In his book, he has, over and over again, reiterated this view.

Subsequently, Inder and I became very close. We found that we were generally on the same wavelength, shared the same views and we worked together towards achieving the same objectives with no personal egos. He frequently recognized my efforts publicly and privately. On my part, I turned to him as a leader of the industry, over issues like giving up Chairmanship of the India PATA Chapter (which had generally been held by the Secretary of the Tourism Ministry) and asking him to take over. This proved to be a good decision, as he provided bold and imaginative leadership. In sum, I really felt that we were partners in tourism, though functioning in different areas.

The book provides great insight into the difficulties of establishing and growing an international business in the days of rigid foreign exchange and taxation constraints, and the narrow perspective of many players. To young businessmen and women listening to our Prime Minister at Davos inviting the world to partner with India, it might be hard to even imagine the hurdles that Inder faced in those early years. It is true to his generous spirit that he has titled his book "All Doors Opened", because that was certainly not the situation. He had to face and overcome many obstacles.

Throughout his professional career, Inder showed great foresight, and that is probably the single most important key to his success. Twenty years before he sold SITA, his Board of Directors had said that the future of tourism as a business was not very optimistic. For two more decades, Inder proved them wrong in the short-term. But sensing that they were correct in the longer term, however, he finally made the painful decision to sell. Once again, foresight and insight proved to be his great strengths.

In spite of the barriers and challenges, tourism is an industry that provided many rewards to those of us fortunate enough to have been involved with it. There is great collegiality and *esprit* among colleagues, both at home and abroad. My lifelong friendship with Inder and Aruna, during which we really became like one family, is just one testament to the lasting bonds of the tourism endeavour.

And along the way, I must admit, there has been quite a bit of fun and even some hi-jinks. Some of these are mentioned in the book for the patient reader!

When I began writing this Foreword, I asked Maureen how she would describe Inder. Pat came the reply: "Gentleman. Absolute and thorough gentleman. Always." This was a good response. Certainly in the many decades of our relationship, I never once heard Inder overstep the bounds of polite and courteous behaviour, which is something one cannot say about many people. Knowing that he was very seriously ill and on the day before he breathed his last, we had planned to visit, but were advised by Arjun that he was in no condition for guests. When we realized there would not be another opportunity, we were devastated.

Inder Sharma was a legend, an icon, a builder and an innovator. By overcoming odds at all stages, seizing opportunities, and serving as an inspiration to so many, he demonstrated that nothing was impossible. For me personally, reading this book has been an emotional experience, as he includes me among the eminent personalities he invited to hold his Som Nath Memorial lectures. My name is listed among those he respected and felt closest to. To me, these mentions are real honours.

It made me very happy when Inder's unique contributions were recognized by the President of India with the Padma Shree Award. This book will surely add to his reputation, and also give the reader a very enjoyable and interesting experience. Reading it, one feels he is, once again, among us.

S.K. Misra

26 January 2018

Editor's Note

The seventies were heady days and I well remember SITA World Travel. Whether you were winging to the moon or taking a slow train to Mumbai, SITA's agents always bestowed the same, smiling attention on all their customers. The fashionable term 'customer service' hadn't yet been coined. But India's premier travel company was already offering the best of it.

Some years ago, I found myself on the top floors of Select CITYWALK at my friend Neeraj's request. Her father, Chairman Inder Sharma of the Select Group, wished to publish his auto-biography. She wanted me to be the first outsider to read it and provide feedback.

Chairman was gentle, smiled sweetly and chatted with me a little about my background. I was a total stranger to him. He had no idea just how good or bad I may be as an editor. And yet, here he was, handing his precious manuscript to me.

I went home with the feeling I was taking on more than I could handle. Here was a giant of the travel and retail industry, a gentle-man of renown and repute, giving a stranger the first, inside look at his life. It was daunting.

There was something else that bothered me too. Chairman Sharma was from the world of business. Of turnovers and balance sheets. I was a current affairs journalist and author. I had certainly filmed and written a lot of business stories over three decades. But what did I really know of commerce? But since I had given Neeraj my word, I settled into a sofa that very evening and turned the first page, expecting to understand little.

It was very late at night when I finally got up. I had rediscovered my favourite SITA within them, I had marveled at an incredible life. I was so engrossed, absorbed and delighted at the writer's guts, gumption and intuition throughout the story of his meteoric creation of an empire that—I read All Doors Opened in one go.

Over the previous four years, he, his executive assistant Mrs. Meera Dua and I, spent many hours up in his office. He was getting frail, but would still insist on doing a fresh read each time, adding details as his memory would allow him, for the next edit. Overall, I didn't have to do much, other than to shuffle paragraphs and correct typing mistakes.

There is a rationale to two patterns in the book: repetitions and upper-case letters or capitals.

Chairman Inder Sharma was particularly keen that his book reflects two things closest to his heart. One was his endless love for his family and friends. Consequently and each time I returned an edit with repetitive paragraphs struck out about a given family member, he would insert them again, insisting firmly but gently that yes, he was aware they were repetitions but that I should leave them that way. As I worked on subsequent edits, I realized that Chairman Sharma tells his life's story like a *'sutradhar'* anyway, like a leisurely narration at his Coffee Club. It was a conversation he wanted with his readers, not a ponderous monologue.

It is in that spirit that readers must take the repetitions. Essentially, they are reaffirmations of just how much he adored the person being described, reiterations of that love.

Similarly, capital letters underlined his utter and sheer reverence for his Guruji.

Chairman Sharma, for all his own towering achievements, wanted to elevate Guruji and many of his loved ones above himself and his own life story. Consequently, he could and would not refer to his mentor and guru even in the third person, without using capitals as a mark of respect.

All Doors Opened is a book that gives hope to the despairing, life to dreams.

It is a book that blows holes into the commonly-held belief that successful magnates must have been born with a silver spoon and are uncaring human beings.

This is a book that teaches and advises readers to protect, nurture and stay firmly grounded to their roots, no matter how humble.

It was, is and will remain an honour to be associated with this book. But I deeply regret that Chairman Sharma will not attend the launch. I had my pen ready for a signed copy.

I thank him and his family for entrusting the story of an extraordinary life to my ordinary hands.

Padma Rao Sundarji

New Delhi
January 2018

Preface

On March 23, 2000, I sold SITA World Travel, one of India's leading travel agencies, to Kuoni, an international travel conglomerate with offices and collaborations all over the world. For someone whose starting salary was one hundred and fifty rupees per month, I sold SITA for a princely amount. At the time of sale, SITA had 28 branches in the country, nine representations overseas, joint collaborations in three SAARC countries namely Sri Lanka, Nepal and Bhutan and a staff strength of over 800.

"So who am I and why did I do this–the largest sale of a Travel Agency?"

Let me introduce myself. I am Inder Sharma.

Someone who was a rather poor student and as I like to put it, someone who graduated gradually. Someone who spent eight years at Delhi University's Hindu College for his final degree: a Master's in Economics. Someone, who never attended a management institute but was yet able to anticipate the changing dynamics of India's travel industry, both internationally and locally. Someone who started his career in 1953 as a Transfer Assistant, a job which was at a monthly salary of Rupees 150/-, just one notch higher than that of a peon; someone, who worked hard: first to convert SITA India from a branch of a wholly US-owned Company to an Indian one and finally end up owning the same in 1963.

Someone who was not only elected President of the Travel Agents Association of India (TAAI) for three terms but was also the first Asian to be elected for a six-year period as President of the World

Association of Travel Agencies (WATA), which is headquartered in Geneva. And subsequently, someone who was the first Indian to be elected the President of the Pacific Asia Travel Association (PATA). Someone who was honoured by several countries for his contribution to Tourism and holds the "Key to City of Manila" and "Keys to Britain". Someone, who interacted with three most powerful ladies of the time: Margaret Thatcher, Prime Minister of England, Imelda Marcos, President of Philippines and Sirimavo Bandaranaike, Prime Minister of Sri Lanka.

Someone who was the first travel professional to receive the Padma Shri Award in 1990 for services to tourism and is, till date, the only travel agent to be honoured thus.

So why did all this happen? Perhaps all the other aspects of my life will hold some answers.

My parents belonged to poor families. My father, the late Rai Sahib, Dr. Mela Ram Sharma, did not have slippers to wear till he was in class IX. Till he joined the Veterinary College in Lahore, all he wore was a handed-down shirt and pyjama. He had been educated throughout on scholarships. A father, who gave his son the first sound and true management guru's mantra, one that I still follow: "When in doubt, treat others the way you would like to be treated."

I was never overly religious in my life. Whatever little religious education I received, was from my simple mother, the late Mrs. Santosh Devi. She had never enjoyed formal higher education. She was religious, but not dogmatic. She taught me a second set of precious mantras. "Give away that which you most wish to receive," she told me. "Recognize the divinity of the Divine." This enabled me to recognize and worship the divinity of my Guruji.

I am fortunate to be married to Aruna, a very simple, dedicated and undemanding lady, who lives for her family, is devoted to our Guruji and enjoys spending most of her time working for the sick and the poor. A qualified medical doctor, who worked for CGHS and since retirement, works in an honorary capacity for the charitable dispensary run by the Delhi Commonwealth Womens' Association. Aruna is a simple, understanding wife, mother and grandmother, always willing to help family members.

I am blessed with two children, my daughter Neeraj and my son Arjun. They are extremely capable and are successfully managing businesses they have built themselves. They are assets to our family. Neeraj is a qualified Chartered Accountant having done her articleship with Mohinder Puri & Co., and Arjun is a graduate from Delhi University. He is a good investor and a perfect public relations person.

Our family's other sources of eternal pleasure are my loving son-in-law, Kavi, an unassuming, simple, highly intelligent, practising Chartered Accountant who is ever willing to lend a helping hand. Kavi is a perfect gentleman, least—in fact, never demanding and always a willing advisor or a helper to all those who seek it. And my daughter-in-law, Jyotsana, who was once in a Hindi movie and is now a doting mother and an animal lover.

And our cup of joy brims over because of our two grand-daughters. Shreya, the older one, graduated from Yale University in 2015 and is a national golf champion. She led the Indian Ladies' Golf team to the Asian Games held in 2010. A young girl endowed with great principles, Shreya helped raising funds to establish a corpus to provide scholarships for the daughters of the caddies at the Delhi Golf Club. She now works in London as an investment advisor with an international Bank of repute. Amaraah, the younger one who bubbles with energy, is only eight. But she already holds an Austrian gold medal in skiing. She attends the British School in Delhi, is very attached to my wife Aruna and loves to mimic my walking with a stick. She also plays golf.

I, Inder Sharma, am someone who, with no knowledge or experience of construction or of real estate, helped build almost three million sq.ft. of covered space with the help of my children and our partner, Yogi Arora. Together, we created Select CITYWALK, a nine-time winner of the coveted award of India's "Most Admired

Mall". This is due to the efforts of CEO Yogeshwar Sharma, Chief Engineer Shashi Sharma, and their team.

I am someone who is very grateful to his friends, some genuine and some pretenders among them. The latter taught me to avoid hangers-on, who only praised one all the time, trying to flatter when there was no genuine reason to do so. I am grateful to my colleagues and friends in the industry who mostly stood by me, but also to many more unknown and known faces. I must also say a big Thank You to many who opposed me, and many more in the industry who pretended to be my friends. By doing so, they taught me to recognize a true friend and avoid the pretenders.

I owe my peace of mind and success to my family, my parents, my sister, my wife, my children and my friends who have all along been supportive of me.

I am someone who believes in what J.J. Irani of Tata Steel once said: "Out of every ten men born in this world, nine work for the tenth." I wanted to be that tenth man.

I am someone who thinks God is the only Divinity and that no human is worthy of being worshipped as a God. And yet, I pray to my Guruji every day, a spiritual teacher who is divinity personified, a reincarnation of Lord Shiva, my Saviour.

So who is Inder Sharma, the person of contradictions that belie his achievements?

I am in my eighties. My life holds a lot of precious memories, memorable incidents and countless wonderful experiences, both good and bad. There are so many 'thank yous' waiting to be rendered, to my family, my friends, industry colleagues and several critics. There are apologies too, to several people I may have offended in life.

On one pleasant evening in my daughter's cottage 'Cloud Nine' in Kasauli, I sipped my Scotch, took in the serene, quiet and somewhat chilly night, gazed at the twinkling stars, felt the chilly breeze and observed how the few clouds on the horizon played hide-and-seek with the full moon. As the lights of Shimla winked in the background, it dawned on me that my life has been the way it was because of one miracle: ALL DOORS OPENED.

It was at 'Cloud Nine' that I took a decision—to dictate my memoirs to my faithful and trusted longtime secretary, Harbhajan Butalia. She helped me a lot, not only by taking long and laborious dictations, but by often reminding me of the important events in my professional life and correcting many of my vague memories. She was an inspirational collaborator. But for her encouragement and constant reminders of correct facts, these memoirs would not have been possible. My wife Aruna, daughter Neeraj and son Arjun constantly urged me to write my life story. Well, here it is and I hope you find it interesting. I urge everyone to keep a diary— you may need it in your old age. I wish I had.

I hope this introduction will answer some questions that must have sprung to your mind by now, put into perspective the contra-dictions that may have struck you, and I hope my story will hold its own guidance and lessons for all of you. Enjoy it.

Contents

Tributes

1 | Let's Set the Ball Rolling...

There can be any number of reasons for writing one's memoirs. Everyone has good, bad and indifferent recollections of one's own life. Everyone is anxious to convey something to those he has interacted with over the course of decades. And like many, *with all modesty, I believe mine holds a message for at least a few.*

There are several other reasons that prompted me to go down memory lane, to dig deep into my emotions and put down my thoughts.

First, I wanted to lay bare my background, childhood, adolescence and my long, struggle-filled professional life. I had a deep desire to reveal several facets of my life that are important to me—the inner secrets of my childhood, my parents and their stoic struggle to provide the very best for the family, my background— coming as I do from a little village in Punjab, my formative years as a student of Hindu College where I was a bit of a rebel, 'graduating gradually' both in studies and in life.

My Roots in Village Lalowal where I Started

Second, I wanted to narrate the story of my accidental entry into the world of travel and tourism.

And third, I wanted to detail the trajectory of my career that saw me ending up as Chairman of one of India's leading travel firms, SITA World Travel. I wanted to describe what led to the honour of being the first Asian to be elected President of the World Association of Travel Agents in Geneva, to share the thrill of being the first Indian to be elected President of PATA, the Pacific Asia Travel Association. I wanted to outline the hard journey that led to the many honours that the Governments of Sri Lanka and Nepal had bestowed upon me graciously and generously. I wanted to share with you my elation at being awarded the 'Keys to Britain' by the British Tourist Authority and the 'Keys to the City of Manila' by Mayor Bhagat Ramon and, the most coveted one being the first Travel personality to receive a Padma Award from the President of India. Finally, the accidental novelty of getting involved in building the 1.3 million sq. ft., much-awarded shopping mall, Select CITYWALK. By the end of this book, you will recognize that mine has been quite a journey, one to remember and share and that it was God's grace and the indulgence of my family and friends that made it happen.

A key motivation for jotting down my memories is to express my gratitude and love to my immediate family—my late mother, Santosh Devi and late father, Rai Sahib Dr. Mela Ram Sharma, my wife Aruna, my daughter Neeraj, my son Arjun, and their respective spouses Kavi and Jyotsana. They have not only been supportive but lovingly tolerant of my whims and fancies. To them and to my two granddaughters Shreya and Amaraah who are my great source of happiness and joy, I wanted to leave some family history in the written word.

I also want to express my personal gratitude towards the travel profession, a vocation that has given me so much in life in terms of livelihood, prosperity, recognition and pride. And I want to acknowledge my several friends and colleagues who tolerated me.

In putting these words down, I want to give something back, to make a constructive contribution through my long professional experience, towards helping young aspirants in the fields of travel, tourism and other service industries. It would be a fulfilment of my dream if the story of my life can help them plan their careers in such a way that they can not only achieve their fullest potential but exceed their own expectations.

Finally, I wanted to pay homage and say *Namaskar* to my Guruji, who showed me the path to inner peace, though frankly, I am still struggling to get there.

It's been a long journey, full of highs and lows, mountains and valleys, twists and turns, several crossroads and literally thousands of incidents, big and small, which played a pivotal role in my life and shaped my personality.

There have been several genuine friends who have helped and encouraged me during the course of my personal and professional life. There have been quite a few 'pretenders' who also taught me good lessons. There have been countless ordinary, faceless people who proved themselves to be anything but ordinary, and they all have a place in my life. So many have opened doors of opportunity for me.

2 | The Beginning—
The Curtain Rises

*Village Wells, White Butter and Paranthas
on Board the Train*

I was born in 1931 in Amritsar, Punjab at my maternal grand-parents' home. My maternal grand-father, Pt. Ramchander, was an estate manager for a very prosperous landlord of Amritsar District. Pt. Ramchander was a gentleman with a modest but comfortable income. For as long back as I can

That's Me

recall, I picture him always with his large *hookah*, bent over his account books, the old-fashioned *pothis*. Villagers would often drop in on him. Dressed in a spotless white *kurta* and *dhoti* but always with a black jacket, he would go out with a walking-stick in hand. My grandmother—his wife—Ishwar Devi, was a very simple lady, whose entire life revolved around looking after the family and cooking for her husband. A Brahmin cooked food for the rest of the family. We ate, sitting on the floor—male members first, the ladies later.

My maternal grandparents were very religious and orthodox. Grandfather would not drink water from taps since their washers were made of leather. His water and that of the whole family, came from a well. It was delivered in metallic pots and stored in earthen pitchers to keep it cool. There were no refrigerators or air-conditioners. Other than Santosh Devi—my mother, Pt. Ramchander and Ishwar Devi had no other daughter. But they had three sons. Vasudev, the eldest, worked in the railways, Mahinderjit owned a cloth shop in Amritsar and the youngest, Roshanlal, retired as Asst. Collector of Customs.

Consequently, my mother's pet name was '*Veeran*', which, in Punjabi, means 'sister'. The family were not rich by today's standards. But they had a decent, middle-class life. Indeed, my mother's maternal home was better off than that of her husband, my father—the late Rai Sahib, Dr. Mela Ram Sharma.

His family hailed from Lalowal, a small Punjab village that nestles on the banks of a canal flowing downstream from a tehsil town called Dhariwal in the state's Gurdaspur district.

Myself, Usha with Mama & Daddy

Given a population of less than 1000 inhabitants, most of whom are Jat Sikhs and Mazhbi Sikhs, Lalowal is a tiny village even today. Ours was and still is the only Brahmin (Hindu) family in the whole village.

Despite the passage of time, I vividly remember Lalowal and my memories usually take me back to the summer vacations when we visited there. As my maternal grandparents lived in nearby Amritsar, we always visited Lalowal during our school vacations, mostly to meet my paternal grandmother, Dhan Devi.

Dhan Devi had become a widow at a very young age. She was a strong-headed lady with very old-fashioned views. She had lost her eyesight in a faulty operation. She spent her last few years with us in New Delhi and really lorded over my mother. Dhan Devi was the archetypal Indian *saas,* the mother-in-law, with all the typical connotations and characteristics that accompany the role.

One evening, when my father came home from office, Dhan Devi met him with a complaint. She told him, that while he was away, my mother—his wife—would invite some gentleman home and that the two would not only talk, but sometimes even sing together. It turned out that she was referring to the radio that my mother used to switch on in the afternoon to listen to the then popular music programs aired by Radio Ceylon. My father could not convince my grandmother of this and continued to be rebuked by her for being a simpleton.

My father had three brothers and two sisters. But my paternal grandfather, Pandit Kanshi Ram—Dhan Devi's husband—died just after the sixth child—my younger aunt, was born. His younger brother—my grand-uncle (whom we treated as and called grandfather) Pt. Kirpa Ram, a bachelor at that time, took three vows at the pyre of his elder brother: (1) that he would stay a bachelor to look after the six young children of his elder brother; (2) that he would never enter the house where his widowed sister-in-law Dhan Devi lived, and (3) that he would never sleep inside a house. He kept these three promises all his life, so much so that whenever he visited my dad in Delhi, he slept outside, in the garden, or under a specially-erected tin-shed, but never inside the house. What character, what will-power for a supposedly 'illiterate', uneducated, poor farmer! We all treated and respected him as our real grandfather. That great-uncle/grandfather Pt. Kirpa Ram—bless his soul—lived to a ripe old age of over 100 years.

My Grand Father Pt. Kirpa Ram

He told us many stories, but one of our favourites was the one of when he attended the 1911 Durbar of King George V in Delhi as a youngster. Pt. Kirpa Ram and his friends had walked all the way from the village to the capital Delhi, traversing a distance of almost 500 kms. They carried bedsheets and slept in temples, *dharamsalas* and other available shelters along the way. They ate there too, and as per his account, had a whale of a time. He was very vague as to the time taken for the whole trip and his recollection varied between 'a couple of days' and 'a month or so'.

My father's oldest brother, Pt. Jai Dayal, played a different role in their lives. It was he who pushed his younger brothers to get an education. Pt. Jai Dayal was only a qualified compounder in the Health Department, but endowed with good knowledge of dispensing medication. Being a dedicated and responsible individual and given those days of very elementary health services, he educated himself and even acted as and called himself a medical doctor in the village. When he retired from the Department, Pt. Jai

Dayal set up a private practice and earned a reasonable income. With it, he goaded and supported three of his brothers—Sukh Dayal, Durga Das and my father, Mela Ram, to pursue higher education.

Sukh Dayal and my father were hard-working. They both went to Lahore, one to pursue an M.B.B.S. and the other, to study veterinary science at the Lahore Veterinary College. Both qualified with good grades and joined their respective branches in the Punjab Government.

Durga Das, on the other hand, quit studies and joined the army. I was told that he died overseas at a very young age, leaving behind a very large family. One of them, Raj Sharma, still lives in the village.

Dr. Sukh Dayal, too, died young. As fate would have it, my father, Mela Ram, was left to raise not only his own two children but to provide moral and financial support to many other relatives. He educated a few, found jobs for several and married off others.

My father was a true family man. And it is to the credit of my mother, Santosh Devi, who was sometimes mistreated by one of his senior relatives, that she never complained, willingly and unquestioningly offering all she had. Santosh Devi, bless her soul, was, however, dearly loved by several members of her husband's family too. The affection they felt for her was hardly surprising. For, no matter what difficulties she encountered, my mother was always there to help others with a smile.

Wells, Mangoes and a Necessary Travel Ritual

Normally and even though these usually took place during my summer school vacation, the visits made by me and my mother to the village would be short and sweet: mere, one-day affairs. Till date, I have never spent a night there.

These visits were an experience. While several memories flash through my mind, I distinctly remember two things.

The first was eating generous doses of fresh, white butter churned from buttermilk by my grandmother. Completely unmindful of any calorie or fat content, I would bury it in sugar and eat a bowlful. It was sheer bliss. But as often happens, bliss can lead to disaster. I paid dearly for such indulgences and my rather wayward eating habits by becoming diabetic at a very young age.

As it was usually summer when we visited, I recollect bathing at the village well. The water that gushed out of the well was so cool and refreshing, that I'd sit under its flow in the small tank for half an hour or more till I started shivering and my body turned almost bluish. The others would have to drag me out of the water.

Then, there were the joys of devouring mangoes by that well and demolishing tasty *paranthas*, which my grandmother fried in pure ghee.

We used to travel by the Frontier Mail, a train that ran from Calcutta to Peshawar, on the North-Western Railway, popularly called NWR. Jokingly, we dubbed it '*Nawai Wayayi* Run', which, in Punjabi, means 'a newly-married wife'. The other popular railway companies known to me were the Bombay Baroda Central Railway (BBC & R) and the Great Indian Peninsula Railway or the GIPR. There were others in South India too.

As a child and after we had moved to Delhi, I was always excited at the thought of eating on a moving train and would insist on my mother packing food to take along. It was fortuitous that the Mail passed through Delhi just around dinner time. As soon as we had settled in the compartment and the train began to move, I would commence an important, on-board ritual—dinner, by unwrapping the *paranthas, aloo sabzi* and pickle that Mother had made. Train journeys, to me, were synonymous with eating—and more eating.

Several years later when I served as the Chairman of UP Tourism for a year, I used to travel from Lucknow to Delhi by night train, bringing with me *kebabs* and *roomali roti* to relish on the train. One day, the distinguished Chairman of ITC told me that he was looking for a *kebab* expert. I referred him to Imtiaz, my favorite *kebab*-maker in Lucknow. Imtiaz was hired by the Maurya and is, today, a legend.

In our childhood, mail trains that also carried passengers, like the Frontier Mail, had dining cars. You either ordered food to be served in your compartment, or, you went to the dining car, properly dressed. There, you ate while being served by white-gloved waiters.

Those were days when the 2nd class train fare from Delhi to Amritsar was the princely sum of Rupees 15/-. Most mail trains had four classes: 1st, 2nd, Inter and 3rd. There was a separate compartment for accompanying servants. Few trains had air-conditioned bogies.

The Lessons of Hardships

As a growing boy, I was privy to my father's narrations of several hardships he had faced in his own childhood. How, as the youngest of four brothers, he always ended up wearing hand-me-down clothes and inherited second, or third-hand books; how he never owned slippers, let alone shoes, before entering class 9.

After class 8, he and his brother, Sukh Dayal, moved to Gurdaspur for their Matriculation. While returning home one night, Dr. Wishwa Nath, the then Chief Medical Officer of Gurdaspur, and father of the famous Punjab Police Officer, Ashwani Kumar, saw the two young boys studying under a street lamp-post. He made inquiries and learned that they were from a village, lived in a hut close to his house all on their own and would study each evening till late in the night under that lamp-post. The kind gentleman took pity on them and asked them to move into one of his servant-quarters. What luxury the two enjoyed for two years!

Several years after my father's death, I visited the bungalow in whose servant-quarters they stayed. It brought tears to my eyes and I cried like a child, thanking the Almighty, Dr. Wishwa Nath and my father. To this day, a visit to Gurdaspur brings back those memories. Many years later, my father built his first house there and named it INDER NIWAS. It was the first house in Gurdaspur with modern toilets with flushes. During World War II, it was requisitioned by the government.

Whenever he recalled his tough life, my father would tell us that "hard times make better people".

"Opportunity lives in the midst of difficulties and it is up to you to grab it," he would conclude firmly.

At that age, I didn't understand such wisdom, of course. It is only in later years that I probed their deeper meaning, appreciated their worth and almost began to worship my father for the kind of person he was and for the struggles, trials and tribulations that he and his family had endured with such stoicism.

At Inder Niwas, Gurdaspur, 2002

It is an undeniable fact that he and his family were poor, really poor. That was the bottom line. I saw this even more clearly as I grew up. And it taught me something very important. That if you have will-power, courage, determination and of course, God's Grace, a lack of money need not be a barrier in life. The important thing is to keep fighting and not give in to despair.

My father, Rai Sahib Dr. Mela Ram Sharma, firmly believed in hope against despair. That one should do his *purushaarth* and leave it to Him to reward us for it.

It has taken me all these decades of my life to realize the true significance of that sentiment.

He was an exceptional man, whose influence on me was not only strong, but almost edifying. As a boy, he had been studious, one who always stood first in class. This is what enabled him to educate himself with scholarships and during his college days, by giving tuition to earn extra money. It was a hard life, and yet he always strove to achieve the best in everything he undertook.

It was my father, Dr. Mela Ram Sharma, who taught me to keep my cool and hold my head high in all situations, including adverse ones. He also imbued in me the desire to appreciate the immeasurable value of a united family. Things were not easy even for our family in those days. But being the kind of person he was, my father sold the two gold medals he had received for exceptional educational results, to raise money for the marriage of a relative's daughter.

Rai Sahib Dr. Mela Ram Sharma
Born: Oct. 04th, 1902. Died: Oct. 14th, 1968

My Father
Rai Sahib Dr. Mela Ram Sharma

Dr. Mela Ram Sharma always helped his family members, be it financially or by getting them jobs. He stood by them—at all times and at all costs.

While studying at the Veterinary College, Lahore from 1921 to 1925, my father or 'Dad' as I called him, had learnt fluent English. There, he mixed with more well-off society—among others, with the Sawhney family, whose two young boys he tutored in mathematics—and acquired finesse in his manners. Rajji Sawhney, the older brother, became one of the highest-ranking Indian naval officers at the time of Independence, while the younger brother, Leslie Sawhney, married JRD Tata's sister. Both always addressed my father as *Masterji*. This interaction with the Sawhney family helped my father's career along in a unique way. From a rustic village boy, he grew to become a soft-spoken and well-educated gentleman, one, who was well-equipped to mix with the highest echelons of society of the time.

Dr. Mela Ram Sharma's career began as a Demonstrator at the Veterinary College, Lahore. Due to his hard work, academic brilliance and the newly-acquired sophistication, he was soon transferred to Shimla as a surgeon in charge of the Veterinary Hospital on Cart Road, a very prestigious post, normally awarded to people with far greater experience and seniority.

Shimla was then the summer capital not only of the Punjab 'Province'—as states were called those days—but also the Government of India. It was, what my grandchildren would today call a 'happening' place.

The post involved dealing with senior officials such as the Viceroy of India, the Governor of Punjab and several princes of northern Indian states who had summer homes—and pet dogs—in Shimla. His work was so highly appreciated that instead of the customary tenure of three years, Dr. Mela Ram served for almost seven in that post.

If my father was an excellent role-model as a parent, one who taught us to keep our heads high in all adversity, my mother, Santosh Devi, more than matched him. You might call mine a blessed childhood.

Santosh Devi was a very gracious, courteous and caring woman who never complained about anything. Though not formally educated to an advanced level, she was a worldly-wise and God-fearing person. It was religiousness, but not dogma or ritualism that marked my mother's spirituality. When my sister got married, my mother owned hardly any jewellery, as it had been either gifted to poor relations or sold to pay for their marriages. So she cheerfully borrowed some from her sisters-in-law, just for the occasion.

In her own quiet way, Santosh Devi, or '*Veeran*' (sister), as her own family called her affectionately, contributed immeasurably towards the unity of our family.

Like many middle-class Indian families, we too, had a domestic help. But like a typical Punjabi lady, my mother would insist on lending a hand: with the cooking and on churning the curd, to

My Mother Mrs Santosh Devi—Fondly Called '*Veeran*'

ensure the butter is always fresh and made at home. Other than her one weakness—a sweet tooth—which I inherited, Santosh Devi was a lady of frugal habits.

Dr. Mela Ram Sharma and Mrs. Santosh Devi Sharma complemented each other and made an excellent couple. As parents of us young Sharmas, they were everything we could ask for—guardians, philosophers and friends. If I have inherited any good *karma*, I owe it to them. It is from them that my younger sister Usha and I received good *sanskars*—values—and learnt the practice of humility, for which we are both forever indebted. Over the years, I have tried to the best of my ability to live by those values. And I dare say it is those values that were of enormous help in getting my grip on life.

On January 1, 1943 and in the glittering Durbar Hall of the Viceroy's Palace (today's Rashtrapati Bhavan) in Delhi, Lord Linlithgow, the then Governor-General of India, bestowed the title of 'Rai Sahib' upon my father, Dr. Mela Ram Sharma.

Forty-seven years later, I was overwhelmed with memories and gratitude towards my father when, in the same Durbar Hall, the

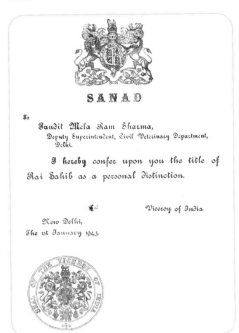

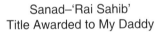

Sanad–'Rai Sahib'
Title Awarded to My Daddy

Padma Shri Award given to Me
by President Venkatraman

President of India, R. Venkataraman in 1990 honoured me with the 'Padma Shri'.

I lost both Dr. Mela Ram Sharma and Mrs. Santosh Devi Sharma—my wonderful parents—when they were both too young to leave us. Still and even in my grief, I remembered what they taught me—to be grateful to God. I was and am, because before they went away, they had at least had the pleasure of seeing me well-settled, in a happy marriage and with two lovely children. Before they said their premature goodbyes, they had also witnessed the unfolding of the birth and growth of SITA World Travel.

It gave them immense pride and happiness. Like all children, I often wish they were alive to see the setting up of Select CITYWALK and the hotels I built in Manesar and Goa. I wish they were there to embrace Shreya and Amaraah. Alas, it happens to all of us. Those who come, have to go—we each have our span of life and no one can change it. We all live according to His Wishes and our *'karmas'*.

3 Early Days—
All about Growing Up

All of us carry memories of our school days. Some of mine are sweet, others I would rather not recollect.

I studied at the Municipal School, popularly called MB School, on Reading Road, today's Mandir Marg, in New Delhi. There, I made some good friends—Balaji Rao, Nirmal Singh Randhawa, Bhagirath Bhalla and Vyas Kakkar. We used to walk together to school playing *Pithoo* along the way—toppling a pile of seven stones with a ball and reconstructing it before the opponent could catch and throw it back at you. What fun those days were.

By then, my father could have easily afforded to send me to a private school. But he wanted his son to grow up—as he did—from the bottom up. So he chose the down-to-earth Municipal School instead.

Up to class V, I was educated in Urdu—the language of the courts and the popular tongue in North India those days. However, our family Panditji convinced my father that being a Brahmin, he ought to ensure that his son learned Hindi and Sanskrit.

Now, I didn't appreciate the sudden change from Urdu to Hindi, but Panditji's wish prevailed. Unfortunately, I learned neither Hindi nor Urdu properly, a shortcoming I carry till date.

With promotion to class VIII came my first bicycle, a Raleigh. What joy it was to whizz through New Delhi's roads at high speed! There was hardly any traffic and the streets were safe. I began to enjoy my rides tremendously. Occasionally, I would take a secret round of Connaught Place.

You have Got to Stand for Something in Life—Else You will Fall for Everything: My 'Slow Graduation'

Connaught Place, or CP, was a unique place. There was two-way traffic and parking in the middle. There were shops like Rankin, Empire Store, Army & Navy Store, Bliss & Cotton, Sahib Singh and Sons, Leela Ram, Kemp & Co., Pandit Bros., Kailash Carpets, Janki Das and several others. Then there were well-known restaurants—Wengers, Davicos, Piccadily and many more. Very few have survived.

If I were asked to describe my school life, I would say it was mostly uneventful. On Fridays, we had a one-hour break to enable Muslim students to offer prayers. That was fun and a bonus for the rest of us. We would often use it to go home for lunch. Or we would pluck 'berberries' on the wooded ridge, right behind the school. Then there was hockey and weekend cricket.

In 1945 at the age of 15, I joined the pre-medical class at Hindu College, then located at Kashmiri Gate. The Gate was an important area between the Walled City and 'Civil Lines', a colony of the elite. Most families had shifted from the walled city to Civil Lines after the Durbar of 1911. The then Viceroy's Secretariat, which is now the office of Delhi's Chief Minister and houses the Delhi Assembly, was close by.

If my school years were uneventful, college life was anything but that. It was an exciting, formative stage in my life, one which played a major role in shaping my personality.

Hindu College was and still is, a reputed institution. My classmates were the likes of Lalit Gujral who later became India's Education Officer in New York, and Surinder Puri, who rose to the rank of Major-General and retired as the head of the Army Dental Corps.

We formed a nice trio and stayed together. We had a few charming girls in our group too.

Studies, in themselves, awoke no great passion in me. I was never a good student, merely an average one. My wide and varied interests of those days can hardly be described as 'scholarly'.

My favorite way to describe those years is by saying "I graduated gradually". It took me eight years in college to complete my studies, culminating in a Master's Degree in *Economics.*

While most students in college got an education, I, in addition, got a wife, who, even today, is trying to educate me.

Aruna's family used to live at Narendra Place on Parliament Street, which is today's Sansad Marg. The multi-storeyed DLF building stands at that spot today. One of her friends and classmates was Nirmal Randhawa, who lived on Hanuman Road. Nirmal's brother, also named Nirmal Singh, was my friend and we used to play hockey together. Nirmal's father, Sardar Deva Singh Randhawa, was a very distinguished income tax lawyer. These friendships were our link. So when I visited my friend Nirmal Singh, Aruna would visit hers—Nirmal Randhawa. While Aruna's family lived on Parliament Street, our family lived on Curzon Road, today's Kasturba Gandhi Marg. Aruna would board her bus at Regal building and I would take the same Gwalior Northern India Transport (GNIT) bus at Scindia House. I would wait at Scindia House bus stop to board the same bus in which Aruna travelled to Lady Hardinge College. The college gate, with its ice-cream carts, was a favorite summer venue for our meetings. We would try out different flavours. And all the while and without knowing it, Aruna's mother was paying the bills. Aruna would take the bills to her for reimbursement. The good lady must have wondered why her daughter was consuming so much ice-cream, even as she paid! I also remember how Aruna's brother Vini, once came after me, brandishing a hockey stick, to save her from what he then referred to as the evil eyes. Those were good days.

Slowly and surely, the developing acquaintance between Aruna and me flowered into a closer friendship. Aruna tells me that what attracted her the most about me were my debating skills and my conduct in the College Parliament, first as a 'Leader of the Opposition' and then as 'Prime Minister'. Our friendship developed slowly, over a period of time and blossomed fully when she joined Lady Hardinge Medical College.

"Politics is perhaps the only profession for which
no preparation is thought necessary."
—Robert Louis Stevenson

I doubt if our venerable politicians would agree with this stark statement.

Politics didn't exactly run in my blood. Nevertheless, I got hooked to politics during my college years and developed a deep interest in student politics. It wasn't unusual. When Gandhiji gave his final call for the Britishers to Quit India on August 9th, 1942, I was still at school. Unknown to my parents, I joined one or two demonstrations, shouting slogans.

Those were heady years. The freedom movement was at its peak. Just months earlier, the British government had attempted to secure Indian cooperation in World War II through a venture named the Cripps Mission. After the Shimla Conference of 1945, at which the Viceroy of India met with major Indian political leaders to reach an agreement on self-rule for India and failed, Congress leaders like Jawaharlal Nehru, Sardar Vallabhbhai Patel, Maulana Azad, the Muslim League's Mohammed Ali Jinnah and Liaquat Ali Khan, Sikh leaders Master Tara Singh and Baldev Singh, Mr. Babasaheb Ambedkar who represented the interests of scheduled castes and many others like Sikandar Hyatt, began to hold frequent talks to plan the strategy for India's Independence.

Given such a charged atmosphere, it was hard for a youngster not to be affected.

Since we had no politicians in the family, I had no political mentor. Yet, I think I possessed an inherent political streak.

I began to take part in the Students' Congress. Later, I made it to the College Parliament. While still at school and without letting on to my parents, I had already taken part in political rallies, shouting 'Congress Zindabad! Freedom is our Birthright', 'Britishers, Quit India!' and all the slogans of the times.

While at college, I would bunk classes, pretending I was attending additional tutorials that got me home late.

In the year 1950, I became the President of the Delhi State Students' Congress. During my tenure, I launched 'Miss a Meal'. The initiative was my attempt to urge students to conserve food grain. Those were the days of food shortages in Bengal and other Provinces, as states were then called.

Giving an NSU Speech—My Student Days

Kashmir was then a hot issue. During my tenure as President, I also led a 'goodwill' mission to the state. And that is where I first met the then *'Sadar-i-Riyasat'* of Kashmir, Dr. Karan Singh, the youngest person ever to head a state. I remember that trip well for some very fiery speeches I delivered to an audience of some thousands in the company of Bakshi Sahib, the Deputy Prime Minister of J&K.

At a preliminary level, I also got involved with the formation of the National Union of Students. But Pt. Jawahar Lal Nehru, who had studied in England, was not in favour of students dabbling in politics. He wanted them to immerse themselves in academics and social and cultural activities instead. So far, this was not the case, because students who were in college or even in school, were mobilized by the Congress party itself for demonstrations and shouting slogans. In fact and even before Partition, the Students' Congress was a wing of the Congress party.

Once, a meeting of student leaders was called in Mumbai and a large gathering assembled at a stadium. The meeting was presided over by Acharya Kripalani and Acharya Narinder Dev. One of the decisions taken was to establish the National Union of Students. It was expected to be actively involved in students' affairs and look after their welfare, but to avoid connections with political parties. Historically speaking and at least in the opinion of many people, this was the right decision, though it resulted in a setback for the Congress party for a period of time.

While Congress gave up student politics, almost demolished the Students' Congress and tried to support the National Union of Students, organizations like Bhartiya Jan Sangh and the Communist Party of India (CPI) continued with their own students' wings. The Jan Sangh was established in 1951 and the CPI was established in 1925. At Delhi University, the Students' Congress was certainly on the decline. When we were directed to help establish the NUS and avoid politics so as not to embarass the newly-elected government, the Students' Congress waned. But the Students' Federation continued to flourish under the leadership of people like Harish Chander. Even independent university presidents and the President of Miranda House, Sheila Dixit, became supporters of the Students' Federation. However, there were two colleges which continued with the Students' Congress for about a year or so: Hindu College and Indraprastha College.

The last meeting was held in Bangalore where, the Students' Congress was finally dissolved. Our train journey from Delhi to Bangalore was eventful. The delegation from Delhi was travelling by 3rd class and we had the Congress flag and the Tricolour flying from our windows, with banners suspended on the sides of the compartment. The train had to pass through the princely State of

Hyderabad to reach Bangalore. (This was before Hyderabad was 'liberated' through what was termed as 'police action').

At the last station before the train entered Hyderabad, police officers approached us. They told us to take down the National Flag so as not to provoke and invite any trouble, while the train was traversing the state of Hyderabad. Young and hot-blooded that we all were, we refused to do so and said, "We will face the opposition". Today one realizes that this bravado was overplayed. We could have attracted an attack on the train, and apart from us, other innocents could also have been hurt. But we stuck to our guns and kept the flags flying. The police decided to have four armed policemen posted in our compartment. We had no trouble.

The Conference was held in Lal Bagh. A decision was taken to dissolve the Students' Congress and to advise students that they should not get involved with any political party until after independence but focus on their academic and student welfare activities instead. Most university unions followed the advice. This is the period when the Communist-dominated Students' Federation and later on, the Jan Sangh-sponsored Vidyarthi Parishad gained strength, while the Students' Congress declined.

During my years dabbling in students' politics, I also took a keen interest in India's parliament. With the help of my father, I often visited parliament sessions. Though I didn't understand much of what was being debated there, those visits motivated me to take even greater interest in the college parliament.

The Hindu College Parliament was presided over by Professor Prem Chand. He was an enigmatic character, a delightful, friendly gentleman who played a pivotal role in the formation and development of my life and personality. He instilled in me great self-confidence.

Prof. Prem Chand had an aristocratic bearing and was very debonair. His was a 'larger-than-life' image and he wore an

Extreme left—Prof. Prem Chand & Myself in Hindu College Days

attitude—that of a multi-faceted, highly colourful personality. The Professor was of striking appearance, tall, thin and a chain smoker. He was never seen without his tin of 555 cigarettes, and travelled in a chauffeur-driven Buick, which, many assumed, was either gifted to him by Lala Bharat Ram of Delhi Cloth Mills, or, won by the Professor himself in a round of Rummy.

He was the only professor I know of, who was allowed to smoke in class, both by Dr. Thadani, the Principal of Hindu College and by Sir Maurice Gwyer, the then Vice-Chancellor of Delhi University and former Chief Justice of India.

Professor Prem Chand taught philosophy, and he always took the last class of the day. His lectures took two to three hours, but his classes were always so well-attended, that they bear testimony to his commanding personality. Even students not studying Philosophy used to attend. He taught in English but also recited Urdu poetry or Hindi Kavita in the class. Students just loved listening to him. I used to visit him at his flat in Connaught Place's C Block to learn the art, yes the art, of public speaking, so that I could represent the college in inter-college debates. He worked hard on me. With my loud voice, gesticulating arms and no respect for time, I was but an average 'public speaker'. Prof. Prem Chand would ask me to speak in front of his long dressing mirror and shout at me for my arm movements. In fact, on two or three occasions, he tied my hands behind me and said: "Learn to speak with your brain first and then your tongue and mouth! Hand and body gestures come later."

Once, he asked me whether I would like a cup of tea. "I don't mind", I said laconically. Pat came the rebuke. Saying one 'didn't mind' was ill-mannered, pompous and suggested that one was doing the extender of the invitation a favour. Say "No, thanks" or "Thanks, I would love one," he told me firmly. I have remembered that all my life. Professor Prem Chand changed my life and I owe him my undying gratitude.

The Professor had a passion for Urdu poetry and *ghazals*. Apart from the occasional *mehfil* at his home, he would occasionally visit GB Road, where some of the best *ghazal* singers of the day lived. But his visits—to what is Delhi's 'red-light' area today, were always strictly for enjoying the music.

When I took my Master's Degree, Professor Prem Chand took me and some of his other favorite students along on one such excursion. We visited a GB Road *kotha*, but he made the purpose of our visit very clear. It was strictly to learn about the fine art of *tehzeeb*, or refinement. We were so scared, that we were literally tongue-tied throughout that visit and never mentioned it to anybody.

If I mastered the art of public speaking and the finer points of debating, I have Prof. Prem Chand to thank for it. He gave me a great deal of his time, moulding me into a 'student politician'. His parting advice to me was to "always listen to your inner voice and decide accordingly". He advised me "to be who you are and say what you feel is right, because those who mind don't matter and those who matter, don't mind." What a wonderful dictum to teach.

I've always been a glib talker. Talking comes easy to me. In 1951, I won almost every inter-college debate and Hindu College there-with the maximum number of inter-college debate trophies ever.

I became a hero of sorts at college and university. It was my first brush with fame of any kind, and an early moment of triumph and glory.

Hindu College was a remarkable institution and the memories of my college life make up a vast and colorful tapestry.

During My M.A. Economics Days

There was Banwari, the cycle-stand attendant, a caring soul and friend to those who interacted with him. If you didn't have money for a cigarette, Banwari was always at hand to lend you one. During exams, you could leave your books or note-books with him and glance through them while on your way to the boys' room.

Perhaps the most important function Banwari rendered was conveying personal messages to one's girlfriend.

Banwari was the safest of couriers, one who never betrayed your trust. It's amazing how some people who may not be rich or famous can nevertheless, leave an impact on those they meet. Banwari was one such being.

Another notable character associated with the College was Mithan Halwai, famed not only for his sweets but also for his *Poori-Aloo*,

Maitherai (fenugreek seeds) *chutney*, and *lassi* (buttermilk). I can recall many a happy moment devouring these delicacies. For four annas, that is for 1/4ᵗʰ of a Rupee, one got two *pooris* and a *kullar*, an earthen mug full of sweet *lassi*.

I remember that my pocket allowance in the first year of my college life was 4 *annas* per day, that is, in today's terms, 25 *paise*, which was later increased to Rupee 1 per day. This substantial increase in allowance meant that I could entertain a friend and occasionally afford to visit the celebrated Carlton Café. I had edged up a rung or two in life. I entertained Aruna on several occasions at Carlton, normally choosing a 'cabin', for the sake of privacy.

In 1950, an organization called the United Nations Students Association of India (UNSA) was formed. It was one led by Hindu College and Delhi University. One of its patrons was Prof. Rishi Ram Gupta and its first President was S.D. Sharma— 'Sati', a dear friend, who later became legal advisor to my companies.

Prof. Gupta was a wonderful teacher and helped—or at least, tried his best to help—improve my English. Then there was Dr. Bhattacharya who taught English and Dr. Bhatia who instructed us in Economics. There were other great professors like Professor Puri for physics, Professor Balkrishan for Biology and several others. They were all luminaries in their own right, highly educated, talented men who were assets to the institution of learning. They loved their profession. But they also loved their students.

College life was busy, colorful and nothing short of an adventure. Unlike St. Stephens, then—and still—our neighbour across the road, Hindu College was at the forefront of national political activity. I held various positions, including those of Manager and Editor of the college magazine and Vice-President of both the English and Punjabi Literary Unions.

But the most important position I held and one very close to my heart, was that of Leader of the Opposition and later, Prime Minister of the College Parliament.

Prem Prakash, Myself, Pandit Nehru, Jagmohan, Aruna & Sheila Ambegaonkar

During my 'prime ministership'—if I may call it that, one of the most distinguished guests I had the pleasure of welcoming was Pamela Mountbatten, daughter of the then Governor-General of India, Lord Mountbatten. Incidentally, Hindu College never had a regular hall. Instead, we had an amphitheatre that lent itself beautifully as a meeting place for parliamentary meetings. Many fiery speeches were delivered there. Some very distinguished freedom fighters addressed the students there. The list included Asaf Ali, Aruna Asaf Ali, Bhulabhai Desai, Acharya Kripalani and several others.

Lighter Moments

Dr. Thadani was the principal of Hindu College at the time. He was a very strict and stern-looking gentleman, always clad in a well-pressed suit. He would get off his car at the gate of the college and walk to his office, a distance of hardly 150–200 yards. His keen eye would survey everything around him as he strode through and he would acknowledge the greetings of the students with what almost looked like an army salute. It was like a Commander reviewing a Guard of Honour.

Upon his retirement, the Head of the English Department, Mr. Bhattacharya, was appointed as Principal. Mr. Bhattacharya lacked Dr. Thadani's polish. He too, decided to continue the tradition of walking from the college gate to his office. But unlike Dr. Thadani, Mr. Bhattacharya constantly bent forward, looking down, almost as though he were searching for something on the ground. One day, I mischievously dropped a one-rupee coin on the ground. When Dr. Bhattacharya came up with his head bent, I walked up to him and, pointing towards the rupee, said, "Sir, this is what you lost and this is what you were looking for—and here it is, Sir!" Politely, he ignored me and walked away.

After 15 minutes and while I was regaling my friends in the college cafe with this incident, a *chaprasi* told me that the Principal wanted to see me. I was scared of course. He could either report me to my father, or expel me or fine me heavily. All three prospects were frightening. I walked into his office. But the perfect, mild-mannered gentlemen that he was, Mr. Bhattacharya said only one thing, "Young man, these are bad manners. You are here not only to get a degree, but to become a gentleman. Don't ever do anything like that again, otherwise I will inform your father." Up to then, I might have been brazening it out but for those few minutes, I was really worried. Thank God, nothing happened, but I never forgot that incident and was always careful about my behaviour.

Even in the pre-independence era when both Hindu College and St. Stephen's College were located at Kashmiri Gate, the two buildings faced each other. This continued even after they shifted to the University campus where they stand today and have been rivals since inception.

Kashmiri Gate was also famous for St. James Church, and of course, for the fierce battle between the British Army and our freedom fighters in 1857. The Mughal army or the 'mutineers', as they were described by the British, were within the Walled City and had fended off the onslaught between Kashmere Gate and Mori Gate. Gen. Nicholson, the British Commander, was at the Ridge and firing cannon shots from there, while the Mughal Army defended the Walled City. Once the Walled City was breached, the British army marched into Delhi and as history would have us believe, a massacre took place.

There are different Kinds of 'Learning Grounds'. The Trick? Learn fast!

The period during which I learnt the most was when I was the Leader of the Opposition in College Parliament. This was an exciting phase of my life, and I dare say it played a role in sharpening my wits. When I lost the election for prime minister-ship to Sheila Ambegaonkar, the point was driven home to me— that the art of baiting, witticisms and possessing a 'gift of the gab' alone, though important items in a politician's tool kit, are not sufficient to succeed in life. This realization has stood me in good stead throughout my life. To broaden my horizon, I tried, over the decades, to study and work hard to expand my knowledge. Again, this was made possible because of the unmitigated encouragement I received from my mentor, Prof. Prem Chand.

'Saat Samundar Paar'—Crossing the Seven Seas

One's first overseas trip is normally a momentous occasion and mine was certainly no exception. It was in August 1951. The fact is, I was a complete 'babe in the woods'. I was only 20 years old, had never been on an aircraft and had never attended a formal party.

And yet, here I was, selected to represent the United Nations Students Association (UNSA) at the 'International Students' Movement for United Nations (ISMUN) Conference in Stockholm.

My father couldn't afford my air ticket. But one of his dear friends, Rai Bahadur Suraj Bhan Jhalani, who was very fond of me, graciously saved the day and bought it for me. I distinctly remember that the total airfare was Rupees 1,827—minus a five percent commission—for a trip on board Air-India's Super Constellation, a four-engined propeller aircraft that flew the route

First Overseas Trip, 1951, Vasudev Mamaji,
Daddy, Mrs. Kaur, Mr. Kaura, Daddy's Friends, Myself, Mama

Delhi-Bombay-Cairo-Rome-Paris-London. I returned on the route Paris-Frankfurt-Rome-Cairo-Delhi. The ticket was sold to me by Harry Kaul, who later became Air-India's Commercial Director.

At the time, Indian travellers on overseas visits were viewed as citizens of the land of Gandhi and Nehru and commanded respect. To be an Indian was a matter of pride: it meant one was coming from a nation that had won freedom from the British by peaceful means. A movement, which had caused ripples in colonies around the world, resulting in freedom for so many other countries like Ceylon (now Sri Lanka), Malaysia, Burma (Myanmar today) and several others.

They say 'travel broadens the mind' and I think this is absolutely true. You learn so much when you step out of your country. Everything is different: the people, their mannerisms, customs, ways of thinking and their behaviour. Even the weather and climatic conditions are a newness. It is only when you travel that you realize just how enormous and complex the world is. That all you took for granted, may not have any relevance whatsoever in another country. You learn to adapt, accept and embrace unique conditions and different circumstances. This is one of the best possible ways of learning and developing your personality. I certainly did.

Hyde Park & More: London! Here I Come!

My first lesson in international travel took place upon my very first arrival at London Airport. The customs officer asked me if I had anything to declare. I told him I had nothing except my clothes. He then asked if I was carrying any presents for anybody. I nodded and told him I had a packet for a friend's uncle. "Do you know what it contains?" he asked. I said no.

"Young man", said the customs officer. "Never carry a sealed packet for anybody unless you have checked what's inside." For a raw twenty-year-old, this was sound advice which has stayed with me till date. I have never, ever carried packages for anyone, without verifying and knowing their contents.

Of course and in retrospect, it was a bit crazy because I was later to take up a profession which would require me to travel frequently and yet, I would never carry even a closed envelope for anybody. There were far too many stories of people caught smuggling or sneaking foreign exchange out of the country in sealed envelopes.

This incident at UK Customs illustrates that if one gets the right advice at the right place and time, it can help one along. Provided one applies one's own common sense and benefits from the lesson.

Even the best advice in the world is useless if we pay no heed to it. I won't boast that I capitalized on all good advice given to me, but much of it did, indeed, help me in the course of my long career.

When I arrived in London, my good friend Prem Prakash's uncle, Mr. Prithvi Chander, for whom I'd carried the package, took me firmly under his wing. He was generous with his time and company and eager to show me the city. In fact and in typical Indian style, I would say he overdid it to the extent that by the end of two days, I was trying to duck him.

On my third day in London, I changed my hostel without informing him. Like anyone at that age, I needed my personal space and privacy to explore London. This was my first overseas foray, and I was keen to experience the city, both by day and night.

An experience of note was the India House celebration on the 9th of August, on the occasion of Mahatma Gandhi's momentous 'Quit India' call of 1942. Mr. Krishna Menon, our High Commissioner, invited me to share the dais with him, as I was the so-called 'Visiting Student Congress Leader'. To say that I was very nervous is to put it very mildly. Here I was, a twenty-year-old with no great experience of anything and certainly no international exposure, sharing a platform with a personality as iconic as Krishna Menon. Boy, was I scared! But thanks to the skill and training imparted by Prof. Prem Chand, I managed an impassioned speech. The day was saved and I got my share of basking in the spotlight. Though only for a short while, I enjoyed it thoroughly.

Country First, Self Later

Deep down, I think most of us Indians are patriots. I, too, had a burning desire to do something symbolic—yes symbolic—for my country, even if it was something stupid.

Driven thus by my strong—if young and immature—sense of patriotism, I took great joy in having my shoes shined by a white man at Trafalgar Square. It was youthful, delirious glee—Ha, ha, you Englishman! Now shining the shoes of a coloured man! An Indian, whose country you ruled for almost 200 years! What malicious pleasure I took in that shoe-shine.

On the more positive side, I gave a five-minute talk on the BBC on the 'Indian Students' Movement', and was paid five Guineas for my effort. This was the first money I had ever earned in my life, and so I can be forgiven for feeling mighty proud of myself. Upon my return to India, I gave the coins to my mother, as the first money I had earned. I also took great pleasure in sharing a stand at the Hyde Park corner to lecture on India. Close by was a Pakistani bellowing on Kashmir. I don't know why I had a larger audience—perhaps because though I was loud, I neither shouted nor used any unparliamentary words.

After my adventures in London, I arrived in Stockholm for the conference. I must describe my preparation for this event.

I had felt that going overseas for the first time merited a new wardrobe. After all, it wasn't something that happened every day. Up to that point in time, I had never owned a suit. So I got myself a three-piece checkered suit of Scottish tweed, a black *sherwani* and a *churidar pyjama*, specially tailored by Loke Nath & Sons of Delhi and Shimla fame. I also bought a *langot*, in the belief that visiting Europe could mean dancing with the girls there, and I wanted to keep myself in check and avoid any sort of embarrassment, if you know what I mean. After all, I was a man, a *young* man. I borrowed Rupees 100 to learn ballroom dancing at a dance school at Metro Hotel. I was all set. No one could accuse me of not taking my foreign trip seriously.

An experience I remember clearly was the formal dinner before the opening of the conference. Faced with an array of knives and forks, I didn't have a clue about how to use them, but did have the good sense to watch my fellow delegates and realize that unlike at home, there were different knives and forks for meat and fish.

Also, I'd never consumed any alcohol stronger than an occasional beer and that too, mixed with lemonade. But at the banquet in Stockholm, the wine was in full flow. I had never tasted wine and knew nothing about the distinction between red and white. Yet again, I observed what the others were doing and ordered my wine accordingly. *Isn't it amazing how effective and useful just simple observation can be?*

For the love of me I don't know why, but I was asked to propose the vote of thanks to the host. I was both surprised and honoured to be given this privilege, and did the needful. My debating skills of the College Parliament came in handy. People were impressed, particularly a local young lady who came up to me to exchange pleasantries. I do remember she was very pretty. We became friends, 'pen-friends', much later.

I participated in the meetings with great gusto. At the closing session, I proposed the name of the President of our Association, Satya Dev Sharma (Sati) for the Presidency of the International Association. 'Sati' was elected. But because we had the same surname, I found everyone congratulating *me* for taking over as president of ISMUN (International Students Movement for UN), which also enjoyed the backing of the UN Headquarters. I had to repeatedly set the record straight and tell them it wasn't I, but the President of our Association's India chapter, the 'other Sharma'.

A few eyebrows were raised. Some people mumbled that they 'didn't know 'that' Sharma and thought they were voting for me. I assured them he deserved the honor.

I sent a cable to Sati in India, to give him this good news. Needless to say, he was thrilled and, I think, grateful too. Sati, his parents and particularly his maternal uncle, who lived in Mathura, genuinely believed that one day, Sati would rise to the stature of a national leader. Sati and I stayed good friends. He became a successful lawyer and my legal consultant, both in my personal life and in business affairs.

But my overseas adventures hadn't ended yet, not by a long shot!

From Stockholm, I travelled to Paris. And was immediately and completely charmed by the city. And who can blame me? Paris and its people—certainly the ladies, have this effect on young men. Instead of the three days I was meant to spend there, I stayed on for almost ten days, enjoying myself thoroughly.

I left France for Frankfurt. Thanks to my delivering lectures on the Indian Students Movement and the national political situation, I earned enough to cover my expenses. Often, I would get a small fee and a stay—free of cost—at a students' hostel. I ate simple food, accepted all invitations, walked around to see the sights and experienced local life. Once again, the lessons Prof. Prem Chand had taught me, came in handy.

In reality, Europe was in the throes of a grim period as it was still recovering from the widespread devastation wrought by the war. Cities had been heavily bombed, and this was the predominant sight, particularly in Germany, which had borne the brunt of destruction. Food was rationed and the most commonly available vegetable was the potato. Eggs were rationed in both Britain and Germany, as were several other commodities.

Yet, my foreign odyssey continued and so did my adventures, since I adapted to alien and diverse conditions in a completely foreign environment quite easily.

A few days in Frankfurt were followed by a week in Italy, with the result that my planned three-week stay in Europe had already stretched into two months.

Then I flew to Cairo. By then I'd earned sufficient money from my lectures, so I could stay on in Egypt for another five days before returning home.

This extended tour meant that when I returned to India, I found myself short of attendance in my M.A. class. Prof. V.K.R.V. Rao, the Dean of the Delhi School of Economics, refused to excuse my absence. The result was that I lost a year.

Needless to say, my father wasn't amused. In fact, he was hopping mad and he had every reason to be. But the thorough gentleman that he was, he eventually forgave me. That's the way he was.

And that's why I consider him to be very special. He was a truly exceptional man who had plenty to give and always did, asking for little in return.

I spent another year at University, hardly attending classes, relying on friends to proxy for me and wasting my time on politics and gossip in the Coffee House where Tahir, a friendly waiter, would ply us with extra cold coffee.

But I didn't pretend to be a serious or diligent student either. I have always maintained that while my college may have failed to give me education—though all there had tried hard to do so, it gave me the most precious gift of self-confidence and my charming, loving and caring wife, Aruna.

At the end of the day, one studies for a couple of alphabets to append to one's name. So in 1953, when Hindu College moved to the University Campus, I decided that the time was now ripe to complete my post-graduate degree in Economics. I did. And since then, carry those two magic letters tagged to my name—An M and an A. I am a Master of Arts in Economics from Delhi University. I studied under people like Dr. V.K.R.V. Rao and Mr. P.N. Dhar, who later worked with Mrs. Indira Gandhi.

4 | Professional Life—Climbing Up the Work Ladder

Rozi Roti ka Sawal—A Question of One's Daily Bread

Starting work for the first time in life is always a momentous occasion. And so it was for me too. My journey had begun. What my future held, I did not know. For now, here was the present and I looked forward to it with excitement and anticipation.

There's a saying that "one is supposed to be perfect on the first day of the job and then show constant improvement."

I don't know whom this wisdom is attributed to. The fact is that when I joined the travel industry, it was only because I was looking for a job. It was not a conscious decision to select this profession. It was to get a job, any job. Plain and simple! It was the *'naukri'* factor and nothing else. Owing to my rather indifferent approach and my poor academic record, my father had become quite disillusioned with me.

Afsar-banu-ya? (shall I be a bureaucrat)

He was reluctant to assist and had told me in no uncertain terms, that he would not help me in getting a job because I had disappointed him deeply, first by not taking up medicine as a career, and then, by not preparing for the IAS (Indian Administrative Service). I have a feeling that what really niggled him was my academic record. Besides, he had been strongly opposed to my political activities.

Some years later, I apologized to him for disappointing him on all those three counts. I told him, that while I could no longer alter my modest academic record, I would promise never to join active politics. And I stuck to my word. And since honesty was paramount for him besides hard work, I assured him I would work diligently and honestly.

I also told him that I hoped I would not be a disappointment to him. I think I was not. Well, once I owned SITA, he was quite happy and satisfied with my achievements.

The year 1953 was a landmark, a crucial turning point in my life. I had finished my Master's in Economics, was a poor student, unwilling to study hard and uninterested in preparing for the IAS entrance exam, something my father had wanted me to do. But good jobs were scarce.

Finally, some wisdom dawned on me. Failure was staring me in my face. There was my poor academic record and there were no great prospects in sight.

One fine morning, I decided to get a grip on myself and look for a job, any job, without my father's help. I stepped out of the comfortzone of a reckless student politician to actually look for work. My professional career, if I may call it that, began in 1953.

Thanks to my friend, Om Wadhwa who was employed with Mercury Travels, I too, applied for a job with the Oberoi concern. Om arranged my interview with Mr. Gautam Khanna, then Managing Director of Mercury Travels and the son-in-law of Mohan Singh Oberoi—or Rai Bahadur, as he was popularly known.

I was selected for the job and joined the organization as a 'transfer assistant', at the princely salary of Rupees 150 per month. I was to replace Om as he was going to USA for further studies.

The job entailed receiving passengers at Palam or Safdarjung Airport and transferring them to their hotels, overseeing their travel documents, arranging for sightseeing with a car and a guide and then transferring them back from their hotel to the airport on their departure. It was one of the lowliest jobs in the organization, just one step above the peon and, since most arrivals and departures were at night, the job involved working till the wee hours.

Being a transfer assistant acted as a springboard; I found myself catapulted into a world of frenzied action. I may have been casual before, but not anymore. Shedding my 'happy-go-lucky' and carefree attitude, I worked my legs off, putting body and soul into the job to be successful. I wanted to prove to myself and most importantly to my family, that I wasn't a failure in life. While my job required doing night shifts, I used the daytime to learn everything I possibly could about travel and tourism. I volunteered to work extra hours without expecting to be remunerated. I was working almost eight hours during the day in the office and many hours through the night, doing transfers.

This had very positive results. Within a short span of time, I learned quite a bit about most aspects of the job except finance. I dare say it must have been that early hard work that helped me move up the ladder.

I soon started attending lectures and seminars on tourism and also on Business Management. I slowly learnt that what lies behind and before us, is a tiny matter compared to what lies within us.

Several years later, I gleaned some information that acted as an enlightening analogy: that the space shuttle uses more fuel during its first three minutes after lift-off, than during its entire voyage around the earth. It is a good lesson for all beginners in life and business. Work hard and put in your best efforts from day one and with good luck, you will sail through your life.

I must confess that I was a bit cocky and thought I knew it all. After all, I'd been the Prime Minister of my College Parliament; President of the Delhi Student's Congress; had represented India overseas on behalf of UNSA (United Nations Students Association of India); and was the only person in Mercury Travels' Delhi office to have voyaged overseas. I was able to talk about foreign countries. So I could be pardoned for thinking of myself in somewhat lofty terms.

In my Mercury Days

'But, for My Own Part, it was all Greek to Me'

However and after those early days of cockiness, reality caught up. I often came crashing to earth. While doing client transfers, I remember not being able to answer some of the rudimentary questions of my clients, on subjects like Delhi's altitude or population. My ego punctured thus, I took a vow to learn as much as I could about the travel industry and my country.

The fact is that I'm still learning, the process has never stopped. Indeed and as far as I am concerned, the process of learning must never stop.

The months that followed were challenging, interesting and formative. And they threw up several incidents. Once, when I was transferring a tourist to Safdarjung Airport to catch a flight to Srinagar, the gentleman asked me what aircraft was being used on that route. I told him it was a DC3. He immediately asked me what that term stood for, and whether it was an American or French plane. I didn't know the answer but I bluffed and it worked.

I glibly declared, "It's American, Sir!" In reality, I was not even aware then, that France produced aircraft.

But the client wasn't done. He then wanted to know how many engines the DC3 had. I was stumped, but told him that one model had two, while another had four. It was my habit of trying to bluff my way through, at work again. Once again, he punctured my ego and said: "Young man, being in this business, you should know about such things."

The DC3 or the 'Dakota', as it was popularly called, had been the work horse of World War II. I learned later that it had only two engines. I was always 'quick on the uptake' and invariably had a pat answer to most queries and comments. This bailed me out of several tight situations. But while being a glib talker is fine, there's no *substitute for hard and sincere work when it comes to doing your job.*

There were other anecdotes too.

While driving in Delhi or to Agra, people would ask me the name of a particular tree. Not having a clue, I would bluff my way through by saying that I knew its Indian/Hindi name. I would then rattle off any Hindi name like *neem* or *pipal*, but not an 'English one'. Sometimes they would catch me out.

One day an elderly couple gave me some useful advice. "Young man," they said, "If you really want to succeed in life, be truthful. Simply say 'I am sorry, I don't know'. And then go out and learn the answers."

This was sound advice and one I follow till date. 'Sorry' is the one good word that can carry you forward in life.

Dear reader, please don't judge me too harshly for my glib talk. Do credit me with the acknowledgement that I was always willing to learn and am still doing so.

"The dictionary is the only place where success comes before work."
—**Mark Twain**

All these early experiences as a transfer assistant were part of my 'learning graph'. They made me realize that there was simply no short cut to hard work, if one had to succeed.

I realized my lack of knowledge of history, geography and religion. But I was keen and determined to prove myself worthy of the job. Soon, I started to love it. The 'icing on the cake' was the increment of Rupees 30 per month, that came my way after three months on the job.

Then one day, there was a chance encounter that led to lifelong devotion. That's about the best way I can put it. A very important incident played a pivotal role in my life and fuelled my enthusiasm to work even harder.

I met a gentleman whom I not only worship till date, but to whom I am grateful for kindling in me both an enthusiasm to work and a self-effacing awareness of my deficiencies. It was Mr. Som Nath Chib, the then Director-General Tourism, who was known as Som Chib to his friends.

One day, Mr. Chib called a meeting of a few select travel agents to discuss the question of facilitation at Palam Airport. Represented at the meeting were Mercury Travels, Tradewings, Orient Express, American Express, Thomas Cook, and—I think—Jeena, because Travel Corporation of India (TCI) hadn't been formed yet.

This was my first official exposure to a senior government official. Up to that point in time, they had usually been 'uncles' or 'aunties', that is friends of my father. Everyone was very reverential to Mr. Chib. But I was totally unaccustomed to such protocol. As a result, I was very blunt, and laboured on about the attitude of the customs and immigration staff at Palam Airport. I probably used

(Late) Mr. Som Nath Chib

some very strong language, bemoaning their lack of knowledge of English and basic good manners, of saying Thank You or Sorry, as the situation may demand. I was certainly not very polite in my description.

I suggested that there was need for a representative of the tourist department to be posted at the airport to facilitate tourists on arrival and, for issuing permission to travel agents to assist through immigration and customs.

In those early days, the Indian immigration authorities thought that every foreigner who visited India was either a spy or a smuggler, some sort of an undesirable character probably arriving in India only to subvert our newly-found freedom.

The immigration desks at our airports were manned by police personnel whose knowledge of English and manners were at best rudimentary, rather than trained, dedicated immigration staff. This resulted in the rather unpleasant situation of travellers being virtually 'interrogated' and subjected to needless harassment and rudeness. Most immigration staff were from Haryana and they wholly lacked finesse. Even if they weren't from that state, at least they sounded very rude and crude. The economy was certainly somewhat restrictive, but the customs authorities adopted a disproportionately authoritative attitude.

They would open several suitcases and rummage through them, which, as you can imagine, was very annoying for passengers. Unfortunately, there were instances when these officials even asked for a gift, with excuses like "I need it for my wife" or "for my daughter or son, etc., who is getting married soon."

I related to Mr. Som Chib my experience with the London customs officer, his discipline and how courteous people had been all over Europe.

Now Mr. Chib was hardly the sort of person who would sit back and listen to someone drone on and on. He didn't suffer fools gladly and was quite famous for speaking his mind. But he heard me out with great patience. I continued my 'lambasting' as though Som Chib were a junior tourism official and personally responsible for all the inconveniences, dirt and other inadequacies of Palam Airport.

Seeing me get emotional, my manager, Rajinder Mohan, who was also present at the meeting, squeezed my hand hard as a warning, but I just went on and on. On leaving the meeting, Mohan whiplashed me verbally. If Mr. Som Chib so much as made a phone call to our boss, Gautam Khanna, I'd be tossed out of the job, he told me, with great annoyance.

For a good week, I felt an invisible Sword of Damocles hanging over my head. The moment soon came. Mr. Som Chib summoned me to his office. My knees felt like jelly and I was literally shivering with worry. Anxious to ensure that I didn't do a grand repeat of my earlier behaviour, my manager Mohan spared no words in emphasizing that I had better be humble and polite. I nodded my head vigorously. Yes, I would behave this time.

Mr. Som Chib was surprisingly relaxed and invited me to share his home-made lunch with him. I was so afraid that I hardly ate or talked. Our conversation was in monosyllables. He was patient, calm, and kind, and I slowly began to relax. Suddenly, he asked me which book I was currently reading. I wasn't an avid reader, definitely not a serious one. As usual, I tried to bluff my way through by naming a frivolous author I'd vaguely heard about.

He then asked me the name of the last book I'd read. I once again fumbled. He then said, "Young man, you're an idiot and a waster." I was livid but stayed calm. Nobody, but *nobody* till date, had ever called me an idiot. Even during the worst of my relationship with my father or bosses, they never used strong language. I swallowed my swollen pride.

Next, Mr. Chib handed me a report prepared by Timothy O' Driscoll, then Director-General of the Irish Tourist Board. He asked me to read the report and discuss it with him after two weeks.

I left his office that was then located in the Taj barracks opposite the Imperial Hotel—on Queensway or, today's Janpath— where Mercury had an office. We used to call Mr. Chib's office a *'Saheliyon ki Bari'* (a house of girlfriends) because except for Mr. Chib and his number two, Mr. Kadapa, the employees were ladies: Anjali Mehta, Vibha Pandhi, Kanta Thakur, Asha Malhotra and several others.

I forgot all about the report. Weeks passed, and I was summoned by Mr. Chib again. The same ritual followed, with the same result. I hadn't read the report, and knew hardly anything about it. Chib raised his voice again but didn't call me an idiot this time. He just asked me to go back and read that report.

In the months that followed, Chib seemed to develop some affection for me. I have often wondered why. This good-natured indulgence of my ways lasted throughout his life. It is for this reason and in honour of his memory, that my Inder Sharma Foundation has held the Chib Memorial Lecture ever since his first death anniversary.

With Vibha and Ram Murthy

We have had 25 such lectures and I feel they are the most fitting tribute to the memory of a thorough professional and an exceptionally fine gentleman who laid the foundation of Indian tourism.

Speakers have included Dr. Karan Singh, Mr. Madhav Rao Scindia, Mr. K.B. Lall, I.C.S., Mr. Abid Hussain, Mr. I.K. Gujral, Mr. S.K. Singh, I.F.S., Mr. Kamal Nath, Mr. Francesco Frangialli, Dy. Secretary-General, World Tourism Organisation, Mr. Salman Khursheed, Mr. Charles Correa, famous architect, Mr. Joop Ave, Minister of Tourism, Post & Telecommunications, Government of Indonesia, Mr. Geoffrey Lipman, President, WTTC, Lord Collin Marshall, Chairman, British Airways, Mr. Doug Fyfe, President & CEO, The Canadian Tourism Commission, Mr. Joseph Frohlick and Dr. Wolfgang Kipps, Chairman & Mg. Director respectively of Schönbrunn Palace, Vienna, Prof. Christine Ennew, Director, Christel De Haan Tourism & Travel Research Institute, Nottingham U.K., Mr. S.K. Misra, who was responsible for developing road tourism in Haryana and is often referred to as the father of domestic tourism, Mr. Martin Brackenburry, Director, Christel De Haan Research Institute, Nottingham University, Mr. Praful Patel, the former Minister of Civil Aviation, Govt. of India, Mr. Jon Hutchison, Former President, PATA, Mr. Renton de Alwis, Chairman, Sri Lanka Tourism Board, Prof. Don Hawkins and several others. After 25 lectures, I had to stop them for lack of interest.

Gradually and through those early interactions, Mr. Chib changed my attitude towards travel and tourism, indeed towards life. *Bless his soul, for, if he hadn't called me an 'idiot', he would never have sparked off the zeal in me to keep learning throughout my life.*

Several years after my first rant about the pathetic state of the immigration officers at the airport, a special cadre of immigration officers was introduced. It consisted of men and women hand-picked and trained to deal with visitors.

Sometime later, I received a promotion and was transferred to Mercury Travels' Calcutta office. My lofty designation was 'Manager, India Tourist Department'. It sounded very impressive. But in reality, there were just three of us in the department—I, my steno-secretary and a peon. I was thrilled at my salary being hiked to Rupees 450 per month, with free board and lodging at the Grand Hotel, Calcutta. Boy, was that something! I thought I'd 'arrived' in life.

I could not spend my entire salary and soon started saving money. By now, I was beginning to enjoy my life and work. My friends and also the ladies around me, thought I must be very senior and very well-paid to be able to stay at the Grand.

My close friend in Calcutta was my colleague, Surinder Singh Chaudhary. We used to have a ball. We would share meals in our rooms, listen to music from 'Scheherazade', the 'open-air' nightclub of the Grand Hotel and host our friends, including some charming ladies. Mr. Mukherjee, Manager of the Calcutta branch of Mercury, was a superb administrator and a gentleman. He too, soon became a good friend and mentor.

Those early years at the Oberoi-owned Mercury Travels left behind some other memories too. I still recall the senior Mrs. Oberoi very fondly. The very distinguished-looking wife of Rai Bahadur Mohan Singh Oberoi was an immensely pious lady, who would read from the Guru Granth Sahib and distribute *prasad* every morning. She had an apartment close to the Mercury office.

One incident is worth recalling. Every afternoon, the peon brought tea for the staff. Every day, he would ask me if I wanted *Sanghara*. I would refuse. To us North Indians, *sanghara* (*singhada*) is a fruit, not something that accompanies afternoon tea. One day, I asked Surinder why people in Calcutta uncommonly ate this fruit with afternoon tea. He laughed and said: "Try for yourself". I relented the next day and ordered a *Sanghara*. To my surprise, it turned out to be nothing but a *samosa*, a snack that is also popular in North India.

The Calcutta of 1954 was a very pleasant city. People were disciplined, they queued up for trams and buses. Yes, the Bengalis chattered loudly, but were always polite. There was the renowned Chowringhee—where the Grand is located, two cinema halls in the immediate neighbourhood and the famous restaurant Firpo's. I was told, that in the olden days, after dismissing the maids on Fridays, the executives of British firms would gather at Firpo's for lunch. It continued to be frequented thus until the 50s. Then there was fashionable Park Street with expensive shops, a few restaurants and night clubs. The famous singer, Usha Uthup, first performed at the open-air Scheherazade Night club at the Grand and later, at a restaurant on Park Street. The famed Magnolia Restaurant even sent its ice-cream to Delhi, where it was sold by vendors. It is in Calcutta that I acquired my first pair of hand-made shoes, crafted by a Chinese shoemaker on Bentinck Street.

I was a devoted employee. To save the company the extra expense of hiring a guide and if time permitted, I would often do the guiding and night transfers myself.

One night, as I made my way to the company car to go to the airport, I found the driver missing. I learned later that he had fallen asleep in a drunken stupor. Instead of hiring a taxi, I decided to simply drive to Dum Dum airport myself and receive the arriving client. As luck would have it, Rai Bahadur Oberoi also arrived on the same flight. By being the manager, chauffeur and transfer assistant rolled in one, I formed a favorable impression on him. Subsequently, I was to always enjoy his blessings and his appreciation.

After a six-month stint in Calcutta, I returned to Delhi in 1956 as Deputy Manager. But now I was a fully-trained travel professional. The job of deputy manager was a well-respected one. Thus began another chapter in my professional life.

I interacted with other travel professionals like Balli Sehgal, Manager of Trade Wings, Behram Dumasia, Manager of Jeena & Company, Mrs. Singh of American Express, Jagdish Baveja, Manager of Pakistan International Airlines, Mr. Palta of Air France, Dilbagh Singh and Narender Nath of KLM and several others. The Manager of the Delhi Mercury branch, Mr. Som Madhok, was my boss.

Life as Deputy Manager of the Delhi branch of Mercury Travel was quite comfortable and easy. I no longer had to do night transfers, but concentrate on handling tourists and in addition, on supervising the air ticketing business. There were several airlines in India. They had not yet been nationalized and Indian Airlines was not formed. They were Deccan Airways, Airways India, Bharat Airways, Himalayan Aviation, Kalinga Airlines, Indian National Airways, Air Services of India, etc. Later, they all merged to form the domestic carrier, Indian Airlines and Air India, the international carrier.

In those days, one had to issue an Exchange Order on airlines to obtain a ticket. The agents were not given ticket stocks. Doing business was cumbersome, slow and tedious. On the international scene too, airlines were not online yet, so one had to make telephonic requests for seats, etc. One consulted the voluminous ABC guide for airline timetables. Airfares had to be calculated based on flights taken. My main duties continued to be the handling of inbound tours; travel responsibility was something I had volunteered to take on in addition. This extra work came in very handy at a later stage, when I began to enlarge the scope of SITA Travel, by which time I had a fair idea of international and domestic air travel and also of handling incoming foreign tourists.

Back in Delhi, life fell into the same old routine. I would arrive at office at 9 am, before most other staff, often when the *chaprasis* (peons) were still dusting the premises. I would go through the incoming mail first. By now, I was supervising the work of others and additionally heading the Incoming Tours Department at the Branch. I learnt most 'ropes' of the trade, developed good relations with airlines, hotels and the Department of Tourism. It was only accounting that I never relished. Even today, it is hard for me to decipher a balance-sheet. Marketing and Public Relations were my forte.

Those were the days of manual typewriters, mostly Remington, handwritten notes and—at best—a teleprinter service. One had to book a trunk call from City A to City B. There were ordinary calls, which could sometimes take a day or two to be put through, and then there were urgent calls, which one would get within a few hours. Lastly, there were immediate calls which could not be person-to-person, but only from the calling number to the called number. Teleprinters were introduced in the mid-fifties and reduced the tedium of written or typed messages. Teleprinters provided a faster and more reliable way to communicate than international calls, which often took more than a day to be put through.

In July 1955, I finally left Mercury Travels. I did so to join SITA World Travel Inc., an American company, then with its headquarters in Palm Springs, California.

I started my life at SITA with the grand title of 'Manager, India'. Yes, "Manager, India"—with a total staff of one assistant-cum-stenographer Mr. Kumar, who was very reluctantly sanctioned only when the head office learnt that I could not type, and a peon. I faced all kinds of questions. Why can't each of us dust his or her own table and the area around it, when we open the office in the morning? Why do we have to serve tea or cold water to visitors? Why don't we have a water-cooler-dispenser? What is a peon and what is his role in the office? All these queries had to be answered.

By 1963, I had progressed to the level of 'Vice President, South Asia'. It sounded like a very high title but was not much to talk about. Still, it looked impressive on a visiting card, especially to the ladies.

5 | SITA: The International Connection

Joining SITA was another momentous development. Or, per-haps—I should call it an accident.

SITA was the brainchild and creation of John C. Dengler, a German immigrant to the United States. He was popularly known as Jack. He was the owner and President of SITA, while his wife Helen, another migrant from Germany, was the Vice-President of SITA, USA. It remained a family-owned corporation till Dengler sold it to Diner's Club Inc. in 1966.

Jack Dengler had started the Company as 'Students International Travel Association' in 1933 in New York. Later, the acronym 'SITA' became the company's official name.

And of course, the jokes came thick and fast. 'Sitting In The Airport', 'Stupid Idiots Travelling Abroad' and 'Sexual Intercourse Training Association' were some of the more interesting ones. In India, people often asked me whether SITA was my mother's or sister's name. (My sister's name is 'Usha'—though married to a gentleman by the name 'Ram', the Goddess Sita's husband—while my mother's was Santosh Devi.)

The company's first tours in the 30s had comprised of students travelling from Columbia University to Europe. On board the ship and in Europe, they attended academic lectures. Originally, they toured Europe by cycle. They also received academic credits and recognition for these tours.

In later years, i.e., after World War II, SITA became a regular tour operator, catering to all sections of travellers. In the United States, it acted as a wholesaler, never dealing directly with a client but always through a retail agent. Slowly and as his business grew, Dengler felt the need to have his own offices overseas to look after SITA tours visiting various countries. The first office was opened in Paris. By 1966, SITA had a presence in Canada, Mexico, Japan, Hong Kong, Thailand, Singapore, Indonesia, Australia, New Zealand, India, Egypt, Italy, France and the UK, sometimes maintaining several offices in one country. It was a truly international travel operator, all 100% of which was owned by the parent company.

My Kingdom and I

I had joined SITA in the later months of 1955 as 'Manager, India', and by 1963 had progressed to 'Vice-President, South Asia'. There were a few notable landmarks to those years.

In 1963, SITA India was converted into an Indian company, and I acquired 25 per cent shares in it. *It was Jack's first collaboration with an employee anywhere.* Then by 1969, I had bought over the entire shareholding of SITA India. It was my own, personal *riyasat* or kingdom, maybe not the biggest or the best, but mine, nevertheless.

But I'm racing ahead now. Before going any further, I must describe my start with SITA. Like many aspects of my life, this, too, had its share of drama.

The Drama

The drama of my joining SITA is worth recalling. I had joined in the latter half of 1955. But the sequence of dramatic events had really begun in February 1955 when I was still with Mercury and when John C. Dengler, President and owner of SITA Inc. visited India.

Jack Dengler's arrival at Palam, 1955. I was still in Mercury.

Mercury Travels was handling his travel arrangements. Gautam Khanna, Managing Director, Mercury Travels, had assigned me the job of personally escorting Dengler on his India tour. Gautam's instructions were to keep him so busy and preoccupied, that he got no opportunity to meet any other travel agent. Gautam wanted SITA's business. So I set about my task very zealously.

It's strange how some things are meant to happen, and that too, at a particular time. You can call it destiny, like I do.

While travelling together, a kind of friendship developed between Dengler and me. While I was always proper and formal, Dengler came across as a very simple and friendly person. In fact, so unassuming that he even washed his own shirts. Those were the days of washable nylon shirts.

By the time we had travelled together for almost two weeks and returned to Delhi, he mentioned to me that he had a desire to open SITA's own offices and operations in India. It was shocking news to me.

As a faithful and loyal employee of Mercury Travels, I took a pronounced stand on the issue and gave him all possible reasons for not opening an office in India. I emphasized the great advantage in his dealing with Mercury Travels as it was a subsidiary of Oberoi Hotels, then the largest hotel chain in India.

Though I wanted to succeed and take up a job with him, hopefully in the USA, I didn't want to do so at the cost of my principles and my loyalties. Therefore, I also reported the matter to my Manager, Rajinder Mohan. On Dengler's last day in Delhi, I was supposed to take him out for dinner to the then famous Moti Mahal restaurant in Darya Ganj, owned by the colourful Kundan Lal, a typical Peshawari gentleman.

If any one single person or restaurant made Tandoori Chicken a global dish, it was Kundan Lal and Moti Mahal. If only he had patented the idea, he would have been a millionaire, instead of dying a disappointed person whom fate cheated of his rightful place in the history of Indian cuisine.

Moti Mahal started as a small *dhaba*, but soon managed to get some open space alongside its location. In spite of Kundan Lal's list of the Who's Who as customers, he could never cover his open space. One dined under a *shamiana*, a cloth tent. Moti Mahal never got a liquor license, but a few faithful customers were served Scotch in tea-cups. It was often said that to be a fully-accredited ambassador to India, one must do three things. Lay a wreath at Mahatma Gandhi's *Samadhi* in the morning, present your credentials to the President of India in the afternoon and dine at Moti Mahal in the evening.

But back to Mr. Dengler.

My manager at Mercury, Mr. Mohan, told me that it would be proper if he, as a senior, took Dengler out to dinner instead. I didn't know it then, but at that dinner meeting, Mohan not only encouraged Dengler to open an office in India but volunteered to personally do so. It is only after I joined SITA as a trainee in the New York office that I saw his letters, which were part of Dengler's India file.

Twists and Turns on the 'Work Highway'

In the meanwhile, plenty was happening. In May 1955, another incident transpired, instigating a change in my professional life.

Gautam Khanna decided to replace Mohan by bringing in R.K. Narpat Singh, who was then working as Deputy General Manager, Thomas Cook India, a reputed and important British travel company, which, at that time, was one of the largest in India.

I was Deputy Manager of Mercury's Delhi Office. But yet again, my basic nature of being over-confident and cocksure of myself, compelled me to stick my neck out. I declared that I should have been given this opportunity to be promoted to the Manager's post, instead of bringing in Narpat Singh.

Admittedly, I had less than two years of work experience under my belt, whereas Narpat Singh, from the Jodhpur royal family, a national squash champion, had considerably wider and longer experience in a much bigger travel company, namely Thomas Cook. He was the better candidate.

I don't really know whether it was luck or stupidity, but I decided to resign from Mercury Travels.

After submitting my papers, I sent a cable to Dengler and informed him that now that I had resigned from my job, I could give him my frank and impartial opinion on the issue of opening a SITA office in India. I also offered my availability and willingness to join him, as I had rendered my resignation.

Incidentally and several years later, Narpat Singh also worked for me at SITA as Vice-President and was attached to my office, as special assistant to Chairman. We became good friends. His wife Neeru was a very good friend of my wife. Neeru was a charming hostess.

We have to remember that in those days, communication was a rather slow business.

A month passed and I had received no response from Dengler. I even sent him an LT cable (Letter Telegram as these were called) but still got no response.

In the meantime, my thirty-day notice period with Mercury Travel had lapsed and I found myself with the dubious distinction of being jobless. I didn't let my father in on the fact that I had resigned from my job.

Fortunately for me, I heard from Dengler in the second week of July. He asked me to appear for a formal interview in New York. All expenses would be paid, and I was to take a PanAm flight. In those days PanAm, an American airline that is now defunct, had its famous "Around the World Services"—PanAm I & PanAm II, one eastwards and the other westwards. Those were the days of two main American carriers covering India, PanAm and TWA (Trans World Airlines or, as it was popularly called, 'Time Wasted Abroad'). Such acronyms were very popular. For example, Pakistan International Airlines or PIA, was called *Pahunch Gaye Inshallah* (Thank God we reached our destination). Air France was referred to as 'Air Chance', Air India as 'Always Impossible', and BOAC—the precursor to British Airways, as 'Better on a Camel'...

Boy, was I thrilled at that invitation to New York! I was over the moon. There was no mention of any salary, but that was an issue I didn't even bother to think about. I thought Americans always paid well.

I applied for my American visa, and learnt, to my surprise, that the American Embassy had already been informed by SITA to issue me a 'work visa'. Incidentally those were the days of McCarthyism and to get a US Visa, one had to take an oath to declare that one was not a member of the Communist Party. The American Embassy was located at Mandi House. The Diplomatic Enclave, a project of Mr. Nehru where the embassy is currently located, was developed much later.

Excitement coursing through my veins, I arrived in New York and was booked into a second-class hotel, Martinique, located near the famous Macy's store. I was interviewed and duly selected for six months of training in America. At the same time, there were two other gentlemen—one from London, whose name I forget and Mr. Kunio Fukeyama from Tokyo—who were being trained for similar job positions in their countries.

But my Mercury years had given me a lot too. Besides gaining an insight into the travel business, I had learnt two important lessons during my two-year stint with Mercury and immediately thereafter.

The team of SITA Inc: Myself, Wildeboker,
Helen & Jack Dengler, Kanio, Chye, Gibson and others

MEET THE SITA "UNITED NATIONS" TEAM
Hand-picked by Jack Dengler

White Sun Guest Ranch in Rancho Mirage, California, hosted a September 28-30,1966, SITA Manager's Conference, and here are most of them gathered around the ranch patio fountain after a lunch break.

Standing, from left Charlie Kwok, Hong Kong; Prayong Somquamkid, Bangkok; Roger Varcoe, Auckland, N.Z.; Jon Ogawa, Tokyo; John Georgandas, Athens; Inder Sharma, New Delhi; Jan Perry, Los Angeles; John McDonald, SITA Headquarters, Rancho Mirage; Robert Chu, Taipei, Taiwan; Tan Chee Chye, Singapore; Lillian Martin, San Francisco; Del Calhoun, Houston; Charles Smith, Melbourne and Warwick Gibson, Sydney, Australia; and David Dengler, Seattle.

Seated from left Jack Dengler, President; Andre Ambron, Miami; Helen Dengler, Public Relations; Joe Mapa, Manila, Philippines; Hilde Boker, Europe; Armin Lehmann, Chicago; Alan Gibson, Toronto; John Crosby, New York; and Malcolm Finnegan, London.

Absent Bill Gentry, Honolulu; Jeanne Winkelstroeter, Tahiti; KonFah Pern, KualaLumpur, Maylasia; Fred Salzer, Nairobi, Kenya; Mounir Habashi, Cairo; Max Spitz, Tel Aviv; George Garabedian, Jerusalem; K.N. Kapoor, Calcutta; Asif Dewjee, Bomhay; and Atam Ram Marwah, Srinagar.

The first was that *you shouldn't limit your efforts to doing just the job assigned to you, but go flat-out to learn and master other aspects of your profession and make yourself more useful to your employer.*

The second lesson which I learned when I was selected to work for SITA and while undergoing my training in New York, was that *loyalty to your organization and employer pays off in the long run.* It may sound old-fashioned, but believe me, I can vouch for this, as this was the basis for my selection by SITA and my being preferred to Mohan, who had considerably more experience than I and had offered to work for SITA.

Come on, Jack!

'Jack'. That is what everyone in SITA affectionately called the owner and the President of the Company, Mr. John C. Dengler. Jack was a simple man, but very intelligent and far-sighted. He recognized the need to have his own offices overseas, in order to ensure that there was uniform handling of customers and business everywhere.

Time flew. After six months, I returned to Delhi and opened the SITA office at Metro Hotel on Queensway—as Janpath was then called—in a 12 × 14 foot room. It was an important milestone in my professional life.

Being a bit of a sentimental fool and even after almost 63 years, I still use the same Godrej table which I had purchased for Rupees 450 for that first office. Unfortunately, the chair, in spite of several repairs, hasn't survived the passage of time. Or, perhaps the actual *kissa kursi ka*—the tale of the chair—is, that I have become too heavy for it.

My neighbours at the Metro Hotel were Pakistan International Airlines, whose manager Jagdish Baveja, is still a dear friend. Later, TCI, too, opened an office at the Hotel. TCI's first Manager in Delhi was Pradeep Virmani, who was later succeeded by Dalip Singh and then Behram Dumasia.

The fact is that we all had very little work in those days and the Metro was the venue of excellent, sexy cabarets. Rehearsals for the shows were held during our lunchtime, so we got several free 'peep-shows' in the bargain.

Now, Jack Dengler was miserly to the point that when I asked for a secretary, I was informed that even the owner, Dengler, did his own typing and made his own coffee. I was taken aback, but I realize now that perhaps all this helped me become more self-reliant. With great difficulty, I got a secretary—as I did not know how to type—and the sanction to hire a peon. However, it was all totally beyond the comprehension of the Human Resources Manager at the HQ of SITA.

I remember how I had to justify the requirement of a peon to the American managers.

Maybe I was too smart for my own good, but as I didn't have a full-time workload on my hands, I offered Headquarters my willingness to escort tour groups. In this way, I accompanied several SITA groups over the years, their countries of origin ranging from Hong Kong to Thailand, Indonesia, Singapore, Malaysia and Nepal. This greatly broadened my horizon and consolidated my work experience. Once again, I had offered to learn beyond the actual duties assigned to me and it was to my benefit.

At around this time, I started 'Delhi Bulletin'. It was to later become a monthly travel magazine, literally India's very first of its kind. Later, it was rechristened 'Indrama' and edited by Ghulam Naqshband, winning several awards in the industry.

In 1964, we moved the SITA office to the Imperial Hotel. I had gone to see Rai Bahadur Oberoi regarding accommodation for our office. Not only did he immediately agree, but even offered me Room No. 50,

Pg 1 of SITA News Letter

With Balli Sehgal, Behram Dumasia, Rajinder Mohan, Mani, Som Madhok, Indira, Aruna and others SITA Delhi, Rm 50, the Imperial

located in a more vantage and prominent spot than the Mercury Travels office itself. Mercury was an Oberoi concern, so I was totally flabbergasted and overwhelmed by such a generous response from Mr. Oberoi. Today, Room 50 is where the famous 'Patiala Peg' bar is located, the one which serves only 'double' drinks.

Several years later, I found myself on the lawns of the Oberoi Hotel in Gopalpur-on-Sea near Puri in Orissa (Today's Odisha). The year was 1986 and I was enjoying a drink with Rai Bahadur Oberoi. I asked him why he'd given SITA preference over Mercury, which was his own company. His answer illustrated very clearly how well-equipped with shrewdness and marketing savvy he was and how adept at recognizing business opportunities that most others wouldn't even dream about.

He told me that during his travels overseas, he had seen that SITA's offices were housed in prestigious hotels around the world, like, for instance, the Imperial in Tokyo, the Raffles in Singapore and the Oriental in Bangkok. All these addresses were mentioned in all SITA tour brochures circulated in America. Hundreds of retail travel agents and thousands of current and potential clients saw these names; such widespread publicity of a hotel by a prestigious tour operator was worth millions. It was like getting excellent visibility free of cost. To say that I was impressed by this line of thinking and logic, is to put it mildly. What a far-sighted and brilliant approach by a marketing guru and hotelier par excellence, one who had just about passed his matriculation and didn't even have a basic degree in marketing or public relations, let alone an advanced one from a management school!

Many years later, we opened an office at the Oberoi Grand in Calcutta too. Again, he gave us space at a better rent than paid by his own Mercury Travels.

> *"If music be the food of love, play on."*
> —**William Shakespeare**

Play on, indeed. *Thoda jashn ho jaaye!* (Let there be some merriment!) Those were the days...

My office at the Imperial Hotel adjoined the famous Tavern restaurant, where there was a jolly session of music and dancing every night. Rather mischievously, I used this 'free' offering of Tavern's music for my own ends. I would sometimes invite good friends like Mani and Behram Dumasia of Jeena & Co. (which later became TCI), Vimi and Som Madhok of Mercury Travels, Darshi and Balli Sehgal of Trade Wings and Mahender Sethi of the Tourism Ministry, among others. We had our own drinks while food was brought in from the famous Kake da Dhaba in Connaught Place. Later, we would dance to the music of Tavern. It was opportunism of a different kind. The fact is that we couldn't afford to visit Tavern that often, but revelled in enjoying these 'freebies'. And a good time was had by all.

"Why, then, the world's mine oyster, which I with sword will open."
—**William Shakespeare**

There's a fair bit of drama involved in the situation and circumstances under which I acquired SITA. It was an adventure in itself. While it was a momentous and joyous event, it was no bed of roses, as I was soon to find out.

If the truth be told, I actually had to borrow money from my father, who, in turn, had to delve into his Provident Fund. This went against my father's grain as he believed that one should never borrow for one's personal needs. But he justified this act by telling himself that he was, after all, doing so only for his son's career.

Now let's go back to what had happened in 1963. At the time, Dengler had given me share-holding of 25 per cent, but in order to protect his own interest so that he didn't suddenly find himself with a new partner in India—should I sell my shares—and on the advice of his bankers, Dengler had placed a restriction, or rather, a business condition in the shareholders' agreement. It stipulated that no shareholder of SITA India could sell his or her shares to an 'outsider', without first giving an opportunity to other existing shareholders to buy the shares at book value. Yes true, *at book value*. The fact is, that without any valuation for goodwill, this was a really low value.

At that time, Dengler's lawyers had wanted to protect his rights and ensure that I did not sell the shares. Of course, at the time, Dengler never visualized that he would ever sell SITA.

In 1966, Dengler sold the company and his entire shareholding in overseas offices to Diner's Club International in the United States.

When he had commenced the process of that sale, the same clause came to my rescue. I exercised my right to buy Dengler's shares, which, at that time were valued only at Rupees 2,25,000. It was a princely sum for me. Still, I exercised that right and bought his shares, paying for them in three instalments.

This stirred a hornet's nest. At first, Dengler was very upset with me. Because my exercising this right emboldened SITA's Manager in Singapore, Tan Chee Chye, to also revolt. Dengler's anger at us was stoked by the fact that Diners Club USA was pressuring him to complete the process under his U.S. agreement, while we both exercised our rights under the local Indian and Singapore agreements respectively. The struggle and impasse lasted about 6 months. During this time, I was frequently harassed by the Managing Director of Diners India, the flamboyant Mr. Kali Modi, younger brother of famous Mr. Russi Modi. Kali had started behaving almost as though he were virtually the new owner of SITA India. During this process, I was invited to Los Angeles for a meeting with Mr. Bloomingdale, then the Chairman of Diners Club International and of the famous Bloomingdale Stores. It was Diners Club that was buying SITA's parent USA company.

I was cajoled, entertained and threatened with serious legal action, if I didn't sell my shares to Diners Club. During that meeting, Bloomingdale, who by the way, was over six foot tall and a towering personality, paced up and down in his penthouse office at Sunset Boulevard, Los Angeles, with a team of his lawyers in attendance. As for me, I pretended to be calm and composed and sounded almost foolishly submissive. But I stood my ground firmly.

I pretended that I was totally ignorant of the legal aspects of such transactions and that I couldn't respond without consulting my lawyers. The meeting ended with Mr. Bloomingdale fuming, his frustrated lawyers simmering and—me smiling all the way home.

After almost six months of uncertainty, the matter came to an end. Favorably for me.

However, in the meantime, as a protective measure and out of fear of things going awry and my losing my identity, I had established a second company called Indrama. This was to ensure that just in case I lost the case, I would be ready with an alternative plan.

Silver Lining on the Cloud

Amidst this rather grim situation, one positive factor did emerge. This fight gave rise to one major and favourable change in the Indian Government's thinking. I had set up Indrama as a tour operator, not a full-fledged travel agency. This meant that we did not have to be recognized by IATA, IAC, Indian Railways or even the Regional Passport Office. But at the time, the classification of 'tour operator' did not exist. With my very good connections with the Ministry of Tourism and in order to receive government accreditation for Indrama, I managed to get the Government of India to, for the first time, create the category and recognize the existence of tour operators, who, unlike travel agents, didn't have to adhere to any rigid requirements.

Thus, Indrama became the first Indian tour operator to be recognized by the Ministry of Tourism and was, therewith, a significant and major trend-setter in the travel industry. The Indian Association of Tour Operators (IATO), is an important branch of the industry.

My eyeball-to-eyeball confrontation with Diners Club had ended in triumph for me. When Diners finally realized that I wasn't the pushover they thought I was and that they could neither browbeat nor purchase me, they allowed Dengler to sell his shares to me and to Chye in Singapore. The one person who could never reconcile to this was Diner's local man, Kali Mody. So narrow-minded was he, that he even refused to talk to me at social functions.

But just when I thought my problems were over, I was confronted with another major one: that of remitting the sale price to Dengler. Those were the years of very strict foreign exchange control by the government. My application went to Mr. Y.T. Shah, Jt. Secretary in the Ministry of Economic Affairs. If ever there was a person whom I would term a negative man, it was Shah. He took the cake. He behaved as though each dollar belonging to India was his personal money and as if anyone who demanded foreign exchange was a cheat and a person of dubious character.

Other than that, Shah was a very efficient and honest civil servant and a stickler for rules.

My application for the remittance of money was initially rejected. Once again, my respected friend and benefactor, Som Chib, came to my rescue. He personally set up an appointment with Shah and finally convinced him. I got the permission to remit the money but not without certain conditions.

Persuading Shah was no mean achievement. Som Chib finally told him that the two of them had a different perspective and way of

Aruna & I with Mrs. & Mr. Y.T. Shah, Secretary, Economic Affairs

viewing issues. He bluntly told Shah that while he saw the 'glass as half-full', Shah saw it as 'half-empty'. That was the first time in my life that I was hearing that expression. And it helped change Shah's mind.

When the permission finally came through, it enabled a wholly foreign-owned company to become a wholly Indian one, but with a rider. The pre-condition was that in the next three financial years, SITA India would earn foreign exchange equivalent to the purchase price.

I'm glad and proud to say that with our fine teamwork and the hard work of my colleagues, notably Ghulam Naqshband and Atam Marwah, we achieved this target in the very first year itself. Very soon, we became one of the leading foreign exchange earners in tourism. In fact, when the annual award for that category was declared, we stood at number one.

The One Dollar Story

As it happened, this wasn't my only run-in with the bureaucrat, Y.T. Shah. I got another dose of his somewhat suspicious nature

Signing the Joint Agreement between Indrama & AVIS USA, Ghulam & I

and belief that he was the sole guardian of India's foreign exchange, when SITA applied for approval of a collaboration with the car rental company, Avis International.

I was able to convince Avis to give me an all-India franchise of self-drive cars at a cost of USD 1 plus profit-sharing. Prior to this and in spite of several efforts, Avis had failed to get government approval. So yet again, I found myself applying to the Ministry of Finance and dealing with Shah.

He told me point blank that a fee of 1 dollar wasn't realistic and was, in fact, some sort of fraud. He believed that I must have paid Avis something overseas. We had a heated argument during which, he came close to calling me a liar and a manipulator. I also lost my cool and said some very harsh things to him. If there is one time in my life that I was rude to a senior officer, it was then. I was hopping mad.

Embroiled in my first stand-off and that, after meeting his conditions, I asked him how he would feel, if I called him a corrupt official who was a master at creating needless hurdles. He was enraged, but finally did permit me to sign the agreement and the matter was resolved.

Unfortunately for me and the Indian travel industry, this venture couldn't take off, as self-driven rental cars were not permitted on Indian roads. Several years later, The Oberoi started the collaboration, but with chauffeur-driven cars. Self-drive cars like Avis and Hertz are still not available in India. More recently, the government has liberalized the laws and now some states including Delhi, do allow self-drive cars.

Yes, later on, Shah and I became good friends with mutual admiration for each other. In fact, SITA became his family's travel agent.

Then Came Western Union

I had better luck with Western Union. It is an interesting story in itself.

It all began when I met with the then President of Western Union at a World Economic Forum regional meeting being held in Hong Kong. Coincidentally, we both happened to be seated at the same table during break-up sessions and lunch breaks. Thrown together thus, we got into a discussion on expanding Western Union's operations to India. The gentleman had been trying to achieve this for the past three years, held some three or four meetings with Indian economic and banking authorities, but failed to get permission to start operations in India.

With typical bravado, I stuck my neck out and told him that while he may have failed in his endeavor for three years, all I wanted was twelve months to get this approval, if he gave me the franchise. So great was his frustration with the Indian bureaucracy that he offered me the franchise for USD 1, provided I got the permission in a year, as I had boasted.

I swung into action. On returning to India, I had a discussion with the concerned authorities in the Ministry of Finance and learnt that the bottleneck in this issue comprised, surprisingly, of the postal authorities and the Reserve Bank of India. With their typical mindset, the postal authorities viewed 'money transfers' as a direct encroachment of money-order transfers, which were their exclusive domain.

The Reserve Bank of India had objections because it felt that money transfer was a banking function, and as such, only banks should be authorized to conduct such activities. Both failed to see the larger picture: to understand the actual mechanics of such a legal money transfer system and the vacuum that existed for such a service. My contention was that it was an independent, legal money transaction system most suited for Indians employed abroad who wanted to send money to their families back home. Due to the foreign exchange restrictions of the day and the high prevailing rate of income-tax, most Indian workers—particularly from Kerala, Goa and Punjab—used to send money to their families through *hawala* transactions, often conducted by fraudulent and illegal touts. Sometimes, the recipients would have to wait for days to receive the money and only after the intermediaries had collected "*service charges*".

It's pertinent and relevant for me to explain exactly how Western Union operates. To put it simply, any individual, anywhere in the world—and there were thousands of franchisees spread across many countries—could just approach a Western Union outlet and send any amount of money, the minimum amount then being USD 100, to friends or relatives anywhere in the world, or vice-versa. I grant that remitting money from India to overseas during that era of foreign exchange restrictions was difficult. But receiving money in India was legitimate, legal and also good for the national exchequer.

The Western Union function was as follows:

After depositing money in the originating country, the depositor was allotted a confidential code number or a phrase, which he then passed on to the recipient. The recipient could walk into any Western Union outlet and on furnishing the code or confidential phrase, get instant cash payment without any service charge. The latter was borne by the remitter.

Let's say, if someone in New York or Dubai walked into a Western Union office and wanted to remit USD 500 to his father or wife in India. On depositing the money, he'd be provided a code name, like for instance, 'red rose'. He would then convey this telephonically or otherwise to the recipient, who would get the equivalent sum in Indian Rupees, literally within minutes.

It took me all of 12 months and several trips to the Reserve Bank of India in Mumbai, and the postal authorities in Delhi, before I achieved success and got the franchise for SITA. I got it for USD 1. I don't mind admitting to a little pride in declaring that this USD 1 was worth its weight in gold, as it paved the way for a major facilitation for Indians receiving remittances from abroad and that too legally, by the safest and fastest way and almost within minutes.

Today, there are literally thousands of Western Union outlets in India, ranging from State Bank of India branches, to major post offices and small entrepreneurs.

I consider Avis and Western Union my humble contributions to Indian tourism and the country's economy.

While on the subject of my 'contributions' to Indian tourism, I'd also like to mention the origin and history of the 'Foreign Travel Tax (FTT)', in which, I played some role.

Tax Bharo, Bhai!

G.S. Sawhney, then Chairman of the Central Board of Excise & Taxation, an official with an open, incisive mind, took a major decision that helped the Indian travel industry.

In 1971, the Government of India decided to levy an additional tax of 12.5 per cent on the value of tickets issued in India for foreign travel. Needless to say, this was a huge blow to the travel industry.

I led an industry delegation to protest against the levy, as it would be highly detrimental for Indian travel agents. We opposed the tax, but the fact was that those were the days of foreign exchange shortages and budget deficits. Every government department was seeking new avenues for additional revenue generation. Sawhney insisted that the tax would be levied. I highlighted the point that foreign airlines would get an unfair benefit from this tax. They could conveniently have Prepaid Ticket Advices issued abroad and thus avoid paying this tax. This would boil down to two distinct factors. One being that Indian agents would lose business in terms of issuing tickets for their clients and the other—that travel with Air-India would become more expensive. It would signal a death knell for Air-India and its agents. Sawhney, an experienced officer, agreed to consider the matter.

Not letting any water flow under my feet, I had three or four focused meetings with Sawhney and kept pressing my point.

It paid dividends. After discreetly checking with other sources including with the then Commercial Director of Air-India, Inder Sethi, and studying the effect on Indian agents, Sawhney decided to change the policy and instead levy a flat 'foreign travel tax' of Rupees 500 on all travel abroad and Rupees 150 for journeys to neighbouring countries.

Without sounding vain, I'd like to say that this was another of my 'humble' contributions to the travel industry.

Coming back to Y.T. Shah in the Ministry of Finance—and to his credit, we became friends. A very good example of our friendship is the manner in which we handled the travel arrangements for his wife who was travelling to Australia.

The then Government of India policy dictated that Indian travellers could only encash travellers' cheques in the country they were allowed to visit, in accordance with the infamous 'P' form. This limitation was clearly endorsed on the travellers' cheques themselves. Therefore, the cheques were only encashable in the country for which they were endorsed. This fact was endorsed on the cheques through a stamp: 'Valid only in...', thus rendering these cheques unusable anywhere else.

We in the travel trade wanted this rule amended. As chance would have it and while *en route* to Australia, Mrs. Shah got stranded in Singapore, where, she couldn't encash her TCs. She contacted her husband and he was very upset with me, since SITA had issued her air tickets and the cheques. I promptly told him that this was a 'case-in-point' of the whole issue of the restricted use of travellers' cheques. I urged him to use his good offices to allow these to be encashed everywhere. Shah agreed and it was done. That's what I call a good working relationship. It was a friendship owed to the one-dollar deals I had signed with Avis and Western Union.

While all this was going on, SITA was prospering and going from strength to strength. I think it is incumbent on me to mention our humble beginnings in Bombay, Calcutta and Madras (respectively

Mumbai, Kolkata and Chennai today). In each of those cities, we had made a small beginning and reached a certain level. Except for Mumbai, we were right at the top of the heap in all other cities.

Thanks to some diligent teamwork by my colleagues, all the offices grew in size and stature despite our humble beginnings. Several people, in fact almost 800 in all, played a pivotal role in SITA's growth. I'm deeply indebted to them till date. Our modest start featured a total staff of just four—myself, Tours Manager Atam Marwah, secretary-cum-general assistant D. Kumar and Bharat Singh, the office boy. All three were the most dedicated, loyal and hard-working colleagues. The children of all three men also worked for SITA in later years.

In the western region, our Regional Manager was Asif Dewjee, who spearheaded our growth in the region with SITA ultimately setting up offices in Mumbai, Pune and Ahmedabad.

The Kolkata Regional Manager was K.N. Kapoor, and under his leadership, SITA Calcutta became one of the top travel offices in eastern India. Kapoor expanded the activities in the eastern region by setting up service offices in Jamshedpur, Bhubaneshwar, Guwahati and an overseas collaboration in Bhutan. In the dragon kingdom, we functioned as Tashi SITA, a joint venture with one of the prominent members of the royal family.

In the north, we had offices in Srinagar, Agra, Jaipur, Kanpur, Varanasi. B.S. Ahuja was our regional in-charge for the north.

In the South, S.K. Nayar played a stellar role in making SITA a predominant travel organization with offices in Trivandrum, Cochin, Hyderabad, Secunderabad, Bangalore ("today Bengaluru") and Vellore. It was under Nayar that my son Arjun had a training stint in Chennai. Nayar was a tough taskmaster. On his first day in the office, Arjun wore Peshawari sandals to work. He was promptly sent back, as the office dress code required wearing proper shoes.

In Delhi, where the team was ably led by Bhim Ahuja, we operated out of the Imperial Hotel until 1970. Since SITA's operations were

25th year of SITA Inc in India 1956 to 1981, Jack Dengler and I

expanding, we moved our office to F-12 Connaught Place, where the ground floor area housed our retail office, while the first and second floors housed our inbound and administrative operations. After some years, we enlarged our operations again. While our Travel Division took up all three floors in the CP office, we hired additional space in Malcha Marg for our Inbound Division, which functioned under the dynamic leadership of Ghulam Naqshband and was ably supported by the marketing-savvy Avinash Anand and several other dedicated, hard-working travel experts.

At the time, SITA was growing—and growing fast.

At our peak, we had 26 offices in India, London, Frankfurt and New York, overseas representatives and three joint ventures in Nepal, Sri Lanka and Bhutan. We were truly well-represented in most SAARC countries.

The Outbound Division was ably handled by the very dynamic Kedar N. Kapoor, with excellent assistance from my daughter, Neeraj, who took full control after Kapoor's death.

Showing the SITA Flag ("I am a SITA fan")
to Jack Dengler at the ASTA conference

On the financial side, I was brilliantly supported by B.R. Kapoor and S.D. Vyas and their highly dedicated team. I've always believed that regardless of one's title at work, one should be a team-builder. All my managers were real team-builders.

It's time to admit that I mostly basked in the glory of my dedicated, selfless, hardworking team. I was the public face, the facilitator and the *Karta* of the united family that was SITA.

Several years later and after SITA was sold to Kuoni, some of these professionals became entrepreneurs in their own right and started a new travel organization, named 'Le Passage to India' (LPTI), which, in a relatively short span of time, has become a leading Indian travel company. LPTI is headed by my son Arjun, whose forte is Inbound Tourism.

Sugar is Sweet, Success Tastes 'Sweeter'

I don't mind admitting now with a lot of pride that we got just rewards for our hard work and professional excellence.

Over the years, we won several awards from airlines for being the most productive travel agency. We won the Ministry of Tourism Award for the highest foreign exchange earnings in the very first year this award was established and we won it again on several subsequent occasions.

SITA's presence was very strong, it was an identifiable and respected brand, and we were almost at the number one position in all Indian regions, except the western region. This was because the western region, notably the cities of Mumbai, Ahmedabad and Pune, had several well-established, older companies with good reputations and loyal clienteles.

But SITA did play an important role in the other three regions.

When it came to establishing new offices, we had a definite business plan. Firstly, the emphasis was on locations needed for servicing inbound tourists, our original and main business. The second criterion was a presence in the metro cities, which were source markets for corporate business travel.

However, we also had offices to service our air cargo customers. And SITA opened offices in off-beat locations too, to cater to our major corporate accounts, such as in Jamshedpur for the TATA Steel account, Kanpur for the Singhanias, Vellore for the Christian Medical College and Hospital, Secunderabad for Bhadrachalam, and so on. We expanded slowly but surely, working to ensure total profitability as a company, even if some of our offices were opened solely to service major, prestigious accounts. We attained respectability and acceptability to the point that several of our offices were officially inaugurated by governors or chief ministers of the states. The Chennai office was inaugurated by the then governor, while the chief ministers graced the occasion when those in Hyderabad, Srinagar and Bhubaneshwar were opened.

Bengaluru and Goa were inaugurated by the then union minister of tourism.

I took a similarly bold decision when it came to overseas collaborations. We established collaboration offices in Sri Lanka with John Keells, the country's largest travel and trading company. In Nepal, we worked with two enterprising individuals from the travel industry—Sharma and Khanal, while in Bhutan, our tie-up was with Tashi, one of the leading business houses of that country. All proved to be landmark decisions and made SITA a truly South Asian company.

SITA's impressive progress and rise was the result of teamwork. I am no IIM graduate, but I managed the company guided by the belief that management is basically common sense. One should listen to one's inner voice. It is better to go wrong with your own instincts than somebody else's. I was working with a homegrown start-up. So I did take risks, but one at a time. I followed the advice of my father and took my work, but not myself, seriously. Consequently, I enjoyed my work.

My father had also told me to be fair in my dealings, work relationships and of course, in life. I tried hard to be.

One needs to pay attention to employees, and to the needs and expectations of customers. I believe that most problems that surface in business can be traced back to the failure of management and leadership.

I had fun while working, I enjoyed partying and revelled in nice company.

I took risks, but one at a time. I tried to be vaguely right, rather than absolutely wrong.

When it came to servicing our customers, we were equally cons-cious of our responsibility since after all, we existed due to their patronage. We always tried to give our customers a fair price, with their interests uppermost in our minds. We never over-charged, nor undersold. We never sold airline tickets or hotel rooms at a discount.

While dealing with foreign or local customers, we provided the best available services and gave value for money. Most importantly, US consumer laws demanded an honest description of our services and we fulfilled that by virtue of our origins. This imbued in all of us the same sense of responsible behavior while dealing with our local customers.

There was to be no overselling, no superlatives to describe our services, nor any undercutting. All this paid us rich dividends, propelled SITA to a first-rate travel brand and gave us the reputation of being consumer-friendly.

I was no mercenary when it came to our profits. I always believed that '*profitability was my birthright as a businessman, but that profiteering was a sin.*'

SITA was always a profitable organization.

We adopted profit-sharing policies with our sales staff but never shared our commission earnings from hotels or airlines with the customer.

In fact, this 'commission' in the travel and tourist business was one of the reasons why I sold SITA in 2000 to Kuoni of Switzerland. Today, such conditions are unheard of. It's the era of net fares, service charges and commissions.

I was taught to protect one's good name, as an impeccable reputation takes a lifetime to build but only 60 seconds to lose.

One person who stood with me like the Rock of Gibraltar during all this time was my friend, guide and philosopher, Mohinder Puri. Technically, he was our auditor. But in reality, he was my mentor in many matters related to my business life. I relied so much on him that I ignored financial management almost totally. He did it all for me. He taught me to be totally

My Friend, Guide & Philosopher, Mohinder Puri

honest with my banker, lawyer and doctor. I owe him a lot. Sadly, he left us at a very young age. He died—literally—on the tennis courts of the Gymkhana Club. Friends like Mohinder are a rare phenomenon. Yes, phenomenon. By a sad twist of fate, I lost another friend, Ashok Prashar of Air India, too, on the Gymkhana's Squash Court.

Do you know what they say about success being a heady affair? Well, of course it can be. Nothing succeeds like success. But our very success threw us a challenge.

In my long business life, one of the most important things I did that stands out in my memory, is the formation of Indrama.

Chris Cross, the then Manager of British Airways India and his Marketing Manager, Dilip Mitra, invited Gautam Khanna, Managing Director of Mercury Travels, Nari Katgara, Director of TCI, Cyrus Guzder, Managing Director of Indtravels and Air Freight, Vinoo Ubhaykar, Managing Director of TradeWings and myself, to a meeting at the Akbar Hotel. It was an ITDC hotel which is now leased to the Ministry of External Affairs, to, among others, temporarily accommodate the South Asia University and its guest house for visiting faculty.

Chris did a thorough evaluation and announced his decision to appoint SITA as British Airways General Sales Agents for a large area in India. This created a furore and one of the biggest rifts ever in the Travel Agents Association of India, pitting me headlong against the rest of TAAI, very vociferously led by Cyrus Guzder, S. Nagarwalla, Karan Sarwal—then of Cox & Kings and, duly supported by the Katgara brothers and several other regional leaders. There was jealousy and a sense of outrage that I, a relative latecomer, had pipped them to the winning post.

Taking a decisive step, I decided to handle this business under the Indrama banner, because SITA, as an IATA recognized company, couldn't be a GSA for any one airline alone. My opponents were vociferous, insisting that I would poach on their business and divert it to SITA. In spite of my full and sincere assurances, I was neither believed nor trusted. Matters came to such a head that TAAI passed a resolution to boycott British Airways. The bad publicity that ensued hurt British Airways—not so much their business, but their pride in 'fair-play', to the extent that the then Managing Director, Sir—later Lord—Colin Marshall flew in for meetings with TAAI and me. He couldn't bring about a *rapprochement*. The result was that Colin advised me to voluntarily give up the GSA of British Airways after a few months. He wanted to save face for both sides.

I don't mind admitting that my professional pride was hurt by this unsavory situation. I challenged TAAI to mention one single incident where we had poached on anyone else's business. To our credit, not one unfair practice was pointed out of which Indrama was guilty. In spite of this, we were forced to give up this GSA position. During this time, I had some rather bitter exchanges with Cyrus Guzder, Karan Sarwal and Jimmy Nagarwalla.

The fact is that this did sour my personal relations with Guzder—whose other qualities I have always respected and admired. He is a very well-read, intelligent scion of a much respected Parsi family. His father, Jimmy Guzder, was a very likeable person and I admired him a lot. Jimmy had a keen and typically Parsi sense of humour.

The buck didn't stop there. TAAI was also able to convince Raghu Rai, then Chairman of Air-India, to withdraw Air-India's support to SITA. On his instructions, a circular was issued by Nani Mittal, a spineless commercial director of Air-India, instructing all its foreign offices not to support SITA by referring any inbound tourist business to us.

Fortunately for me, all the foreign managers privately refused to accept this directive. They took it as an insult to their independence. However, many, if not all senior Indian officials, followed these instructions.

We suffered a bit. Raghu Rai and I had some rather bitter and impolite verbal exchanges. It was unsavoury, I thought, for the Chairman of Air-India to intervene on behalf of one side, particularly when Air India had nothing to do with the issue. But SITA was, by then too important and respected a travel agency to be ignored. Our hard work, ethics and professionalism ensured that we hardly lost any business.

SITA was soon appointed sole handling agents for Orchid Holidays of Thai Airways and for SpeedBird Holidays of British Airways. All this triggered fresh protest, but we overcame all such petty-minded objections this time. It was business rivalry and we stood our ground.

SITA Outbound—Providing Easy Passage

Call it astute business sense, good training or whatever, but I had a long-term vision for SITA, and this played a role in the company's overall success.

In 1974, I acquired a 25 per cent shareholding in UP Hotels (the Clarks Group) from the Gupta family, and entered the company's Board of Directors. I worked in close cooperation with the Gupta family for a short period of time. But I soon realized that their style of working wasn't exactly what I expected of a professional company. Their approach and style was family, rather than profession-oriented. So I parted ways with the company in a graceful manner and we are still good friends.

Part of this same long-term vision for SITA was my desire to partner Thomas Cook, which, at that time, was the market leader.

Thomas Cook was weak in the inbound segment, which happened to be SITA's strength. Our asset was our network of offices. Thomas Cook's strength was foreign exchange and the business of corporate houses. It held the potential of an ideal partnership.

I started negotiations in 1979 with Ralph Kantor, Director and later with Sir John Cockney, Chairman, Thomas Cook. The negotiations went on for almost a year and the final understanding was, that Thomas Cook would first create an Indian company and

SITA would then acquire 26 per cent shares in that company. And Thomas Cook would have the same stakes in SITA, with a view to ultimately merge the two. The deal also stipulated that I would be the chairman of the Indian company, and in addition, be on the company's UK Board. This understanding was informally solemnized at a luncheon meeting at the company's London Headquarters, when I shook hands with Sir John Cockney.

In 1980, Kantor and Pradeep Madhavji, the latter then the commercial manager of Thomas Cook India and previously a banker, came for a formal meeting. In my opinion, Madhavji sabotaged the deal and it fell through. He later became head of Thomas Cook India. It's a matter of noteworthy interest that history was going to reverse itself. Ashwini Kakkar, then Chairperson of Thomas Cook India, tried to negotiate the sale of SITA to Thomas Cook in the year 2000, but once again, the deal fell through.

By now, you may have observed that I've always been a bit of a renegade in virtually all aspects of my life. My outspoken nature and somewhat carefree attitude made me speak my mind out on several occasions and ruffled several feathers. That's the way I've always been. Direct, blunt and somewhat brash. But honest—so I believe—and lucky.

> *"Pray you now, forget and forgive."*
> —**'King Lear', William Shakespeare**

Maybe I'm being a little too harsh on myself. Sure, I may have rubbed a lot of people up the wrong way, but I have no regrets, because all my statements and gestures were in response to given professional situations as they unfolded, at that particular time. They were never meant to hurt anyone at a personal level. I have hardly ever borne any personal malice towards anyone and this is true even today. I firmly believe that 'differences of opinion' should never be allowed to transcend personal relationships. Even now, I have an occasional drink with Karan Sarwal and his wife at the Delhi Gymkhana. I would often walk up at an industry function and shake hands with Cyrus Guzder. Vasant Kotak's wife Nirmala is a good friend of my wife Aruna.

If my buying SITA was a momentous, eventful and colourful story, my selling the company was equally dramatic in its own way. And also very poignant.

It's time for me to share with you the entire scenario and circumstances surrounding the sale of my beloved company, which, to me, was like a third child.

The sale of SITA in 2001 was like a particularly tempestuous episode in the long drama of my life. But to understand it, one must take the story back in time a bit.

In 1994, Hans Lerch, then Director of Kuoni, had approached me, first in a sort of roundabout manner, and then, at a lunch at the Oberoi in New Delhi. He finally posed a direct question: Would I be interested in selling SITA? At that particular moment I laughed it off as a joke. My response was: "Hans, you cannot afford to buy SITA."

This was not in monetary terms, but in terms of sentiments. SITA was like a child to me whom I had nurtured from birth.

So much for that conversation with Hans Lerch. It was soon put on the back-burner and forgotten.

Seven years later at a Delhi travel seminar, my daughter Neeraj and I happened to be chatting with Ranjit Malkani, Head of SOTC Kuoni in India. At the time, the market was rife with rumours that Kuoni was buying TCI. On the spur of the moment and in sheer jest, I mentioned to Ranjit that it was believed that they were buying TCI and if that was so, I asked why had they overlooked SITA? Believe me and I swear, at that time it was meant purely as a joke. As it happened, my 'joke' paved the way for the sale of SITA.

Ranjit immediately responded to my statement by pointing out that seven years ago, Hans Lerch had indeed approached me about purchasing SITA and that I had refused his offer.

I concurred with him. Indeed I had refused, I told Ranjit. But over these years, a lot of water had flown under the Yamuna bridge. I remarked that the travel industry and its marketing dynamics had changed dramatically.

For me, some significant changes had occurred at a personal level too, but most importantly, at a professional level.

At the personal level, I could very well foresee that my two children, Neeraj and Arjun, both—if I may say so—endowed with strong personalities and both capable of taking SITA to greater heights, may just not be able to work together as a team, because of their radically different views and personalities.

I don't want to dwell further on this subject except to mention that if they were to work as a team in any business, it would be an unbeatable combination. They have proved this in handling Select CITYWALK, our new venture in partnership with Mr. Yog Raj Arora and his family.

More importantly, I had my own personal theory and vision of the travel industry, internationally and in India. I didn't have to be a genius to foresee that the dynamics of distribution channels, systems and technology were changing the industry and would continue to do so, while the role of travel agents would diminish. Given the strong differences that had emerged between airlines and travel agents' associations in different parts of the world on the subject of reduction of agents' commissions, I could foresee a somewhat different scenario than the one that had allowed SITA to flourish.

With airlines having registered periodical loss-making years, I could foresee that the travel agent, the middle man in the marketing and distribution network, would take a hit. Airlines and their marketing staff would become more aggressive in seeking direct sales. I predicted that technology would change the entire methodology of ticketing from B2B to B2C. As such, travel agents would find themselves increasingly side-lined and their role reduced. As it happens, an agent's commission is almost negligible today. Way back then, I foresaw that big business houses would demand sharing of commissions to reduce their travel costs. I could visualize the scenario and saw that the entry of electronic ticketing would bypass agents.

In a nutshell, the travel business which, in terms of volume, accounted for almost 80 per cent of SITA's turnover, would become less remunerative. The fact is that at that stage, SITA wasn't merely a tour operator. Had it been that, changes such as these wouldn't have mattered that much. SITA was a composite organization, dealing in virtually all aspects and segments of the travel trade—air tickets, tours, rail bookings, shipping, air freight, cargo, customs-clearance, transportation, you name it. It was a truly multi-faceted, composite travel identity, and a major one at that, with 26 offices and an 800-strong workforce. Here's a quote from the minutes of SITA's Board of Directors' Annual Report of 1980, almost 20 years before the company's sale.

"The Directors felt that the future of travel and tourism is not too optimistic. In the field of travel and air-cargo, unhealthy and sometimes unethical competition is growing. There are demands of longer periods of credit by passengers and cargo customers. The cost of financing has increased and, therefore, profitability is likely to be affected. In the field of inbound tourism, the margin of profit is shrinking."

This showed the foresight of the management 20 years ahead of time. It was this scenario, firmly etched in my mind and this vision, that prompted me to consider selling SITA.

I must mention that there was another personal reason. It is *my firm belief and conviction that be it politics or business, one should quit when the curtain call is at its loudest, and not wait for 'catcalls'.*

The stage was set for a deal with Kuoni. Ranjit and I started working on a war-footing to complete all formalities and legal work within the stipulated time-frame, while keeping the whole affair a secret. I truly appreciate the graciousness shown by both Ranjit and Hans, who was by now Chairman of Kuoni, to concede to most of our demands, whether related to the price, or the future of SITA's staff. The deal was completed in the shortest possible time, and signed at the Oberoi, Mumbai in 2001.

I can be forgiven for getting a bit emotional when I disclose that all three of us, Neeraj, Arjun and I, were in tears at the signing and hugged one another. You can well imagine our feelings at that moment. I felt I had lost my third child—that is how much SITA had meant to me. I felt as though I had betrayed the trust of 800 odd employees, who over a period of 50 years, had built up one of India's finest and most respected organizations. In modern business lingo—a brand equity. I don't mind admitting to a little pride when I'm still recognized as the former owner of SITA.

That night, and for several nights later, I couldn't sleep. I felt ridden with guilt. To this day, narrating this story chokes me.

But, emotions apart, I've been proven right, both in family and business circumstances. It was the toughest of tough decisions, but I'm glad I had the courage and foresight to take it.

I also realized that maybe I was putting a roadblock in my children's lives and their careers. By sheer dint of hard work and some very bold decisions, my son Arjun achieved great success and he heads TUI and Le Passage to India, the largest inbound travel management company today.

Neeraj suffered a bit. She had quit the travel industry. It had been a hard decision, as she not only looked after SITA's internal branches but was also the first—and youngest ever—woman President of the Travel Agents' Association of India. She took a break to research and write her book on her Kailash Mansarovar trip which she left midway, to return to support me and join hands to complete the construction of Select CITYWALK.

Today, both Neeraj and Arjun along with Yogiji, supervise the management of Select CITYWALK. The day-to-day management is overseen by professionals like Yogeshwar Sharma, Shashi Sharma, Srinivas and a team of young managers. The quality of their management is reflected in the fact that for the past eight years, the Mall has won over 78 awards, including the 10th CNBC Awaaz Real Estate Award for 'The Retail Mall of the Decade', and consecutively for the past eight years, the Image's 'Most Admired Shopping Centre of the Year in India'.

Simultaneously, Neeraj also devoted time to groom her daughter into a very sensible and balanced teenager. Shreya is a national level golfer. She became the National Ladies Golf Champion and has won both the Sri Lanka and North India Golf Championships. She also led India as the Captain of the Indian Golf team to the Asian Games in China. My other granddaughter, Amaraah, is a skiing gold medalist. With two such talented grandchildren, what more can one ask for?

In their own way, both Neeraj and Arjun are remarkable children and I thank God for His blessings. God and my Guruji have been more than kind to Aruna and me.

6 | The Travel Industry: Playing Field, Battlefield

As you can see, my professional life virtually revolved around SITA. First, by joining it as an employee. Then, by climbing up the ladder. Next, by buying the Indian part of the company and running it for 45 years. And finally, by selling it on 23rd March 2001 and bowing out of the hardcore travel business.

While SITA India was my company and of course my business mainstay, I was, nevertheless, very aware of what was going on around me and intensely involved with the travel industry, both in India and overseas.

SITA India had been established on 23rd March, 1955.

In the mid-50s, L.K. Jha, Economic Secretary, had talked about the travel industry's 'multiplier effect' and its various benefits to the nation. When I was made to read the paper by Som Chib in the late fifties, it triggered my interest. In the years that ensued, I began to understand what it meant.

For instance, I became a great advocate of the Tourism Satellite Accounting (TSA) system. The TSA is a standard statistical framework and one of the main devices for measuring the economic effects of tourism. The only officer who supported me on this issue was senior bureaucrat, Amitabh Kant. Kant is the author of a successful book and was the key brains behind the 'Incredible India' and 'God's Own Country' campaigns which branded India and Kerala as leading tourism destinations respectively. It is not a joke but absolutely true that one Director-General, Tourism asked me: "Inder, why use a satellite to prepare tourism statistics when we are already doing so manually with almost 90% near-accuracy?" I just laughed and walked away.

To start with and like many at the time, I thought international tourism was a luxury industry, catering mainly to elite Americans and Europeans. I felt it was purely elitist. And domestic tourism did not figure anywhere in my scheme of things either. When I joined SITA, my perception broadened a bit. I began to understand tourism's importance for the preservation of culture, heritage, arts, etc. and its huge scope for creating employment.

However, in those days, the main issue was tourism's capacity to earn foreign exchange. In 1953, India's share in world tourism was less than 0.04% and stayed at about the same level for several years. Even in 2013 and as per United Nations World Tourism Organization (UNWTO) figures, our share was only 4.1% and 5.1% for international tourist arrivals and international tourism receipts respectively. It was distinguished and eminent people like S.N. Chib, S.K. Misra, Billo Goswami, Nitish Sen Gupta and Vinod Duggal, to name a few, who helped me realize the true importance of the tourism industry. I learnt to look beyond mere numbers and dollars. My subsequent international experience with global organizations like the Pacific Asia Travel Association (PATA), the World Association of Travel Agencies (WATA) and others, educated me further.

Ralph Waldo Emerson had said, *"Though we travel the world over to find the beautiful, we must carry it with us or we find it not."*

By the time I left the industry in 2001, I think it is reasonable to say that I had a fair amount of experience. I could articulate the true importance of travel and tourism. *This industry gave me a broad perspective beyond mere numbers, it taught me that mere numbers mean nothing. It is the number of tourists multiplied by the nights spent in a destination and further multiplied by the amount of money spent per night, which matters.*

Of course and in the final analysis, what ultimately matters is what all this does to the host economy and its tourism assets. Our mute monuments are our treasures and true reflections of our living culture and social fibre. Yet, the entire emphasis was on international tourism, with nobody taking domestic tourism seriously. The millions who travel for holidays and on pilgrimages were never mentioned. Partially, this was due to the fact that at that time, earning foreign exchange was of paramount importance.

I was ambitious and wanted to be in the limelight. I had a desire to learn and tourism turned out to be a good teacher. It definitely taught me a lot about human nature, most importantly, the expectations of one's customers. I soon learnt that tourism is show business and all the players, be they individuals or corporations or, the state itself, are all on stage primarily to show off. It is all about fulfilling an individual's curiosity—his desire to explore and in a few cases, to learn.

During this period, the very structure of the travel industry had changed. What was once elitist in nature was now no longer so.

Today, tourism around the world is basically an open house with millions of tourists and literally thousands of intermediaries. Of course, this broadening of the base is a good thing because the industry is a means of livelihood for millions across India too.

As estimated by organizations like the World Travel & Tourism Council (WTTC) and the Pacific Asia Travel Association (PATA), millions of Indians have—either directly or indirectly—found work due to tourism. For the purist, the 'quality' of tourism may have suffered in this process. But there is no denying that the quantity has increased. In this aspect, the role of industry associations is also important. These represent the collective view and wisdom.

The first such travel association that I joined was the Travel Agents Association of India (TAAI).

TAAI—A Story of Ageing Warriors

When it comes to my professional life, you might say I've had a long and strong association with associations. It has been enduring and endearing, certainly with some setbacks, but mostly satisfying. I have always, right from my student days, enjoyed taking active part in associations, be these cultural or professional.

I had a long and somewhat eventful relationship with TAAI. Having attended over 40 conventions, I feel I'm entitled to freely and frankly comment and pass an opinion on this Association. Like for all chroniclers of history and particular events, this is *my* version of what transpired. I am sure some will disagree and others will endorse my observations and views. It is history as this 'historian' sees it. But then, isn't historical narrative always so? Take the Indian uprising of 1857. For the English, it was mutiny. But for Indian historians, it was a battle for freedom.

To begin with, TAAI concentrated more on tourism-related issues than on travel, both international and domestic, though matters relating to airlines' commissions structures did feature at most annual conventions.

I'd like to go back to my first TAAI conference in 1957 in Jaipur. I was still a newcomer to the industry and quite a greenhorn. This convention is one I distinctly remember, particularly an incident involving two respected gentlemen.

It so happened that Shyam Poddar, owner of the Orient Express, and Gautam Khanna, Managing Director, Mercury Travels, fell out over some small issue and developed personal differences. Gautam was always a teaser and Shyam a sensitive, self-made man. As a result of their differences, Shyam resigned from TAAI, taking some of us by surprise. Personally, I felt this was not good for the image of the Association. So I am happy to report that several years later, I was instrumental in convincing Shyam to rejoin the Association. Such incidents are considered trivial, but I believe they have an important bearing on the health of the industry. Sometimes, all it takes is a little individual effort to massage some egos and tide things over, if only to ensure overall good for the industry.

The next conference was in 1959 in Mussoorie, when Gautam Khanna was the President. TAAI had the honour of welcoming Prime Minister Jawaharlal Nehru to the meet. People of my generation would know, that Mr. Nehru hardly ever wrote or prepared his speeches. He used to speak extempore. And what an orator he was.

I thought it significant that the sum total of his observations was, surprisingly, that tourism was not a core economic activity, but a peripheral one. PM Nehru was more philosophical than specific. "This is a free country and foreign visitors can go where they like", he said, adding that "he could not understand why travel agents want to organize their trips and wrap them up in cotton wool." While studying at Cambridge in 1910, a time when a voyager did not even need a passport to traverse frontiers, it is true that Nehru himself had travelled in that fashion. But though times have changed drastically, it is unfortunate that this view prevails to a great extent in some quarters, even today.

It was not until 1960, at the Darjeeling Conference under the Presidentship of Allan Currimbhoy, the head of Tradewings, that I started taking an active and somewhat vociferous part in the convention's proceedings. In particular, I remember one conversation with Allan, a wonderful, tall, US-educated gentleman with great understanding and human qualities.

After a reception at the Darjeeling Club, we took a walk to the Mount View Hotel. (Incidentally, the hotel later burnt down and never rebuilt by the Oberois. I still wonder why.) Allan's first advice to me was: "Mere loud talk isn't enough. There should be substance in what you say." Being young and brash, I told him in my typically forthright manner, that the way in which I speak was my normal style which had evolved in that way, because I had been actively involved in college politics. And that, as we all know, politics is all about talking a lot. Whether I convinced Allan or not, I don't know. The fact is that I was young, extremely carefree in my outlook and always quick on the trigger.

The Darjeeling conference gave me some confidence and turned out to be a handy and useful curtain-raiser for me. I began to articulate my thoughts and take active part in the deliberations of TAAI, both at regional and national level. In the beginning, I was in awe of stalwarts like Allan Currimbhoy, Jimmy Guzder of Air Freight, Nari Katgara of Jeena & Co., Gautam Khanna of Mercury Travels and Vinoo Ubhayakar of Asiatic Travels, all of whom except Vinoo, were owners of their companies, while I was—a mere employee.

In due course of time, I became President of the Northern Region and in 1961, a member of the TAAI Managing Committee. Jimmy Guzder was the President.

At Madras TAAI with Sardar Ujjal Singh, Governor of Tamil Nadu, Nari Katgara, Parikh & I

One incident springs to mind. At that time, many prominent members of the TAAI Managing Committee were from the western region. Consequently, most conversations took place in

Gujarati—at least, the heated ones. It so happened once that an argument broke out and a few choice expletives were heard. I was shocked. After the meeting, I went up to Vasant Kotak and brought this to his notice. He was quite amused and told me this was normal Bombay/Parsi talk, and nothing serious. That there was something in it that even a Punjabi could learn!

There can be endless debate about the success of TAAI meetings. Personally, I feel that the success of any meet depends on whether it manages to fulfill its objectives or not. At several annual conferences, very relevant topics pertaining to travel and tourism were discussed. Many issues were raised and debated, some were resolved, some continued to defy solution. Topics such as—"Domestic Tourism: a Sleeping Giant" (in 1977), "Optimising Foreign Exchange Earnings" (in 1987) and "Tourism is Export" (in 1996) are but a few examples of very crucial issues of those times. This clearly illustrates how TAAI was at the forefront of many aspects of tourism and concentrated on key and relevant subjects, a concerted focus for which many ministers, officials and other travel organizations later claimed credit.

Convention in Kathmandu: My tenure as President of TAAI was an eventful and important phase in my career. There was no shortage of drama.

At the meet held in Kathmandu in 1969, I was told that there was a certain protocol involved and that TAAI must recognize and greet members of the Nepal royal family, when they arrived at the meet. The family had interest in hotels like Soaltee, Annapurna, travel agencies like Yeti Travels and others. Some of the royals were involved in the tourism business. The million-dollar question was: How was I to recognize them? A special signal was thought of. I was told that a local gentleman, Jyoti Khanna, was willing to stand at the door with a red handkerchief to give me a warning. The red handkerchief was to be the signal that a member of the royal family had arrived. It was all quite simple. As it happened, one of our own members who was standing near the door accidentally

Introducing H.H. Prince of Nepal to Vasant Kotak, Vinoo,
Pesi Master, Welinker at TAAI KTM

took out his handkerchief, without knowing about the 'signal'. It
was also red. This is it, I thought and promptly announced the
arrival of His Royal Highness. In fact, there had been no princely
arrival at that moment. And I, was the cause, for much mirth at
that meeting.

Also during the Kathmandu meet, His Majesty, King Mahendra,
very graciously hosted a reception for the delegates. I did not
know whether liquor would be served at the reception, so I did
what I thought was the smart thing to do. I had two quick ones
on my own. Though I got slightly tipsy, I just about made it to the
reception in time. As TAAI President, I was asked to introduce the
important delegates to His Majesty. His Majesty was in a special
room while all the delegates were in the main hall. It meant my
repeatedly going out, picking up a few delegates and escorting
them in to introduce to His Majesty. There was a mad rush to
shake hands with the King so I thought the best thing would be,
to request him to come out and mingle with all the delegates. His

Majesty was a very gracious, informal and polite host. He agreed, very happily. But while making this request and urging him to the outer hall, I had touched his elbow. My touching the royal elbow turned into a protocol issue. Next morning, I was reprimanded by Shri Raj Bahadur, our then Ambassador to Nepal, for this act of discourtesy. In Nepal the monarch was considered an *Avatar*, the reincarnation of Lord Shiva, and so could not be touched by mere mortals.

At the Delhi Convention in 1973 and under the Presidency of Mr. L.G. Ramamurthi, TAAI invited the Deputy Prime Minister, Morarji Desai. The Association was hoping that tourism would be declared an export industry and accorded the same tax incentives and other fiscal benefits as the export sector. However, things didn't exactly go according to plan.

Desai was somewhat of a 'no-nonsense man' and didn't mince his words. He almost shouted at the gathering and asked which 'tangible goods' were being exported by the tourism sector. He declared that tourism was not even an 'industry' and that therefore no concessions could be given to it. He felt that tourism existed only for the rich and didn't cater to the poor. These were his views, and he articulated them in his usual, blunt and strong manner and with the full weight of his authority as Deputy Prime Minister.

People may accuse me of being the 'judge, jury and hangman', but I'd like to proclaim loud and clear that for a very long time, justice had not been done to the tourism industry. It's a deplorable fact and a rather sad state of affairs, but as it happens, the industry got its due recognition as an export industry only in 1998 when my daughter, Neeraj was the TAAI President.

Tourism has been a major foreign exchange earner, but also a very large employment generator. In 2013, it was estimated to have created one in every eleven jobs as per WTTC statistics and directly and indirectly, a total of 266 million jobs worldwide.

We at SITA did our bit. After Morarji's speech, SITA took out three advertisements that, according to us, were pertinent to the situation on hand. The advertisements had very catchy headings. One ran: 'Imports That Earn Foreign Exchange'. The second showed a minaret of the Taj Mahal as a chimney, and was titled 'Tourism: A Smokeless Industry'. A third ran: 'A Past that Pays for Our Future'. These ads were designed by Mr. Suhel Seth, a name to be reckoned with in the field of advertising today.

All these advertisements were suitably illustrated. These ads were more than just ads. They were strong statements of facts, illustrating the benefits of tourism. Unfortunately and like most true, strong statements, they were largely ignored by the 'powers-that-be'.

It is human nature to jump onto centrestage and take credit. A lot of people, particularly in the government, take credit for various initiatives. Yes, there were certainly several initiatives by the Ministry of Tourism, which was always very supportive. But true genius lay in the memorandums submitted by the industry itself.

I must also give credit where it is due. Often, sympathetic senior officials did encourage the industry to raise some points so that they could initiate action. There has always been a good relationship between the industry and the department of tourism. But as I said, not all bureaucrats and ministers took up cudgels on behalf of the industry. Some ministers like Purshotam Kaushik, could not even understand what marketing meant. He barely understood selling.

TAAI and FHRAI addressed issues that were of importance to their members and to the industry as a whole.

Today TAAI has lost its relevance as the chief voice of Indian tourism, and it is IATO and the PATA India Chapter that are at the forefront. In different ways, they all serve the industry.

'United We Fall, Divided We Stand'

At the risk of sounding prosaic, I do feel that this sub-heading is one good way of summing up and describing the Indian travel industry. I've always felt that a collective and joint effort would have achieved much more for all segments, than was actually achieved. But then, as we all know, unity has never been a strong point with us Indians. Usually two Indians have three opinions, whereas three Japanese have one opinion.

Talking of divisions, I must mention one particular incident, or rather, situation.

Bobby Kooka, Air India's Commercial Director and an icon in his own right, felt that the Indian travel industry was talking in different voices. So he and Chib, the then DG Tourism, decided to take matters in their hands and do something constructive.

The fact is that travel agents and hoteliers had their own agendas and demands. In those days, earning foreign earnings was the main issue for the entire travel industry. Agents said that they earned 100 per cent of the foreign exchange emanating from tourism, while hoteliers claimed the same. Both Chib and Kooka decided to bring the two segments together. So a joint Travel Agents Association of India and Federation of Hotel & Restaurants Association of India meet, a 'historic' event you might say, was held in Srinagar.

Several important industry members attended the meet. They included JRD Tata, Knut Hammarskjold, Director-General IATA, Marvin Plake, Head of PATA and leading hoteliers and travel agents. Unfortunately, the meet failed, as we could not bridge the differences. Agents wanted full credit for the foreign exchange earned as they were the first recipients of the same, while hoteliers wanted hotels to get the credit for 90% of the earnings, conceding only 10% for the travel agents. Both sides could never see eye-to-eye.

That fact speaks for itself. This crucial standoff and this state of affairs of the industry haven't changed much. In fact, the situation has become significantly worse today, given that there is a plethora of associations of hoteliers, travel agents and tour operators.

On a lighter note, I'd like to narrate an incident during that meet, involving my good, senior friend, the irrepressible Late Ram Pershad of Ambassador Hotel, Delhi.

In his typically direct manner, Ram asked the Chair, Mr. Vasant Kotak, who was then President of TAAI, to define the difference between an 'agent' and a *dalal*. With my wits about me, I spoke up and told him that it was actually quite simple. If the principals are 'respectable', we were their 'agents' and if they are of the *kotha* variety, we were their *dalals*. There was laughter all around.

Since that day, I called Ram Pershad 'Sir' and he called me 'Guruji'. Incidentally we were the Co-Chairmen at that particular convention.

In my life, I have committed many blunders. Some, of course, were very small in nature, while others were more impactful. One of those I committed within TAAI was to challenge the supremacy of the western region, which resulted in my fighting an election for the post of TAAI President in 1979. I had already served three successful terms and yet decided to oppose Pesi Master, a thorough gentleman, who deserved to be the president. On that occasion, I was being plain greedy and self-centered. We both got an equal number of votes and Vinoo Ubhayakar, the gentleman that he was, refused to cast his casting vote as President. This division actually had the whole of the western region pitted against the other three regions. Pesi withdrew.

Later I felt my behaviour had been unbecoming and regretted it deeply. I apologised to Pesi. The fact is that while he had acted like a gentleman, I had been petty. That was the long and short of it.

As TAAI grew in stature to become an important body both for tourism and travel-related fields, it was increasingly sought after. Everybody scrambled to be part of it. In 1988, there was a demand from tour operators to be made voting members. The TAAI criteria for membership stated that active membership was open only to those companies that were recognized by at least two of the following: IATA, Indian Airlines, the Railways, the Tourism Department and the Passport Office. The tour operators said they did not need to be recognized by any of these bodies except for the Ministry of Tourism. But TAAI was opposed to the prospect of tour operators becoming active TAAI members with voting rights. There was an undercurrent of tension and of personality clashes.

As a responsible member of TAAI, I wanted to contribute my bit towards this important issue, and believe me, it certainly was an important issue. I felt that tour operators had a point. Using my rather copious persuasive powers, I was able to convince Ram Kohli—later one of the founders and president of IATO—to cooperate. To his credit, he accompanied me to Bombay to meet the TAAI President in order to try to resolve this issue. The likes of Vinoo and Gautam also supported the cause of tour operators. But the western region and the then President, Mahender Sanghi and later Vinod Kothari, didn't agree.

I believe this was a defining moment in the history of the Indian travel industry. If TAAI had agreed to take in tour operators as voting members, perhaps IATO would have never been formed. Similarly, the Travel Agents Federation of India (TAFI) may have also not been conceived, if TAAI had accepted agents not recognized by IATA as members.

TAFI was born because some hypocritical TAAI members, who, though themselves discounting and acting as consolidators for smaller agents, opposed the membership of non-IATA consolidators and agents indulging in discounting.

In this way, the hypocrisy and the narrow-mindedness of the TAAI leadership of the time, led to the creation of these two organizations that are, today, probably more relevant than TAAI itself.

One day, when the history of the Indian travel industry is chronicled, these facts will be significant.

You might call it protectionism, lack of foresight or anything you want to, but this is how the situation unfolded. While TAAI has undisputed status in the tourism sector, I feel it lost out to IATO, which has become the voice of tour operators handling foreign clients. Similarly, TAFI is as important as TAAI, if not more. To put it bluntly, I feel TAAI is on the decline. *According to me, those who do not learn from the past, and those who live in the past, both have no future.*

At a personal level, I was a very proud father when my daughter, Neeraj Ghei, became the youngest TAAI President from 1997–1999, the only woman to achieve such a distinction so far. That apart, her conduct and handling of this important assignment is a matter of joy, satisfaction and pride to me. Similarly, my son Arjun was elected Chairman of the World Travel Tourism Council, India and also President of IATO.

There is an abundance of travel organizations today, all supposedly representing different aspects of the industry. There is the Domestic Tour Operators' Association, there is Adventure Tour Operators and there is yet another for handling conferences, conventions and meetings. I wonder whether they all serve their purpose or, whether there is, at times a duplication and at others, a conflict of ideas. Or, perhaps these groups merely provide for many more individuals to call themselves presidents and secretaries.

Be that as it may, there is an urgent need for an umbrella organization—a united voice of and for, the entire tourism industry, something along the lines of what Bobby Kooka and Chib had envisaged. It is only then that politicians, government officials and society as a whole, will recognize the importance of this industry.

One, that could perhaps be an all-encompassing Federation of Indian Travel. The abbreviation 'FITT' would be an appropriate acronym, if you consider that FAITH was formed to resolve tourism industry issues and that its core member associations consist of FHRAI (Federation of Hotel and Restaurant Associations of India), HAI (Hotel Association of India), IATO (Indian Association of Tour Operators), TAAI (Travel Agents Association of India), TAFI (Travel Agents Federation of India), ADTOI (Association of Domestic Tour Operators of India), ICPB (India Convention Promotion Bureau) and IHHA (Indian Heritage Hotels Association). As things stand, the ITTA (Indian Tourist Transporters Association) may still not be fully fit to take on the myriad problems that the industry is confronted with.

7 | PATA: An Umbrella Association

During the course of my career, I've had a long association with associations.

The first one that I joined was Caravan, where Ghulam Naqshband was very active. This was when I was in my last year of high school. Pamela Mountbatten was the Patron.

An undoubted highlight for me was my close association with PATA (Pacific Asia Travel Association), which, at that time, was considered a unique and very important body for the travel industry.

As in most cases and just like historians, I have my own interpretation of events that may vary from those of others. So and with my apologies, here are my recollections and my version.

SITA India joined PATA in 1964. I was the designated representative of SITA India. Before that, I used to attend as a representative of SITA-USA. Like many others in the industry, my sole objective then was to make business contacts and seek business both at the Travel Marts and the Conventions. And indeed PATA turned out to be very useful for business in those days. Today, and since I have retired from the active travel business, PATA is more like an Old Boys' Club for me and my wife, Aruna. We have several good and close friends from all over the world whom we enjoy meeting. Friends like Chuck Gee, Dean Emeritus of the School of Travel Industry Management at the University of Hawaii, Tan Chee Chye from Singapore, Tunku Iskandar from Malaysia, Gloria Henderson from Honolulu and many others.

PATA's earlier avatar, PITA, was formed at a meeting held in Honolulu in 1952. It was attended by 87 delegates, mostly from Hawaii and other Pacific areas. At that time, the Association was christened the Pacific Interim Travel Association—PITA. To begin with, the geographical boundaries of PITA were made up of only the Pacific Rim countries. Its main purpose was to attract mainland American tourists to destinations like Honolulu, Japan and the Pacific Region.

Shyam Poddar of Orient Express had missed the Honolulu meeting because his PanAm flight was delayed, otherwise an Indian would have also been the signatory to the formation declaration that was filed with the authorities.

In March 1953 and at a conference held in Hawaii, its name was changed to encompass the entire Asian Region. It was now to be called the 'Pacific Asia Travel Association', PATA for short.

It was much later that PATA's annual conferences became enlarged industry conclaves, where seminars were held and important industry matters discussed. From a body that focused mainly on the Pacific Area, PATA had now become a great organization, an invaluable source of tourism information and a major and important platform for the travel industry.

My involvement with PATA also spawned in me a certain respect for the Association. It is unique and differs from other organizations in that it is one of the very few with members from not just one, but virtually all segments of the travel and tourism industry. National tourism boards, airlines and shipping companies, travel agents, tour operators, hotels, service providers like convention centers, credit card companies, educational institutions and many others are allied to PATA. It is a comprehensive representation of the entire industry and addresses issues faced by all segments. Among the several great assets of the organization have been its various educational programs, task forces and lately, its statistics division. PATA Meets and Travel Marts have proved to be very beneficial for all branches of the industry.

Started in 1978, the PATA Travel Marts are among the body's most successful activities, living up to their high-utility status, especially for ASEAN countries. With the industry now broad-based, there are many more such events, but the PATA Marts were trendsetters, continued to play a major role in tourism and for a few years, contributed handsomely towards PATA's revenues. Gerry Picolla made the PATA Travel Mart a great success in the entire Pacific region.

Two Marts have been held in Delhi—in 1966 and 1993—and a third in Hyderabad in 2008. Bangalore hosted the last one in September 2015.

I don't think I'm being outlandish in stating that in one way or the other, India always makes 'news'. A case in point is India's entry into PATA; an eventful affair in itself, and a part of history worth knowing. A great deal of effort and lobbying went into this, and in the end, it was a close affair. India was then not eligible as a member-state, because we are geographically located outside the originally demarcated area of the Pacific Ocean countries, which determined the original boundaries of PATA.

It was at the Sydney Conference in 1964, and basically owing to the efforts and initiative of people like Som Chib, then DG Tourism and Bobby Kooka, then Commercial Director of Air India, that we managed to become members. Our membership was approved by a single vote.

That single vote, too, has an interesting tale around it.

Ram Pershad, whose company was only the GSA of Egypt's United Arab Airlines (EgyptAir from 1971 onwards), cast his vote as a representative of that airline in the absence of the airline's official delegate. That did the trick and India was officially elected as a member.

While India's entry was a matter of great joy and satisfaction to the entire national travel industry, it was especially significant because it also meant that PATA eventually enlarged its geographical membership base to include the Indian sub-continent in 1974. This was a major step, and one with clear implications.

Countries like Burma, Bangladesh, Sri Lanka, Pakistan, and later even Afghanistan, became eligible for membership because of India's entry.

Some individuals of PATA deserve a place in my personal 'Hall of Fame'.

There was Marvin Plake, who played a significant role in laying the foundation of PATA. Plake was a firm man with rigid views. Another gentleman to play a key role in the body was Ken Chamberlain, who broad-based and liberalized PATA and brought other segments into its fold. They both served as Executive Vice Presidents of PATA. Another PATA staff member I must single out for credit is Gerald Picolla, or Gerry as he was called, who as a Director of PATA, enlarged the PATA Marts and made them very meaningful and significant events. In recent years, John Kowadsky provided PATA with a useful statistical base. His forecasts are fairly accurate. But his talents, in my opinion, have not been fully appreciated by many. Sheila Leong was another key staff member—helpful, patient and very hardworking.

My active involvement in PATA grew when I was first elected to the Board of Directors, and then later in 1993, as its President. The current equivalent designation is Chairman, while the President is the CEO and a paid member of the staff.

I won't deny the fact that becoming the first Indian President of PATA wasn't just an important milestone in my professional life, but also one that gave me a sense of great satisfaction and pride. In Honolulu, I had the privilege of inviting no less a person than Margaret Thatcher as a keynote speaker.

As part of the preparation for the Meet, we had been looking for a keynote speaker. The initial names suggested included the former President of the Soviet Union, Mr. Mikhail Gorbachev and the former President of Sony, both of whom normally demanded a hefty fee for speaking at such forums. The hosts, Hawaii and PATA, didn't have such funds.

I suggested we invite Mrs. Thatcher and asked my dear friend, Sir Colin Marshall, later Lord Marshall, then the Managing-Director of British Airways, to approach her. Colin tracked her down and contacted her. Thatcher agreed to come.

I then asked Colin if BA would fly Mrs. Thatcher down to Honolulu. Colin agreed.

But after receiving Thatcher's commitment, Colin told me that she charged a hefty fee for such events and that PATA would have to pay. I told him that PATA had no money to do so and that BA would have to.

Colin was shocked, saying that he had presumed PATA would pay. But now, he had invited her and she had accepted. The die was cast. The question of payment hadn't figured at all. As a good friend, he agreed to my request and finally declared that British Airways would fly her to Honolulu. I don't know if BA also paid her fees or not, but Mrs. Thatcher was personally escorted to Honolulu by Lord King, then Chairman of British Airways.

Let's face it. It isn't every day in one's life that one gets to meet and spend some time with someone of Mrs. Thatcher's status. I was very honoured. Contrary to her reputation of being an Iron Lady, I found her very unassuming and unpretentious. Over a very pleasant, one-on-one breakfast meeting with her, I answered all her queries about PATA and filled her in on all relevant details. We even discussed Indian politics, and politicians, about whom she was not only well-informed but had her own strong—and not necessarily very flattering—views.

To say that I enjoyed and cherished my tenure as President of PATA is an understatement. One of the major landmarks and achievements, where I played an important role was the entry of the People's Republic of China as a full member—without Taiwan having to resign under Chinese pressure.

Taiwan was already a full member of good standing. But the People's Republic of China had made it a condition that Taiwan, that was listed as 'Republic of China' in the PATA Roster, must be expelled. There was strong support for Taiwan within PATA. Taiwan was an active member and had always been very supportive of the organization. It was an effort to find a solution, whereby the People's Republic of China could become a member without losing Taiwan.

The solution was found. It was resolved to list Taiwan as Chinese Taipei instead of 'Republic of China'. Joop Ave, the then Minister of Tourism of Indonesia, my successor as President of PATA and a good personal friend, used all his diplomatic channels to convince both the countries. Stanley Yen, a very well-respected gentleman and another close, personal friend in the Taiwan hospitality industry, convinced his government not to resign.

To persuade PRC, I had to make two trips at my own expense, to talk to Chairman Li, of the China National Tourism Corporation. It was at a meeting held in Monte Carlo that the negotiations finally attained fruition.

Immediately after the meeting and with tears in his eyes, my dear friend Stanley handed in his personal resignation, as he felt Taiwan had been let down. But the Government of Taiwan continued as a member. What could have become a crisis was amicably resolved, thanks to my friend Stanley's magnanimous nature.

China is one of the biggest supporters of PATA today.

Troubled Waters

There was hardly a time when there wasn't a ripple or two in the waters.

During my tenure, a crisis brewed. It had to do with India hosting a PATA Travel Mart.

Picolla, staff director in charge of the Mart, and no great admirer of India, threatened to resign unless the venue of the Mart was not shifted away from Delhi. His contention was that the venue, the Indira Gandhi Stadium, was not of international standards. He was not wrong, but it was a matter of prestige for me and the Ministry of Tourism.

As a person who has spent virtually his whole life in the travel business, I'd like to proclaim loudly and clearly that when it comes to national interests, the travel industry is second to none.

When the Delhi Mart's future became uncertain, naturally, neither I, as President of PATA, nor any of my Indian colleagues in the industry, were going to just sit back and allow this to happen. We rolled up our sleeves and swung into action.

Yogesh Chandra was the Director-General of Tourism at that time. The then Cabinet Secretary, Raja Gopalan, was an alumnus of Hindu College, and had been junior to me. Together, we three forged a powerful team. We used our good offices to put pressure on the Ministry of External Affairs to lobby with the member-governments not to support the cancellation. I did the same with other industry voting members. The effort worked and the Mart was held at the Indira Gandhi Stadium in Delhi. The venue itself wasn't in a state of preparedness for the event, but it was spruced up at the intervention of the Cabinet Secretary and the then DG Tourism. Thanks to our teamwork, the Mart was a success.

Then, there were other stand-offs.

At the international level, Doug Fyfe, the Deputy Tourism Minister of Canada, had an argument with me at the Hong Kong Conference and walked out of the meeting, threatening to pull Canada out of PATA. As they say, one is always wiser after an event, and so it was with me. I realised that Doug did, indeed, have a point, and that I and Lakshman Ratnapala, the then Executive Director, had been rather authoritative, if not downright dictatorial, in our dealing with him.

While acknowledging this at the end of my year as President, I gave Doug the annual President's Award. I felt he had taught me a good lesson on how to conduct international meetings at an organization of such diversified membership.

PATA Manila, 1983: Thanking Imelda Marcos
at the Presidential Palace on behalf of PATA

At the Manila meeting held some years later, he returned the favor. He gave me the President's Award for my continuous efforts at PATA. In doing so he said that like me, he had also learned how to conduct himself among equals in an international meet. We became the best of friends.

To my great honour and privilege, I also received the PATA Life Membership Award in 1995, being then only the second Indian— after Nari Katgara—from the industry to be honoured thus.

India's membership at PATA also had a significant impact on the Indian travel industry as a whole. Till the PATA India Chapter was set up in 1974, most Indian travel associations such as TAAI, IATO, FHRAI, etc. were sectoral by nature. The PATA India Chapter not only brought all the industry segments together, but also involved in a very direct fashion, the Ministry of Tourism both at the central and state level. This was a very significant change and welcome development.

Incidentally, another 'first' for me was being elected Chairman of the PATA India Chapter. This was thanks to the statesmanship of S.K. Misra, (Chappy to his friends) then Secretary, Tourism. I was and still am, the only person from the private sector to hold this position. In the normal course, it is always either the Secretary or Director-General Tourism, who are Chapter Presidents.

My Dear Friend Mr. S.K. Misra

Whenever PATA's Board of Directors met, I always tried to do something special, something unusual for my friends. The first trip that I organized was to Rajasthan. They visited Jaipur, Ajmer, Jodhpur and travelled right up to the Pakistan border. On a full moon night, they were regaled with music, dance and festivities by local artistes and spent the night in the desert in tents. They all talk about that trip even today. Unfortunately I could not accompany them as I was unwell, but my wife Aruna did, and told me how much everybody enjoyed themselves and how grateful they were. Ever since then and whenever there is a major PATA event in India, I organize such excursions to unusual places for these leaders of PATA and their spouses.

Our next such trip was to the languid backwaters of Kerala, where the hotel we stayed in put on a terrific and professional show of Indian hospitality. This time, we arranged a mock Hindu wedding of all the couples. The ladies wore *sarees* and the men *kurta-pyjamas*, some even trying *dhotis*. Those who were "married" by the priest around a holy fire were Sue and John Rowe from Australia, Gloria and Hal Henderson from Honolulu and Millie and Tan Chee Chye from Singapore. They immensely enjoyed the ceremony and the cocktail reception that followed. I was the acting father of all the bridegrooms and Aruna the acting mother to all the brides. It was great fun.

The next trip we organized was to Punjab and Himachal Pradesh and the participants were again the Rowes, the Hendersons, the Chyes, Maneesah and Tunku Iskandar (popularly known as TI) from Malaysia and Aruna and myself. We travelled to Amritsar, the former princely states of Kapurthala and Patiala in Punjab, and finally to Shimla, the former summer capital of British India (and now that of Himachal Pradesh). At the Golden Temple in Amritsar, there were sobering moments. I narrated the terrible story of the Jalianwalla Bagh massacre and my friends were aghast at General Dyer's ordering the firing and killing of so many innocent people. That wanton massacre was avenged some years later by Shaheed (Martyr) Udham Singh, who had been greatly influenced by Shaheed Bhagat Singh. On March 13, 1940, Udham Singh shot and killed Gen. Dyer.

On one evening, we took the group to the Indo-Pak Wagah border to witness the thunderous closing-of-the-gate ceremony. They were so enthused by the latter that T.I. and Chye decided to recommend holding a similar ceremony on the Singapore/Malaysia border to their respective governments. Then, there was dinner at the famous *Bhrawan da dhaaba* of Amritsar. They enjoyed the *dal makhni, tandoori paranthas* and other vegetarian delicacies. Shimla was the pinnacle of that trip. There, they stayed at Wildflower Hall, the former summer residence of the British chiefs of army, enjoyed Shimla's balmy weather, witnessed a cultural programme at the Gaiety Theater on Shimla's famous Mall and then dropped in at the former Viceregal's Lodge, now the Cecil Hotel. They were awed to learn that this is where Rai Bahadur Mohan Singh Oberoi had begun his working life, after mortgaging and selling his wife's jewellery.

Currently, PATA is emerging from a period of crisis and is trying to restructure itself to meet the new challenges and requirements of its membership. These are necessitated by the changed circumstances and the manner in which business information is now distributed. In fact, technology has changed the entire distribution network. Business is now being conducted more and more with the help of the electronic media. As an old-fashioned marketing man, I still feel that one-on-one personal contacts will never lose their relevance. But I do wish that PATA Marts were organized with the same enthusiasm as those originally undertaken by Gerald Picolla, who was the V.P. Marketing. The first ever PATA Travel Mart held in Manila in 1978, was a huge success.

During my professional career I have been involved with several other industry associations, such as the American Society of Travel Agents (ASTA), whose Indian chapter I headed as President. I was and still am a very enthusiastic member of the SKAL Club, basically a social club of senior travel professionals. I served as the President of its Delhi and national chapters. I also served as Chairman of tourism sub-committees, at both the PHD Chamber of Commerce and FICCI. Both have honoured me with their 'Life Time Achievement' awards. In short, I continue to nurse my passion for interacting with other professionals and propagating travel and tourism.

8th Asian SKAL Assembly, Colombo, Sri Lanka 27–28 Sep., 1979

Lately, I have taken a backseat, but my children continue to do their bit.

I believe that the world is a stage and we all are players. And since that is so, why not play one's part well, or at least to the best of one's ability?

Apart from professional organizations, I have also been involved with social and religious organizations like the Chinmaya Mission and the Mother's Ashram. I am involved with Rotary, having served as the President of the Delhi Mid-Town Club. My niche contribution was to arrange, with the help of Vinod Duggal, a former Commissioner M.C.D., and Ramesh Chandra, a former Secretary, Health, Delhi State, a permanent location for the club's charitable dispensary at Dakshin Puri. As a Trustee of RNIPC (Rotarian Naqshband's Institute for the Physically Challenged), I provide support and sometimes even equipment to the physically-challenged. I try, in a very small way, to be a responsible citizen.

Recently my wife donated an ambulance to The Salvation Army Macrobert Hospital in Dhariwal. To honour the memory of my father and on my birthday in 2016, my daughter donated a laparoscopy machine to the Macrobert Hospital in Dhariwal and on Aruna's birthday, an ultrasound machine to the Delhi Common-wealth Women's Association-managed charitable dispensary in Zamrudpur, Delhi. That's where Aruna volunteers five days a week to look after poor patients, and has been doing so, for the past 25 years.

8 | WATA—A Rather Exclusive Body

I did mention my long association with associations.

The story continues.

In the late seventies and under my stewardship, SITA joined the World Association of Travel Agents (WATA) which has its head-quarters in Geneva.

WATA is a somewhat exclusive club, into which entry of new members is difficult. It isn't for everyone. Membership is normally limited to one member per country or major city. TCI was the existing Indian member for Bombay and Delhi. Surprisingly—and yes, it really happened—TCI opposed SITA's entry.

This aroused a sense of combativeness in me. Being opposed, I went hammer-and-tongs to get what I wanted. With great determination and vehemence, I lobbied hard for our entry. After two years of fierce international lobbying, SITA was admitted as a full member. Even more surprisingly, TCI resigned in protest. Several years later, TCI re-applied for membership. As ex-President of WATA, I endorsed and supported TCI's bid and they were re-inducted as members.

Without going overboard, I must say I couldn't have proved my liberal outlook in a better fashion.

I became the president of the body in 1981. As such and because it is an organization with its headquarters in Switzerland, I had to sign certain documents with the concerned Swiss Authorities and banks. Lo and behold! Some six months after I'd innocently signed those WATA–related papers, I had the dubious pleasure of a visit from the Enforcement Directorate, Ministry of Finance. The Raiding Officer, one Mr. Kaul, asked me if I had a Swiss bank account. Having such an account was strictly illegal and invited heavy penalties. I laughed and denied it. Next, the Inspecting Officer asked me to furnish an affidavit to this effect, which I happily did. Then and in a very authoritative and menacing voice, he rattled off the dates on which I was in Switzerland, and the name of the bank where I was a co-signatory to a bank account.

Initially, I was shell-shocked and scared.

It then dawned on me that all this drama obviously had to do with my signing documents of WATA-related bank accounts and other official communication as President of WATA! I laughed the matter off and things were cleared up. But not before a lot of explanations and a raid on my office by the Directorate.

This was a setback to my pride and a complete shock to SITA's foreign collaborators and also to SITA USA, which had majority shares in the Indian company and which we still treated as a headquarter of sorts. It was beyond their comprehension that business premises could be raided without valid reason and files and records carried away for checking. Such things never happened in the United States or any other country where SITA had offices.

During that period, I had to visit Geneva at least three times a year to participate in WATA's Executive Committee meetings. These repeated visits just to Switzerland and nowhere else, had also aroused Mr. Kaul's interest and suspicion about my activities. He was convinced I had some business interest in Switzerland and therefore must have a Swiss bank account.

Without in any way trying to sound vain, I'd like to mention that I was the first—and so far the only—Asian to be elected President of WATA. This post was prestigious, challenging and professionally very satisfying. I served as President for six years. It gave

Speaking at WATA Manila, October 1983

me a lot of experience in dealing with the travel industry at the global level. I also made good friends in various countries. The experience stood me in good stead when I later became the first Indian President of PATA.

Also highly satisfying were the personal experiences. At the Manila WATA meet, I had the great privilege of meeting and dancing with Imelda Marcos, wife of the Philippines President, famous or rather notorious, for her 3000 pairs of shoes and several thousand dresses. I was given the 'Key to the City of Manila' by Ramon Bhagat Singh, the then Mayor of Manila. This was a prestigious civil honour. But more was to follow. Some years later, I was honoured with the 'Keys to Britain' award by the British Tourist Authority. The presentation ceremony was held at the Tower of London. I have also been honored by the governments of Nepal and Sri Lanka for my services to promote tourism to their countries.

During these frequent visits to Geneva, I developed a taste for Swiss chocolate from a famous shop. This love for Swiss chocolate, combined with my passion for Indian sweets, was responsible for my developing diabetes at a young age. Names elude me but I enjoyed lovely meals in good Swiss restaurants, particularly one near the main railway station, whose name slips my mind. The other favorite was one in the old part of a Swiss city, near a 15th century armoury. It was famous for its steak, baked potatoes and fondue. All fattening, all delicious.

It was on my last visit to Geneva as President of WATA, that my left toe was hurt and started bleeding. I returned to India, but the wound became gangrenous and my toe had to be amputated. At the same time, I was detected with neuropathy in my feet and legs, a condition I still suffer. What a heavy price for that early love for Swiss chocolate!

9 | The Indian Tourist Product

(There's something in it for everyone)

The Origins of Travel

In order to do justice to a subject like tourism, it is important to start by tracing one's steps, as far back in time as possible.

People have travelled since the days of Adam and Eve. Over millions of years, the only things that changed are their motivation and the infrastructure for tourism. Hordes of people have walked,

At Taj Mahal: Did we both make Indian Tourism?

ridden horses, elephants, camels, taken bullock-carts, trains or—in more recent times—flown from place to place and continue to do so. Be it to look for food, more hospitable habitats or, greener pastures for cattle: mankind has always been on the move. Today's travel trade personnel who pour over detailed itineraries may be surprised and amused to know, that the earliest form of travel was an exercise aimed solely at accessing food and seeking shelter. People were hunters, food-gatherers and travelled in search of sustenance and habitats. Call them migrants or visitors or tourists and unlike their counterparts today who hit the road to hunt—at best—for the best beaches, superior education, the most interesting monuments or, the pleasure of eating at the best restaurants, early man wandered primarily in search of nourishment. Gradually, travel began to revolve around waging war and invading new territories. This phase was invariably followed by an urge to expand one's own horizons and explore the world. Chengiz Khan, Roman emperors, Alexander: they all crossed frontiers, not as tourists, but invaders. The resistance they faced was not from immigration or customs, but from the locals. These warriors crossed borders not for personal pleasure, but for the headiness of conquest. India, too, received its share of such 'tourists' during its early history, most of them from our northwestern frontiers.

Most travel for leisure and pleasure started only within the last century. No passports were issued prior to 1914, because there was no such thing as organized overseas travel. People crossed frontiers with ease. There were no long queues for immigration, no baggage search at customs, no visas, no health certificates.

Gradually, distances shrank, travel time reduced and the desire to visit new destinations grew.

Definition of a Tourist

Who is a tourist? What are the accepted national and international norms and definitions of a tourist? Before we go further, it's important to analyse those parameters.

The current UN definition of an international visitor is as follows:

"The term 'visitor' describes any person visiting a country other than that in which he has his usual place of residence, for any reason other than following an occupation remunerated from within the country visited."

The definition covers temporary visitors who spend at least 24 hours in the country they are visiting, and the purpose of whose journey can be classified under one of the following headings:

a) Leisure (recreation, holiday, health, study, religion and sport)
b) Business, family, mission, meeting.

Temporary visitors who spend less than 24 hours in the country visited, such as travellers on cruises taking day-long excursions at various ports of call, are 'excursionists'.

India as a country is a superb tourist product. It has something to offer all year round and the range of its offerings is vast and varied. Its history stretches back to thousands of years. It has a mosaic of different cultures. Buddhism, Hinduism, Sikhism, Jainism, Christianity, Judaism, Islam, Zoroastrianism—almost all world religions are represented here along with their places of worship. It is this combination of its prehistoric culture and its innumerable religions that makes India such an intricate mosaic, a well-knit tapestry.

India: 'Khandani' Hosts

Tourism isn't new to India. Indeed, Indian travel vistas are among the most ancient in the world and India can well and truly be called the 'original host'.

The first visitors to the country were the likes of Hiuen Tsang and Fa Hien, ancient Chinese explorers who opened a window to the country and shed early light on it. Following in the trail of such illustrious travellers were students and scholars who visited centers of learning like Taxila, Nalanda and later, Sarnath.

India was perceived as the 'Golden Bird', and as word spread about its uniqueness, the country found itself playing host to a series of successive dynasties. First came the Aryans who thundered down the passes of the North-West Frontier Province. Then came Alexander The Great in 326 BC, with his formidable armies, some of whom stayed back and settled in northern India. They were followed by the Gaznis, Ghoris, and other tribes, culminating in the arrival of the Mughals. They all came over land.

Later, the sea also provided easy passage to India. Following the visit of Vasco Da Gama in May 1498, Europeans discovered the sea route to India. Then came the Portuguese, Dutch, French and finally, the English. The last expanded their influence by employing war-diplomacy and occasionally, deceit too.

While all this was going on, Indians were travelling domestically for religious purposes. Hindus, the original inhabitants, travelled to the four *Dhams,* i.e. Badrinath, Dwarka, Puri and Rameshwaram. Later, Sikhs, Buddhists and Jains too, began to undertake similar visits to their holy shrines. These pilgrimages were the first and most major form of travel within the country.

Pilgrimage tourism has been around literally for centuries. It would not be blasé on my part to say that Shankaracharya was probably the first travel agent and hotelier in India. He motivated people to travel on pilgrimage to the four *Dhams*. He established *dharamshalas*, which can be called the fore-runners to hotels. *Pandas* (priests) were probably the original inbound tour operators. But even spiritual leaders like Gautama Buddha, Mahavira, Sri Guru Nanak Dev Ji and several others were great voyagers themselves. Their travels added distinct dimensions to their personalities and ways of thinking. They set up places of worship and learning all over the country. This resulted in the establishment of several pilgrimage centers such as Haridwar, Mathura, Ayodhya, Banaras, Bodh Gaya, Sabarimala, Amritsar and others all over the country. It also led to the establishment of places of learning such as Nalanda and Varanasi.

But there are some unfortunate aspects to our history. Some Muslim rulers plundered and destroyed these places of learning and ancient archaeology. Further, it is equally sad to note that India has not—and still doesn't—take sufficient advantage of its invaluable holy sites linked with the lives and times of religious leaders such as Lord Buddha and Lord Mahavira. The only exception, perhaps, is the Golden Temple in Amritsar, that attracts 5.5 crore (55 million) visitors per year and is beautifully maintained by the Sikh community.

Gaya's Mahabodhi Temple Complex (where the Buddha attained enlightenment) is a very valuable religious site. Sarnath (where he gave his first sermon), Kushinagar (where he achieved salvation) and several other Buddhist sites spread across the country offer unlimited pilgrimage opportunities to followers of the faith.

Enhanced connectivity, infrastructure development, availability of decent, mid-level accommodation and adequate information dissemination could make India a Mecca for Buddhist tourists and generate growth in the inflow of short-haul tourists from neighbouring South and Southeast Asian countries.

The National Council of Applied Economic Research (NCAER) 2003 Survey on domestic tourism presented some interesting facts regarding places visited by pilgrims who combine religion with leisure. It identified Tirupathi and Sabarimala as major domestic pilgrim centers in South India and Vaishno Devi and Haridwar in north India. In eastern India, Puri and Bodh Gaya were pre-dominant. Also very important were Ajmer-e-Sharif, Shirdi and Amritsar in western and northern India.

Given this backdrop of antiquity and old traditions, India should be at the forefront of the domestic tourism industry.

In recent times, former Secretary, Haryana Tourism, S.K. Misra, was the great initiator of domestic and highway tourism. Mr. Misra—or, Chappy to his friends—can be truly called the 'Father of Domestic Tourism', just as Som Chib is always referred to as the 'Father of

India's International Tourism'. Haryana developed facilities for tourism by road by setting up several guest houses, restaurants etc. along the highways. Highway tourism is important and can provide empowerment to thousands. Take the Delhi-Amritsar highway. It has *dhabas*—cheap eating places—every 50 kms or so, providing employment to young boys from the neighbouring villages and a hot and nourishing meal to long-distance drivers.

However, as far as international visitors are concerned, we are yet to achieve our full potential. Sadly, I daresay we have not done so by a long shot! While we are—and should be—proud of our past heritage and achievements in various fields, we cannot and should not be totally ignorant of our shortcomings. We have one of the world's finest tourist products, but at the same time, we are rather poor planners and indifferent marketers of this product because we lack the infrastructure and the right approach to promote the country and service foreign tourists. Despite moralistic slogans like *Athithi Devo Bhava* (the guest is God), a Sanskrit phrase first revived and articulated by Dr. Karan Singh, we haven't stopped taking tourists for a ride and shortchanging them.

The formal organization of Indian tourism didn't happen overnight. Various committees were formed and entrusted with specific tasks. Tourism, as an organized activity, became a more serious and formal entity when the thrust was on earning foreign exchange. It took a long time to comprehend the multiplier effect of tourist expenditure upon the market economy. It is only lately that the vast employment potential of tourism has begun to be understood.

The industry developed gradually. In 1960, we received 123,095 foreign tourists, a figure which represented but 0.18% of the global market share. An important factor to be considered is that in the interim, not only have foreign tourist arrivals increased but so also have our earnings from foreign exchange. However, the relevant question is: Has our share of the global world business increased correspondingly or not? It hasn't. India's market share in terms of percentage, still hovers at around 2.9%, as per UNWTO.

Challenge of Half Million
(foreign tourist arrivals)

Government Apathy

It doesn't take a genius to see that India has been lagging behind. Why? What's the problem? The main problem as I see it, is the fact that the Government of India in its 'totality', has never treated the tourism sector as an important economic activity or industry. Most politicians and opinion-makers of all political parties consider tourism a 'luxury' or an 'elitist' activity. They forget that pilgrims and those who undertake *Bharat Darshan* (tour of India) are also tourists. The budget allotment for the tourism sector in the sixties was rather inadequate. Though it has improved today, it is still not very large. It took the government a long time to even create a separate ministry for tourism. The scenario was not very positive. I don't think I am being overly harsh in stating that the tourism sector has received nothing other than step-motherly treatment both from the Prime Minister's office as well as the Planning Commission. Tourism is mentioned in some plans, but never as a major generator of employment, a foreign exchange earner and an important activity that promotes handicrafts, cuisine, culture, heritage, monuments and the overall environment. Yes, this would all be possible if tourism were genuinely and professionally managed.

Let's be honest. Nothing concrete has been done to encourage the industry. In 69 years of annual budget speeches, I don't think tourism has been mentioned more than five or six times, and that too, in just a few lines. Even over the last few years, during which eminent economist Dr. Manmohan Singh was the Prime Minister, not much was done. The Planning Commission referred to tourism for the first time in 1974. Till then, tourism was not even a part of the Five-Year-Plans. Still and like in many other economic fields, I have hopes in both Mr. Narendra Modi and Mr. Rahul Gandhi, as they are both far-sighted.

Toothless Tiger

The main problem, as I see it, is the inability of the Ministry of Tourism to both create and deliver a product. It carries a millstone around its neck, since it has to depend on several central and state ministries. This, in effect, makes it a 'toothless tiger'.

Also and since tourism is a 'state subject', various states feel they need not conform to the general rules and refuse to play ball. There is no cohesion, which is very detrimental. Given India's huge size, federal structure and cultural diversity, what is required is team work among the ministries and the states. That has been happening of late. But it totally depends on individuals, both at the central and state level. The centre can only advise the states and do precious little else. Even political heavyweights like Dr. Karan Singh, the late Madhav Rao Scindia, and the silent but solid worker Jagmohan, could not fully achieve their objectives.

The dismal situation has been further compounded by the fact that there is no dedicated tourism cadre, and most of the staff is constantly shifting. Imagine a situation where a bureaucrat has spent five years looking after coal and mining or agriculture and suddenly finds himself steering tourism-related decisions. Tourism requires less governance and more creative and promotional work. It requires a dedicated team with aptitude, knowledge and flair for international competitiveness. I am sorry to say this but I have known some of our tourist officers posted abroad—many could not even manage a knife and fork, let alone stay sober at a cocktail reception.

National Tourism Board

So what's needed? There is one possible answer.

There should be an independent and autonomous body dedicated solely to tourism, something along the lines of the Indian Railway Board. This need for an exclusive Board is something that was recommended over the years, including by the Mohd. Yunus Committee. It is a matter that has been debated since the early eighties. Even distinguished civil servants like Som Chib, who literally established the Department of Tourism, was mindful of this issue and outlined it in his essays. The Board should be an autonomous body with representatives from the private and public sectors. The private sector representatives should be handpicked, and their selection based on their proven track record, performance and not on their gift-of-the-gab, or, in deference to a particular office they may be holding in travel associations, or even out of political considerations.

Keeping in mind their experience and background, their expertise should be utilized to the maximum. This will not only yield concrete results but also lead to greater cohesion between the industry and government. It is time our tourism planners took full advantage of the experienced professionals in the industry.

Many Hands Make Light Work

The adage is undoubtedly true. But unfortunately and in the case of the tourism industry, it's more a case of 'many hands, many problems'. The real strength of tourism lies in the hands of the private sector, the sector that ultimately delivers the promised-and-paid-for services. This sector includes hotels, tour operators, guides, even shopkeepers and civil society.

In India's case and in the early days, TAAI (Travel Agents Association of India) and FHRAI (The Federation of Hotel & Restaurants Association of India) were the only cogent bodies to be involved in discussions on promoting and representing the industry.

Today, too many trade associations have jammed the highway. Now, there are a dozen bodies representing agents, hotels, airlines, domestic agents, adventure tour operators, the conventions business, etc. Sadly and by each working to promote its own, individual, vested interests, they have together totally bifurcated the industry. There should be a confederation of all these bodies, so that collective work can be done. I believe that the PATA (India) Chapter can step in and provide leadership because, apart from the well-represented private sector, the Government of India and state governments are also among its members. WTTC (World Travel & Tourism Council) was another suitable body to take the lead, but unfortunately, it became a 'rich man's club' and faded away. TAAI, TAFI (Travel Agents Federation of India) and HAI (Hoteliers Association of India) can do a lot, but some of their work tends to duplicate that of others. This is why there is an urgent need for one supreme organization, to deal with the field of tourism.

According to me, there's no alternative to hard work to make a tourist destination successful, and most importantly, economically profitable for the host country. It requires an effort at national level, not from the sector alone. It needs coordination of various segments both in the Government—at the Centre and in the states—and between the public and private sectors. Tourism encompasses a very complex tapestry of areas and needs a proper, fully-professional delivery system.

In a semi-federal country of our size, crafting a common national policy is difficult, but not an entirely impossible task. We have states managed by different political parties, each with its own 'vote-catching' agenda. Politicians are more concerned with projects that get them votes in this or the next election. They claim to want to serve their constituency and will find every reason to demand funds to promote it. This is why I laugh whenever I recall what Piloo Mody once said: if you want tourism to grow, you should give voting rights to tourists!

Another disconcerting aspect is the way we deal with shopping. Most countries receiving tourists depend heavily on shopping, to not only generate foreign exchange but also enhance the scope of developing their products, mostly handicrafts. Shopping by tourists is akin to the export of goods, an area which generates employment, earns money and has its own multiplier effect. Selling to tourists is export at its best. The state emporiums are useful, as are tourist shops. But I know from reliable sources and much in the way it began in Thailand, that tourist groups in India, too, are literally 'sold', or 'promoted', to shopkeepers. This evil exists in most tourist-recipient countries, but in our case it's blatant and very common. Many shopkeepers literally 'buy' the visit of tourists to their shop, whether the visitors buy anything or not. This evil must be stopped by persuasion or by law. The day is not far when like in Thailand, group visits to shops will be auctioned by tour operators. The shop that proves the highest 'bidder' will have the group of tourists visiting its premises.

10 | Tourism 2020 Vision

The United Nations World Tourism Organization's (UNWTO) Tourism 2020 Vision, outlines the development of tourism for the first 20 years of the new millennium. Essential features of the Tourism 2020 Vision are, its quantitative forecast covering a 25 years period with 1995 as the base and its forecasts for 2010 and 2020.

Although the evolution of tourism in the last few years has been irregular, UNWTO, for the moment, adheres to its long-term prediction. The underlying structural trends of the forecast are believed not to have changed significantly. Experience shows that in the short term, periods of faster growth (1995, 1996, 2000) alternate with periods of slow growth (2001 to 2003). While the pace of growth till 2000 actually exceeded the Tourism 2020 Vision forecast, it is generally expected that the current slowdown will be compensated in the medium to long-term.

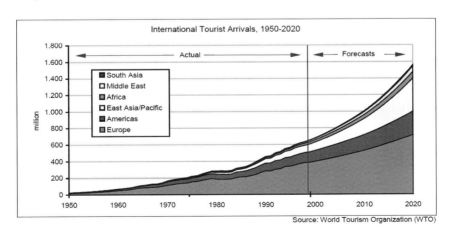

Source: World Tourism Organization (WTO)

UNWTO's Tourism 2020 Vision predicts that worldwide, international arrivals will touch nearly 1.6 billion by the year 2020. Of these, 1.2 billion will be intra-regional, while 378 million will be arrivals of long-haul travellers.

The curve of total tourist arrivals by region shows that by 2020, the top three receiving regions will be Europe (717 million tourists), East Asia and Asia-Pacific (397 million) and the Americas (282 million), followed by Africa, the Middle East and South Asia.

East Asia and Asia Pacific, the Middle East and Africa are forecast to record growths at rates of over 5 percent per year, compared to the world average of 4.1 per cent. The more mature regions, Europe and the Americas, are anticipated to show lower than average growth rates. Europe will maintain the highest share of world arrivals, although there will be a decline from 60 percent in 1995 to about 46 percent in 2020.

All these figures tell their own stories. And make it abundantly clear that India is lagging behind when it comes to optimizing our tourism.

So I'd like to give a clarion call and suggest that the time has come for the Government of India to become more proactive and assist hoteliers and tour operators to create an environment in which they can offer more realistic and affordable prices. And also ensure that the hotel industry, in fact no one, has to face bureaucratic hurdles—read an 'Inspector Raj'—in building and operating hotels. Is a Statutory Tourist Board the answer? Maybe. I doubt it, but let's examine the pros and cons.

We need to 'look beyond' and broaden our general outlook. Products like wellness tourism, adventure and wildlife tourism, home-stay tourism, tourism to our hill stations, particularly in the North-East to name just a few, need more attention in order to be properly developed and marketed.

One could create several other niches, such as the cuisine, fashion and festivals of India, which could all be marketed and promoted all over the world. All these areas hold potential and can become valuable instruments in our toolkit. Another segment of note is VFR (Visiting Friends and Relatives) traffic. The new generation of Indians no longer believes in staying with uncles and aunts but prefers to check into hotels and see the country. They want to see areas that they had missed visiting in their childhood, before their families migrated from India. They now have the urge to see more of the country and—the money to spend.

When I was Chairman of the U.P. Tourism Corporation, I once brought up the subject of assisting UP natives who had migrated overseas and were now returning to trace their ancestry in India. I floated the idea at a staff meeting but it never took off. To date, thousands of people of Indian origin settled in far-off places remain as keen as ever, to come in search of their roots. Since they are all doing well, they would spend money on a decent holiday while on such a trip too.

Paradise Lost! Well, Almost…

Those of you who've seen India's North East will agree that it has a lot to offer to visitors. With distinct cultures and traditions of its own, this region holds great promise and potential, but remains largely untapped because of very poor connectivity. Our hill towns like Shimla, Mussoorie, Nainital and Darjeeling have been ruined because of ill-planned commercialization and over-urbanization. The only three good examples are Ranikhet, Kasauli and to some extent, Ooty, all of which have maintained their original character. The credit for this should go to the Indian Army that has managed and tended to Ranikhet and Kasauli. It's very fortunate that our civil society isn't involved in administering these places. These venues clearly prove that we can keep our cities clean as long as politicians are not administering them.

I don't want to sound like a prophet of doom, but do want to call a spade a spade. I'm afraid that Goa, our most popular resort-destination for leisure and pleasure tourism, may be heading towards disaster, thanks to uncontrolled activity on the beaches. I'm afraid this region sometimes also features in the news for criminal activities like sex tourism. For the past five to six years, I have maintained that all this can and will spoil Goa.

One of the most important segments/products of the travel and tourism industry is MICE (Meetings, Incentives, Conferences, Exhibitions). This segment deserves our full attention because its yields are multi-layered and sizeable. It's been acknowledged the world over, that MICE business paves the way for increased tourist business. Let's not forget that visiting business delegates also 'double-up' as genuine tourists after their business is over. Further and while a person is attending a conference, the spouse is sightseeing and shopping. This segment is an important economic contributor with a high multiplier impact. It promotes and stimulates tourism and generates revenue for airlines, convention centers, hotels, restaurants, shops, surface transportation and entertainment spots. The global MICE industry is estimated to be about US $ 280 billion with around 400,000 major conferences held annually around the world. (*Source:* ICCA HQ).

Here too, we have lagged behind. The sad truth is that India doesn't have even one convention and exhibition centre of inter-national standards. Pragati Maidan, which is supposed to be our main exhibition grounds complex, is so located that when the India International Trade Fair is held every November, traffic conditions in Delhi become chaotic. The ground situation is then anything but 'user-friendly'. The Hyderabad Convention Centre is of medium size and has only one hotel with about 290 rooms attached to it. The Bangalore Centre is certainly better. But none of these are exhibition-cum-convention centers of international standards. Furthermore, we host all conferences during what is already the peak tourist season. All other countries host such events during their off-season. They use this segment of tourism as a filler for the off-season.

So much for 'ground' realities! Now let's get airborne.

I don't have to elaborate too much on the important and pivotal role played by national carriers and Air India is no exception. One can go on and on about its quality levels. Ghulam Nabi Azad, during his tenure as Civil Aviation Minister, took a bold step by constituting a common board for Air India and Indian Airlines. Mr. Azad was a visionary and a very practical and 'down-to-earth' administrator. After the two airlines had been nationalized, this was the first time that a common board was established with a majority of non-official members. Mr. Azad had probably visualized a day when these two airlines would merge and re-emerge as a strong entity in the international aviation sector. I'm not sure if he envisaged the ultimate privatization of these two companies, but he definitely wanted to bring in a fresh approach and thought process, and reduce bureaucratic influence. He appointed Russi Mody as Chairperson, and the private sector representatives on the board included eminent persons like Mr. Pallam Raju—later a Cabinet Minister, Mr. Suresh Keshvani, Mr. K.L. Dutt, Mr. Ajit Kerkar, the then M.D. of the Taj Group, retired Air Marshall Sharma of HAL, and myself.

Unfortunately, a short while later, the Minister was transferred from the Civil Aviation Ministry—possibly—for political reasons, and a very fine administrator and source of strength and inspiration was lost. Shortly thereafter, the airline's board was dismantled by the then Minister of Civil Aviation.

Lightning may not strike twice in the same place, but history definitely repeats itself. Civil Aviation Minister Praful Patel wanted to do a lot for the betterment of our national carriers, but it was a classic case of 'too little, too late'. The two airlines have merged but losses continue to plague them. Firstly, because the merger was done without advance planning and proper 'step-by-step' integration and secondly, because they are managed by bureaucrats who scurry to various '*Bhavans*' immediately and at the drop of a hat, when summoned by politicians who have their offices there.

Those years on the common board set up by Mr. Azad were like a double-edged sword for me. While they were years of learning, they also had their share of frustration. I learnt on two fronts. One, when Russi Mody advised me to make my correspondence brief. I also learnt that when dealing with bureaucrats, everything has to be appended with volumes of figures, statistics and backgrounders. Balancing all this wasn't easy. Those years were frustrating, but they certainly enriched my wisdom.

I remember an occasion when Anant Kumar, the then Minister of Civil Aviation and Culture was supposed to arrive for a meeting at 4 p.m. Russi Mody was to fly back to Calcutta after the meeting. The Minister showed up at 7 p.m. and Russi missed his flight. I was to make a presentation on the merger, but was so enraged that I made remarks that were found unpalatable by the Minister. The next morning the board was dissolved and since then, the airlines are back in the hands of politicians and bureaucrats. Need I say more?

Though in an era when the Indian public sector was being expanded, India Tourism Development Corporation (ITDC) came about primarily because of the visionary civil servant, Som Nath Chib's dissatisfaction with the working and output of the state-owned Department of Audio-Visual Publicity (DAVP), which was the sole producer of the department's promotional material. Chib wanted a separate body that was focused upon and specialized in producing good promotional literature. The second reason for its inception was to manage Ashok Hotel, which had been acquired by the government shortly before, in order to house delegates to the UNESCO conference who had been invited by the Congress leader and then education minister, Maulana Azad.

Ashok Hotel has an interesting story. It was originally to be built and managed by a private company. Ram Pershad of Hotel Ambassador of New Delhi along with the Maharaja of Kashmir— who was *Sadar-i-Riyasat* of Kashmir State—and the rulers of two other princely states were the main promoters, had bought the land and construction commenced slowly. I have been told that Pandit Jawaharlal Nehru used to stroll past the construction site every other day on his daily walk, and must have taken note of it. Then, Maulana Azad, who was not so well-versed in handling a modern conference, was sent to a UNESCO forum as the leader of the Indian delegation. There, he invited UNESCO to hold its next annual conference in Delhi. When Pandit Nehru came to know about it, he was delighted but inquired where the hundreds of delegates would stay. The simpleton that he was, Maulana *Sahib* said that they could be housed in places like the Western Court and a few other small state government guest houses. The sophisticate, Pandit Nehru, was shocked and put his foot down. But he did note with concern that we needed proper hotels of international standards. It is said that he then decided to acquire the building under construction, the same that he passed by on his walks. It is thus that the under-construction Ashok was taken over by the Hotel Corporation. A nice hall for holding parties and other conference facilities were added to its plan. That was also the time when the old Janpath was planned.

Originally, ITDC comprised three different corporations. One dealt with accommodation in hotels, the second, with the production of promotional and publicity material and the third, with transportation. I served on the board of the last along with Bobby Kooka. Later, all three were merged to form ITDC, the India Tourism Development Corporation. And finally, ITDC was set up to also manage a fleet of government vehicles for tourism. Thus, the new corporation took over Ashok Hotel and accommodated delegates for the UNESCO meet there.

The Man Behind the Wheel: Training Qualified Staff

While talking about the Indian tourism industry, let's not forget the 'human resource' factor, which, in my opinion, is a key issue.

Any growth of the tourism sector and enhanced development of infrastructural facilities is bound to underline the crucial need for trained human resources. Tourism is a highly professional industry and needs professional human resources. I believe that it is of paramount importance that this crucial aspect isn't neglected.

A recent study conducted by Market Pulse on behalf of the Tourism Ministry has predicted that by 2020, the total qualified manpower requirement in the travel and tourism sector will be around 6,472,000 persons, of which 3,500,000 will be needed in the hotel sub-sector, 2,730,000 in the restaurant sub-sector, and 242,000 in travel operations.

To educate and train students in the hospitality industry, the first catering institute was established at Pusa in Delhi and the second one in Bombay. The latter was headed by a popular and very professional lady, Mrs. Lilavati Munshi. Mr. Ajit Kerkar of the Taj Mahal group and Mr. Bikki Oberoi of Oberoi Hotels also started training schools both for in-house training and outside students. Travel agencies like Trade-Wings and SITA too, set up training schools or academies, for instructing travel agency staff.

Today, several such institutes have sprung up all over the country.

11 | Market Pulse Survey

Bill Gates once said: "What I do best is share my enthusiasm". In a small way, I tried to do exactly that, in the hope that it will serve as encouragement to the Indian travel industry's decision-makers, and, as inspiration to those aspiring to make this industry their means of livelihood. While we have good catering institutes in both the private and public sectors, our institutes for travel and tourism don't amount to much. Lately, tourism institutes have been established, for example in Gwalior, Noida, and a few other places. Tourism is also a stream offered by some universities in Kurukshetra, Noida, Himachal Pradesh. But very little research is encouraged or undertaken here.

I've said this before and I am saying it again. I feel that the presence of too many trade associations has caused serious roadblocks all over the world. There was WTTC which was rather exclusive and for the 'big boys' only, though they had the charming and efficient Priya Paul as President. There's PATA, which, though represented by all segments of the industry, is still government-dominated. In our own, very own, *Bharat*, we have TAAI, IATO, TAFI, ADTOI, FHRAI and various other associations. These should all merge on one common platform, while retaining their individual identities.

The tourism industry is referred to as a 'service industry', which it is indeed. But we seem to be missing out on the full meaning of the word, 'service'. Service depends on people who actively serve. Plain and simple. The people involved in the industry perform as per their training. There's no shortage of highly efficient staff in the industry, but I do feel that greater and sustained training is still needed. This is particularly true in segments like airport immigration, tourist police and government and private organizations directly involved with tourism, particularly in the recruitment and training of tourist guides.

'Privatization' seems to be viewed almost as a slur in the Indian tourism and aviation industries. The moment this word surfaces, all hell breaks loose. It's a typical case of '*babus*' not wishing to let go of their '*babudom*', their little empires.

An immediate start should be made by privatizing the maintenance and upkeep of some of our national monuments. The government should surely protect all monuments and restore them. But it must consider privatizing the visitation passage of the tourist. Consider also—cafes, souvenir shops and toilets on a commercial basis but subject to supervision. However, I advocate and back dual entry pricing, one for the local tourist and the other for foreigners. Why not? These are standing testimonies to our own heritage and we should be able to visit them at a lower cost, if not for free. Many European monuments follow the same pattern, so I don't have a problem with that aspect. It will not only increase business, but also help in protecting our ancient buildings. Two excellent examples are London's Tower Bridge and Vienna's Schönbrunn Palace— well-preserved monuments that also make money.

Now let's come to pricing. This is a tricky one. Pricing, in general, is never easy to define. There are many who feel that Indian tourism in general, and hotels in particular, are overpriced and don't provide full value-for-money. But I am of the opinion that one can't generalize about their pricing. The entire industry isn't expensive, especially when we consider the plethora of 'low-budget' accommodation and transportation also available in India. Yes, deluxe hotels may be considered somewhat expensive, but this is due to factors like the cost of land, delays in permissions and—the '*Inspector Raj*'. Still, even these hotels compare favorably with other tourist destinations. Give value for money, not *freebies*.

12 | The Need of the Hour— An Independent Tourist Board

The subject of how the government should promote tourism has been a matter of debate since the early eighties. The first committee to cogently take note of the new economic phenomenon of tourism, was established in 1946 under the Chairmanship of Sir John Sergeant, Secretary, Education. The committee could not complete its work due to its transitional nature, but did submit an interim report in May 1947. As a result of the committee's recommendations, the government for the first time, set up a small tourist department under the Ministry of Transport in 1949. In 1951, the Ministry established four regional offices in Delhi, Bombay, Calcutta and Madras. Mr. Sehgal, an ICS Officer, was the first Secretary and Som Nath Chib, who came from All-India Radio, was the Deputy Secretary in charge of Tourism.

In 1949, the Estimates committee of Parliament had recommended the setting up of a separate Department of Tourism. It was finally established in March 1957. Som Nath Chib, as the first Director-General Tourism, soon discovered, that in order to promote tourism as a major economic activity, the existing administrative framework was inadequate. By the mid-sixties, he was already disillusioned—and so were others—with the administrative structure in the Department of Tourism. In 1968–69, the Indian Institute of Public Administration (IIPA) submitted a detailed report on the subject. Later, a UNDP Group of Experts led by Dr. Timothy O'Driscoll, the Executive Director of the European Travel Commission and a former Director-General of the Irish

Tourism Board, reviewed the submission. The experts submitted their findings in 1971. *Inter alia*, they stated: *"The authority and the resources of the national tourism organization in India depend on the governmental view of the importance of tourism to the national economy, and control of tourism potential."*

The UNDP group pointed out that there are several patterns in the world. There are countries like Britain, Ireland, Sri Lanka, Singapore, Thailand, etc. which established autonomous organizations as statutory bodies. In Australia and New Zealand, there are non-statutory travel commissions but their autonomy is fully respected by convention. They also noted that there were official tourist organizations in several countries. After careful examination of all pros and cons, UNDP recommended the setting-up of a non-statutory 'International Tourist Commission'. We continued with a government department, which was later upgraded to a full-fledged ministry. Mr. Chib recruited mostly ladies with a good family background, well-educated, presentable and those who could articulate well. He was very particular about education and personality. Soon, there were two groups in the department.

The subject was further examined in very great depth by the International Committee of Tourism set up by the Planning Commission, under the chairmanship of Md. Yunus. It was a committee which included several senior civil servants like S.K. Misra, eminent educationist Dr. Kapila Vatsayan, K.L. Thapar of the Railway Board, Dr. K.B. Lal, former Commerce Secretary and ambassador of CEE, Dr. B. Venkatraman, former secretary, tourism, Rajan Jetley who was the Managing Director of Air India, Mr. R.K. Puri of Railways (as Member Secretary) and others from the public sector. The private sector was represented by people like Mr. Gautam Khanna of the Oberoi, Mr. Ajit Kerkar of the Taj Group and myself.

We all felt that the existing organizational structure of the Department of Tourism was inadequate and recommended the establishment of a Statutory Board on the lines of the Railway

Board. Diplomatically or tactically, hidden in our recommendation was a desire to have an All-India Tourist Service encompassing even the states.

In a report submitted in May 1988 to the then Prime Minister, Mr. Rajiv Gandhi on the subject of tourism, it was once again pointed out that 'the existing organizational structure of the Department of Tourism is inadequate to cater to the emerging role of tourism as an important stimulus of economic growth and social integration. It is also not capable of moulding itself into a marketing and developmental institution with well-defined targets.' It went on to recommend that 'the Secretariat and operational wings of Ministry of Tourism should be organized on the pattern of the Railway Board.' It recommended that there was no need to segregate the identities of the Secretary and the Director-General.

The second recommendation was implemented and the post of Director-General abolished; the dynamic Vinod Duggal was the last to hold that position. But nothing has been done about the first important recommendation. Though the D-G's post was removed, vested interests have ensured the continuation of the Ministry of Tourism.

No steps were taken on other recommendations either, particularly one of the most important ones pertaining to the setting up of a 'National Tourism Board'. The bureaucrats were not willing to let go of their hold. The IAS lobby wanted to retain the job that entailed foreign travel, within its own fold.

The recommendation stated, "the newly established APEX body called the 'National Tourism Board' will, among several things, formulate tourism policy, draw up prospective plans and monitor tourism projects and scales." It advised constituting a specialized management cadre for tourism called, 'The Indian Tourist Service'.

These findings and developments speak for themselves. What further testimony is required and what greater frustration can the industry face than to see that in all these long years, these urgently-needed steps have not been taken? Little has happened to improve matters. Once in a while, you get an enthusiastic officer—and matters move. Otherwise, tourism continues to suffer due to a lack of understanding of this economic activity by '*babus*' used to serving in the districts with a stick in hand. Many still lack the basic sophistication needed at international level.

Admittedly, not all problems related to tourism will be solved by a statutory board. But independent personnel to manage the same would certainly streamline overall functions and ensure cohesion, efficiency and continuity. Today, each minister and secretary has his or her own view on tourism and its promotion, sometimes with their own agendas in mind. We need a national tourism policy and a permanent, suitably select cadre, to promote and manage tourism. We do not need a change of Secretary every two years, only to see that yet another new tourism policy is being formulated. We need a national tourism policy that is followed over a long period and has some actions or goals in mind—be these numbers, or the number of nights spent in India or, the amount of foreign exchange earned. Are we going to cater to the normal foreigner who likes a drink with his meal, an air-conditioned bus or a car, a guide who speaks his language, or not? We also need a policy and infrastructure for our domestic tourist. We need to cater to Gujarati vegetarians and their meal preferences as much as to non-vegetarian Punjabis or fish-eating Bengalis.

Therefore, I continue to press for the establishment of an independent tourism board, something that I had first advocated during the period of Dr. Karan Singh's stewardship of the Ministry. He tried too, but the bureaucracy managed to negate his proposals by their delaying tactics, which have succeeded all these years. One post less of secretary, additional secretary and a few other official designations is a sacrifice that the lobby will not allow.

It's a sad story, but unfortunately, a true one. I say this with a profound sense of regret.

13 | The Five 'A's

According to me, there's no bypassing hard work to make a tourist destination successful, and most importantly, economically profitable for the host country. It is a national effort and a national responsibility. It needs the coordination of various segments both in the government at the Centre and in the States and—the private sector. Tourism encompasses a very complex product and demands professionalism for delivering tourism-related services to the end consumer. These services are so stratified, varied and diverse that you need a professional to coordinate various segments and provide an end-product to the full satisfaction of the customer. An officer trained only to follow fixed rules and regulations cannot be suitable to undertake professional and competitive business. This is a business that requires special knowledge: the ability to deal with finance, adaptability and the capability to deal with foreigners.

Having stated the obvious, I'd like to point out that in this context, the key factors for a given tourist destination are:

1. Accessibility,
2. Acceptability,
3. Affordability,
4. Accountability, and
5. Audit.

These are the 5 'A's.

Accessibility: The distance or proximity and the accessibility of a given location are extremely important. How far is the destination from its source markets? Most European countries are in close proximity, while India is a long-haul destination.

How well are those source markets connected to the various gateways of the country where the destination is located?

How long does the travel from those markets take? How well connected are the air/sea/rail and road gateways to the leading tourist sites within the country? How much time and money will it take to travel to and within those sites?

As far as connectivity is concerned, aviation has played a major role. When one discusses aviation, the stellar role played by Mr. JRD Tata must be mentioned. JRD, as he was popularly known, acquired his flying licence on 10th February, 1929. He qualified from the Aero Club of India and Burma and six weeks later, joined hands with Nevil Vincent to float India's first airline. First, the Tata Group wrote to the central government about plying the airline between Karachi and Bombay. While the Indian Government was examining the proposal, Imperial Airways, a British Company, landed in Karachi with India's first airmail service. Imperial Airways was later merged with British Overseas Airways Corporation (BOAC).

Back to JRD and his flying career. He first landed in Ahmedabad for refuelling and to deliver eight pounds of mail. A bullock-cart creaked across the runway with gallons of petrol to refuel the small aircraft. JRD then landed in Bombay with 56 pounds of mail. Several years later, Rafi Ahmed Kidwai, as Civil Aviation Minister in Nehru's cabinet, started the night airmail service. Four planes commenced their journey from Calcutta (now Kolkata), Bombay (now Mumbai), Madras (now Chennai), and Delhi. These met in Nagpur, exchanged their mail and returned to their bases. You got your letter the next day. Before this service, the normal airmail letter from Delhi to Madras would take at least three days.

These factors play an important role in the success or failure of tourism destinations.

International airline frequencies depend on bilateral air agreements. It is an inter-disciplinary effort on part of all governments. In the early years, we were very restricted in granting traffic rights to foreign carriers because we were protecting Air India. However and under Praful Patel's stewardship, we liberalized our policies.

Some thought they were too liberal, while others even alleged some 'deals'. I think it was foresight.

Liberalization has helped not only inbound tourism but also the Indian traveller, both domestic and international. Foreign relations play some part, but these are mostly commercial decisions and factors that depend on the growth of infrastructure, such as air, sea, rail and importantly, road connectivity. Successful tourist destinations like France or Spain are close to their source markets and very easily accessible, while we are not. We mostly depend on arrivals by air. Except for Buddhists or Hindus, most of our neighbours in Sri Lanka, Pakistan, Bangladesh, Nepal or even Thailand, all want to travel to Europe. London, Paris, Berlin and Rome remain their preferred venues.

As for the accessibility of tourist attractions within India, we have made significant progress in all fields. We now have more flights to more stations, such as Khajuraho, Dehradun, Aurangabad, Manali, to name just a few. Our railways have introduced new routes and trains—the Maharaja Express is a good example. As for our surface transportation, we have improved in that area too, with more regional permits being issued for tourist coaches and cars. More non-tourist centers are now connected by road and covered by state-run and private bus companies. Slowly, our barriers are coming down.

Acceptability: It is important to know exactly how attractive, accessible and popular our tourist sites are. While these may be very important in our national psyche, what matters is whether tourists—both international and domestic, the ultimate consumers—like these or not and how they rate them. How convenient and consumer-friendly are our airports, railway stations, bus stops and tourist monuments? How comfortable do we make the visits of tourists to our monuments? How easily available are the means to visit those locations? How acceptable, price-wise and location-wise, are our hotels and boarding houses? These are all important factors to determine success. *It is consumer demand and consumer satisfaction that leads to acceptability.* But we waver from the sublime to the ridiculous. Our Taj Mahal draws millions, but our dirt, congestion and poverty are found unacceptable.

Affordability: Once a consumer has accepted India as a favourable destination and there is 'accessibility', to and within the country, *it becomes extremely important to ensure that the product is affordable.* Everyone involved in any business will vouch for the fact that 'costs' and 'pricing' are crucial factors for success. We need to ask ourselves whether our tourist services are favorably priced. There have been some complaints about Indian hotels of international standards being over-priced, though this is not necessarily true.

People also complain about the lack of clean and safe budget accommodation. But whether these grouses are actual or perceived, there is no denying that overpricing of hotels, restaurants and surface transportation all impact our tourism negatively. In this, the government has a major role to play, for it is the government that dominates the transportation by air, rail and also imposes various restrictions and taxes on surface transportation, which makes travel inconvenient and sometimes costly. Land prices and the number of permits required to build and operate hotels, are nightmarish. The number of taxes, both central and state, on hotels and modes of transportation like buses and cars, are rather high. Some municipalities and local bodies add their own taxes. Then there is the '*Inspector Raj*', which is rampant in most cities. In short, what is needed is a balanced approach to taxation on pricing, whether it is aimed at the international or domestic tourist. Hotels and transport services should not be considered the 'golden goose' by the authorities, particularly inspectors. *The client must feel that he is getting 'Value for Money'.* No one likes to be cheated and certainly not while on a pleasure or leisure holiday, whether within or outside one's own country.

Accountability: There was a famous Hollywood movie titled 'Who's Minding the Store?' That is a question I have often asked, in regard to the Indian tourism industry. While we have a full-fledged tourism minister at the Centre and in most states, the fact is that they have little authority and no clear accountability. Everyone passes the buck to other ministries and departments. No one likes to be held accountable for anything. This hardly helps. In order to have a clear and transparent system of accountability that directs both credit and blame to the correct address, I must stress again as in Chapter XII, that what is needed is the establishment of an Indian Tourism Board, like the Railway Board, with a dedicated cadre of its own. This should function both at the centre and state level and be endowed with the authority to frame rules and laws required for promoting safe and economically viable tourism. *The union cabinet must declare and elevate tourism to a national priority.* Finally, the industry also requires an ombudsman, one who will ensure that the customer gets proper service. Civic authorities have to be accountable for the behavior of service providers like taxi drivers, travel agents and hoteliers and most importantly, shopkeepers. *Particularly those who are expected to look after tourists should be of high moral fibre and legally accountable.* They often try to over-charge a foreign tourist.

Audit: Auditing and identifying revenue tourism and tourists are both very important. The distinction between international travellers who are businessmen and those who are backpackers must be made, since each need a different marketing approach and different infrastructure. The spectrum is wide. Similarly, in the domestic tourism market, 'yuppies' and rich businessmen each require different infrastructure, one that is, in turn, absolutely unlike the needs of pilgrim tourists. *How much and what kind of investment is needed and should be made, depends on the socio-economic returns of tourism.* Exit polls and constant consumer feedback are essential methods for evaluating a service effectively.

Tourism: From the Red Fort

The only way to put a system in place to properly evaluate consumer feedback is by adopting a National Tourism Policy. *And that, in turn, can only be achieved by setting up a National Tourism Board.*

All this may sound very simplistic. But let's not forget that nations with successful tourism industries like Spain, France and now China, have been taking these measures. If tourism is to become genuinely relevant, socio-economic activity, then we must adopt these five 'A's to achieve some meaningful success. I am told by a very important authority that in China, tourism is discussed at the level of the top, national policy-making body, the Central Council of the Party. I wonder if our cabinet has ever discussed tourism. It rarely finds a mention, either from the ramparts of the Red Fort (when prime ministers make their annual Independence Day speeches) or even during Budget discussions. Recently, Prime Minister Modi did mention tourism in one of his speeches, though not at an important or relevant economic forum so far. This author has hopes from Mr. Modi.

Bouquets and Brickbats

It is important and graceful to give credit where it's due. I'd like to mention that the Ministry of Tourism has been very supportive on the whole and I've had the privilege of working with several officials who were dynamic and genuinely wanted to promote tourism. This was also true of some ministers like Shri Raj Bahadur, Dr. Karan Singh, Madhav Rao Scindia and Ghulam Nabi Azad, all of whom really worked hard to make tourism a national priority. Lately, I found out that Mr. Mahesh Sharma is also a keen player, one instilled with a great desire to promote tourism.

Dr. Karan Singh was very pro-tourism. And with his vast knowledge of Indian scriptures and his imposing personality, he projected India in a very good light around the world. He was the first person who tried to establish a National Tourism Board, but as usual, the bureaucracy frustrated his efforts. Dr. Singh was very supportive of hoteliers and travel agents.

Mr. Azad was a very astute and practical administrator, who skillfully managed limited resources as Minister of Tourism and Civil Aviation. He is the one who, after the nationalization of Air India, established a Board of Directors with several independent Directors, with Mr. Russi Mody as the Chairman. I was appointed to the Boards of both Air India and Indian Airlines.

At the other end of the spectrum and as I've mentioned earlier, we had the likes of Purshottam Kaushik, who once, in all earnestness, asked me to describe the role of travel agents and tour operators in attracting foreign tourists to India. He actually asked me that. Those were the days when all expenses in foreign currency were under close scrutiny. Somehow managing to keep a straight face, I explained to him that travel agents and tour operators were the 'links' between the foreign tour operators who promoted India, and the country itself. I also pointed out to him quite solemnly, that we were the ones who delivered the various services and products promised to the consumer. That in fact, we were the ones who actually '*delivered*'.

The good minister then went off on another tangent and questioned me about the role of the overseas India Tourist Offices.

Again and in all sincerity, I gave him a brief description and explained their useful role. His verbal response was an "Ah".

Then, in *shudh* Hindi, he passed the judgement.

He declared that "if what you tell me is right, we should either close our overseas Government Tourist Offices, or stop wasting foreign exchange by permitting tour operators to go abroad for promotional activities."

By now I'd had enough. The blunt man that I am, I retorted in equally *shudh* Hindi:

"Sir, you need to study at a tourism *paathshaala.*"

He got upset and told me *"Aap angreziwale Bharat ko nahi samajhte!"* (You English-speaking people—a euphemism for the 'elite'—do not understand India). I just said "Thank you, Sir", and left.

He later complained to the Secretary about me. However, the complaint only served as a recommendation letter.

Fortunately, Purshottam Kaushik remained minister for only a short while. Before he could do greater damage to the Ministry of Tourism and therewith to tourism in India, his term came to an end.

14 | Reflections: This, That & the Other

I will let you in on a little secret. That is, if it can be called one at all.

Many people think I've been something of a 'go-getter', 'ambitious' and 'decisive' in achieving my goals. But the fact is that I am plain lucky, one who is blessed by God.

The only thing that I have done is to try, as far as humanly possible, to be fair and ethical. And with God's grace, I dare say I have managed to do so quite well.

I went all the way from being a transfer assistant, to someone who was the first and till date, the only one to get a Padma Shri for services to tourism. I was the first Indian to be elected President of PATA, the Pacific Asia Travel Association and the first Asian to be elected for three terms as the President of WATA, the World Association of Travel Agencies headquartered in Geneva. I was also the first travel agent to serve on the Board of Directors of Air-India and Indian Airlines, to have served as the Chairman of the State Tourism Corporation and to have had the distinction of receiving the Keys to Britain and to the City of Manila. This was because while I set my sights on the stars, my feet were always firmly on the ground. Or so I think.

I took risks, but one at a time. I worked for a homegrown startup. For me, it was better to go wrong with my own instincts than to be right with someone else's. I listened to my inner voice and followed my Dad's advice that "when in doubt, treat others the way you would want them to treat you."

I'm not saying I've been a saint. Just that I've mostly tried to play the game by the rule-book.

When I look back on the trials and tribulations of my life, I do believe I have plenty to reflect upon. I've covered a fair bit of ground as far as my work is concerned. The overriding urges were first, to survive and then, to succeed. These were my primeval instincts and objectives.

Of course, things changed as I grew older and became more senior in life and the industry. On the whole, it's been one hell of a joyride, with its fair share of vicissitudes, ups and downs, joys and sorrows and plenty of drama and excitement.

Today, I'm glad I was part of that joyride. One thing is for sure, if I had my life to live again, I would still love to be in the travel industry. I guess once it gets into your blood, you're hooked for several lives.

Like everything else, there can be different ways to describe the travel industry. Basically, it's a glamorous odyssey. That's life in this business. After all, it is travel we're talking about and travel is glamorous. But before you get very excited, let me tell you that this isn't the whole story. There's no such thing as a free lunch, and this applies to the travel industry too. The fact is that you have to work hard to succeed. Don't expect easy pickings, because there aren't any. Don't expect to be spoon-fed, because it won't happen.

Going back in time—and I know that we 'oldies' always say that but indulge me anyway, those were good days.

There were very few successful travel agents at the top and business lines were more clearly drawn. We competed fiercely with one another, but were also friends. There was good spirit all around. There was decency. During the days of foreign exchange shortage, we even went to the extent of jointly hosting cocktail receptions to drum up business. In later years, I missed that feeling of camaraderie.

My message to the present generation is: *Compete, but don't lose sight of human relationships. Business tussles should not become personal differences.*

My strong faith in God helped me to listen to my 'inner voice', or 'gut feeling', and it is that which has always guided me.

For me, it has always been a case of the 'man behind the machine'. That's what counts. The personal touch and personal interface is very important in the travel industry, in fact in any service industry. Relationships are important, and it's amazing how much business can be generated because of one's personal character and approach to life. *If you want to achieve real success in your business, make sure your personal presence is permanently imprinted in all your dealings. Be fair. Compete, but with dignity and not with malice.*

You'll find that this personal touch can become a 'Midas' touch.

As you can see by now, my life hasn't exactly been a bed of roses. It's been eventful, meaningful and joyous, but it hasn't all been an 'easy passage'.

In spite of the various difficulties I encountered, I don't mind admitting that life in the travel trade spoilt me. But I never got totally carried away. I never forgot that my family had humble beginnings. This realization played a pivotal and stabilizing role in my life. My parents' humble background always brought me down to earth and kept me grounded. Their teachings made me humble—and I believe I am so.

Noted management guru Kenneth Blanchard said, *"The key to successful leadership is influence, not authority."*

I've learnt that teamwork is all-important. It is the essence of success. One must pay attention to one's people. I treated my colleagues with great respect. I was mostly a patient listener, very conscious of my shortcomings and never hesitated to apologize. I could see for myself that this had a very good overall effect on everyone.

I surrounded myself with excellent staff for the simple reason that I needed them. I influenced them, moulded them, but never abused my authority. I dare say I created a good image for SITA, and backed it up to the best of my ability.

The Gospel says: *"It is more blessed to give than to receive."*

Well, I have a simple business philosophy. Give your clients value for their money, and a little extra if you can. It never hurts. In fact, it pays in the long run. Goodwill earned in business reaps rich rewards. As the saying in Hindi goes: *'Ash bhi, Cash bhi.' (fun and—money too!)*

And now let's talk about the wild side of life!

I believe in the philosophy: 'Work hard, party hard'. While all walks of life have their share of entertainment and parties, perhaps none have more than the travel industry.

'Yours truly' has been at the forefront in this area.

Business meant entertaining and parties, and believe me, there were more than should be deemed proper. To say that I indulged myself is to put it very mildly. I over-ate and over-drank and—paid the price.

Diabetes got hold of me and has stayed with me as a faithful but unwanted companion. But, putting aside my personal health woes, parties and social functions did play an important role in life.

At parties, you are on display and people watch and judge you by your behavior. This means that how you and your spouse conduct yourself at parties, is extremely important both in the short and long term. Parties can be used as a means of promoting your own image and that of your company. They are an important part of what is now known as 'networking'. In my case, it did place a lot of strain on my wife Aruna, as she was working full-time as a doctor in the Central Government Health Service (CGHS) and had two kids to look after. Well, we survived.

We at SITA never parted with any commissions. Therefore, public relations demanded that I and my senior staff cultivate and establish personal rapport with important clients. There was no better way than to invite them over for tea, dinner or cocktails (my cocktail parties were usually restricted to 15–20 guests at a time, while a maximum of three couples were invited to our dinners). We had a dining table for 8 persons only and people enjoyed sit-down dinners more than the impersonality of large gatherings.

The Power of Advertisement, Humour and Humility: Air-India and Mr. JRD Tata, Two Class Acts

One can't help feeling sometimes that we are captive audiences to the advertising juggernaut. It is almost overpowering. But that's the way things are. No matter which field of work we're involved in, we can't escape the presence and power of advertising. I am told that the very word 'advertising' evokes strong reactions.

According to George Orwell, "advertising is the rattling of a stick inside a swill bucket". H.G. Wells called advertising "legalized lying". And according to Stephen Leacock, "advertising may be described as the science of arresting the human intelligence long enough to get money from it."

The first advertising campaign that impressed me was Air-India's, created by S.K. 'Bobby' Kooka, a genius who gave Air-India its mascot, the Maharaja. Look closely and the Maharaja could be a mustachioed JRD, as Mr. Tata was always addressed by Bobby Kooka.

If there was one thing about Air-India that made people smile, it was their advertisements. Bobby and Air-India, both equally knew how to take digs at themselves. The Air-India hoarding more or less permanently located at Kemp's Corner in Mumbai, was always a traffic stopper, a trend-setter in its own right. You might say that those were Air-India's glorious days. They had billboards at Piccadilly Circus in London and in all other major metros worldwide.

Kooka's campaigns not only had generous doses of humour, but often created controversies.

One of the Air-India advertisements that really made waves showed a mustached *paan-waala* serving a *paan* (the Indian betel leaf digestive) and declaring, 'You Beatles are Nuts'. It was smart word-play. This was during the Beatles' heyday but they just laughed about it.

Another advertisement caused a flutter and almost created a diplomatic impasse between India and the UK. The British government protested and the Indian government had to do some explaining.

In anticipation of getting their first Boeing, the hoarding read 'We are expecting' and showed a lady seated on a rocking chair, knitting baby socks. It just so happened that at that particular time, the British Queen was expecting a child. But it was a well-guarded secret. The British were in turmoil over how the news could possibly have leaked. Fortunately, everyone eventually saw the lighter side and the uproar ended.

How I wish Air-India would reprint their booklet, 'Foolishly Yours'. This was a booklet placed in the aircraft to introduce passengers to Air-India and the facilities on board in a humorous way. It was Bobby Kooka at his best. It took a dig at all and sundry, including at the nationalization of the airline itself. Unfortunately, it was withdrawn by the authorities, reflecting humorlessness, insecurity and an inferiority complex.

The power of publicity and advertising is clear for all of us to see. Campaigns like Amul's or, that of Nirma washing powder and the latest ones on 'Incredible India' are very important for an organization's success and growth in a competitive marketplace. During my long career, I've seen several advertising and promotional campaigns and have no hesitation in saying that in the field of tourism, one can single out the 'Incredible India' campaign as among the best and most powerful ones. Its nearest rival is Malaysia's 'Truly Asia'.

Within our own ambit, we too made a mark.

As I mentioned earlier, our SITA ads were useful for the travel industry on the whole, because through them, we sent out the right signals about the industry's enormous contribution to the country and its economy. They were very apt and pertinent to the character of the tourism industry, and we at SITA were proud of them. Our advertising consultant too, was great.

Mind you, we also had our share of problems, like for instance, when we came up with an advertisement which ran: "SITA is a 'four-letter' word".

The other one was 'Do it with SITA'.

These drew considerable protests and we had to withdraw them.

Coming back to Air-India, there is no doubt that it was ranked as one of the better airlines of the world. The first Asian carrier to fly across the Atlantic and the first to order the Boeing 747, its service, both on the ground and in the air, was amongst the best in the world.

While reminiscing about Air-India, I can never forget nor live down one incident.

In the early sixties and as the young, over-enthusiastic manager of the American travel firm SITA, I once escorted a group of American travel agents from Cairo to Bombay, for a familiarization tour of India. The tour was jointly sponsored and hosted by the Tourist Office, Air-India and SITA. I was the tour director.

When we were about to board the Air-India flight in Cairo, the ground staff came to me and informed me that due to over-booking, they were one seat short in First Class and whether I would mind travelling in Economy.

Full of a totally false sense of importance, I vehemently refused. When I was on the verge of making a scene, I was given a first class boarding pass. I felt that I had asserted my importance.

After about an hour of the flight, it was time for the meal service. As I was enjoying my aperitif, I saw Mr. J.R.D. Tata come out of the cockpit and walk towards the rear end of the aircraft, the Economy section.

I was shocked. On enquiring from the flight crew, I was told that Mr. Tata was seated in Economy because there was no seat in First Class. It dawned on me that it was I and my inflated ego, who had insisted upon and taken that last First Class seat, even though I was a non-revenue passenger and merely a tour escort.

I got up, walked back to the Economy section and went up to Mr. Tata. I apologized profusely for my behaviour. In fact, I was literally in tears. I was utterly ashamed of myself. To use an Indian phrase, I wished the ground would open up and swallow me. After listening to me patiently, he put his hand on my shoulder and said, "Young man, go and sit in your seat. You are escorting a group of American tour operators who bring business to my airline. I need you both."

By now I was literally begging him to relent and change seats. Finally, he agreed. But I continued to feel deeply ashamed of my behaviour and have, till date, never quite lived down that incident.

It was a lesson in humility—that people do business with people they like, whom they trust, and those who make them feel special, those who treat others like VIPs.

J.R.D. TATA's Autographed Picture,
Celebrating 50 Years of Air India

Years later and during a conference in Kashmir, I reminded Mr. Tata of the incident.

He laughed. "Mr. Sharma", he said, "For my airline and if need be, I would do it again. Air-India is my favorite baby." Mr. Tata obliged and honoured me with an autographed photo of himself, posing with the aircraft that took Air-India's famous first flight from Karachi to Bombay.

Today, I'm sorry to say that Air-India's stock has sunk dramatically and the company lacks the sophistication and courage that it had back then, to be able to laugh at itself and make gentle fun of others, without offending anyone.

In my opinion, Air-India in its heyday was a class act and India's first, truly international brand. Today, some call it the country's laughing stock. It lacks leadership and that can never come from our *babus,* or *netas,* no matter how smart they think they may be. Neither will they ever stop milking the airline. Today, you find every other official being upgraded to First Class, making revenue passengers uncomfortable.

Ideals, Heroes and a Look in the Mirror

The greater the various pressures, pulls and intrigues of the travel industry, the more I realized and appreciated my parents' character. At a personal level, I admire people who are unpretentious and down-to-earth. I inherited this from my parents. My father was a humble man and that humility means a lot to me.

But there are some people outside the travel industry whom I have admired greatly too.

Sardar Patel and his clear vision was one such person.

He was a strong and straightforward leader. He created a unified India. He was responsible for the accession of princely states to the Republic of India. (The only one that Pt. Jawaharlal Nehru handled was that of Kashmir and it is still a mess).

Nehru, though a man with a vision, was idealistic. He judged others by his own high and honest standards, but was no match to Sardar as an administrator. I also hold great respect and admiration for the likes of JRD Tata, Bobby Kooka, G.D. Birla, S.N. Chib, S.K. Misra and Jack Dengler.

Speaking of myself, it would be correct to say that I am shy in some ways. Only in some ways. That's my nature.

But, I'm also quite perceptive—*haha!*—and in my own way, a fairly good judge of people, especially in business dealings. Without in any way trying to blow my own trumpet, I think this was clearly reflected in the kind of talent I attracted to join SITA.

I want to mention that when he initially joined us, I paid Ghulam Naqshband, Executive Director, a salary higher than my own, though I was the company's Managing Director. In fact, Dengler, who was the Chairman of SITA at that time, questioned my decision and asked that if Naqshband was so important and useful, why have me in the job? I explained to him the strength of our combination. Ghulam and I complemented each other's professional qualities and were thus an ideal team. I can hardly over-emphasize the importance of teamwork for an organization's success.

A great and singular honour that came my way was my being awarded the Padma Shri in 1990. I was humbled at this great recognition and also a little surprised that I had been singled out for such a prestigious award.

It seems as though two things had gone in my favour. One was SITA's unblemished record in all financial and taxation matters. The other was the general view that while I raised several issues on several platforms, my viewpoint was always totally focused on the most relevant matters on hand and never carried ulterior motives. I have a very strong feeling that S.K. Misra, the former Secretary, also had a lot to do with my getting the Padma award.

Nevertheless and whatever the reasons behind my selection, it was flattering and wonderful to be bestowed with such an honour.

Life in general, may be beautiful, but it isn't a picnic. We all know that good and bad times are part and parcel of life. I've seen bad times in my day and have been confronted with my share of problems and tensions. There have been hurdles of all kinds and innumerable business hassles, which are only to be expected.

There's a proverb that runs: "Life is not about holding a good hand; life is about playing a poor hand well."

I don't think I did anything exceptional, but did try my best to solve all the problems I faced as effectively as possible, by playing well, the one hand I held.

Nehru said: "The policy of being too cautious is the greatest risk of all."

Though I am and have been a fairly cautious person, I always ventured out of the block. This helped my cause. I have never wasted money. I don't know if I would have achieved more if I were adventurous by nature and had taken more risks, but I am a very satisfied man, as far as my business and personal lives are concerned. God has been very kind to me and friends have been very generous and forgiving.

Today, I enjoy the good reputation of having created Select CITYWALK, the prestigious shopping mall in Saket, Delhi, which has won several awards, including the Best Mall in India, several times over.

I must admit that true credit for the same should go to Mr. Yograj Arora, our partner, my two children, Neeraj Ghei and Arjun Sharma and the most dedicated and professional team lead by Yogeshwar Sharma, Shashi Sharma, Srinivas and members of our marketing team, the maintenance team and the whole staff.

Now, my only contribution is to hoist the national flag at the Select CITYWALK Mall twice a year—on Republic Day and

Independence Day and, at the annual event we hold to honour the Kargil martyrs. I do so each time with a sense of fulfillment and pride.

Of Tandoors and Poetry in Delirium, Friends and Racists

In 1964, the New York World Fair was being held for the third time. An Indian *restaurateur* had taken space to sell Indian food. It was the Gaylord-Kwality combine, *i.e.* Messrs Ghai & Lamba. Kanwar Behl flew to New York on behalf of Gaylord to open the restaurant. He ran into a peculiar problem. Kanwar wanted to set up an open-air *tandoor* (clay oven) in their restaurant, that was also to be used during the exhibition. But at that point in time, there were very few Indian restaurants in New York and certainly none with a *tandoor*. Further, New York's health and fire authorities felt that chicken and other dishes prepared in the rustic oven would be carcinogenic due to the smoke and therewith dangerous for human consumption. They also felt that the *tandoor* itself was a fire hazard.

In a nutshell, the restaurateurs were not getting the required permission to set up the *tandoor* for the dishes that were to be the main attraction of the Indian restaurant.

I happened to be in New York on a training trip. When Kanwar mentioned all this to me, I volunteered to help, not because I had any influence or friends in high places in New York, but only because the daughter of the New York Mayor of the time, worked at SITA New York, where I was also employed.

I mentioned this problem and requested her for an appointment with her father. Her father was kind enough to grant me one.

I explained to him the entire process and tried to assure him that a *tandoor* was not any more dangerous or carcinogenic than an open air bar-be-que or a coal grill. Fortunately, he was convinced.

Permission was granted and the first *tandoor* installed in New York. Since then, several Indian restaurants have opened up with *tandoors* in their kitchens.

Today, there are Indian *tandoori* restaurants in most major cities of the United States.

Dreams......

In 1966, I had an unusual experience. I was hospitalized at the Tirath Ram hospital in Delhi for the removal of my appendix.

The operation was a success. But unfortunately and just on the day I was going to be discharged, I had a fever. The doctors diagnosed it as an infection and retained me in hospital to treat it. On the second day, the fever rose further and remained high for several days.

My father-in-law, Dr. Ram Labhaya, was a consultant in the eye department of the same hospital and so had all his friends and colleagues looking after me. Even specialists from Chandigarh were consulted.

But in spite of their best efforts, my fever would just not come down. After several days, my family got very worried. Many of my family members would spend nights with me in the hospital.

One night, when my wife Aruna was staying with me, I had a unique experience. In my sleep, I began to mutter Urdu poetry.

I was told later that it was the *kalam*, the poetry of Bahadurshah Zafar, the last Mughal Emperor, that I recited. Apparently, I was half-asleep but I still kept up the recitation. Aruna tried to rouse me, to talk to me. But as she and the others told me later, I was only semi-conscious.

Frantically, she called the nurse. The doctors too came in. I was aware of none of these comings-and-goings. They would each try to talk to me, but as soon as they stopped, I would start reciting Zafar's poetry again.

Apparently, I kept asking Aruna why they were all disturbing me, while I was talking to Zafar *Sahab*, who was standing right there, in person, and why the doctors kept telling me that there was no one in the room? Why were they not paying respects to the King?

Finally, the doctors gave me a strong sedative and sent me into a deep sleep.

Next morning when Aruna narrated the incident, I was puzzled. I told her that I had been fast asleep, had indeed dreamt of Zafar, but no more. However, I insisted that I could not have recited his poetry as I didn't remember it.

The doctors, too, corroborated what Aruna said: that I had indeed recited Urdu poetry for half-an-hour or so, till I was administered the sedative that induced sleep.

Surprisingly and even after I was discharged and went home, I could not recollect Zafar's 'Diwan' (collection of poetry).

Since that incident, I have read a large portion of Zafar's *Diwan*.

> *"Kitna hai badnaseeb Zafar dafan ke liye*
> *do gaz zameen bhi na mili kue-yaar mein."*

("How ill-fated Zafar is that he was not even granted two yards of earth for his grave in his beloved land.")

Those famous words that the emperor, who was exiled and imprisoned in Burma, wrote during his last days in his cell, brought it all back. When I was in Rangoon, I visited the emperor's grave. And as long as I was in Rangoon, the poetry lingered.

Though I cannot remember Zafar's verses any more, my recollection of these incidents are vivid. But do I have an explanation? Of course not.

Friends....

My very good friend Prem Prakash, started his professional career as a stills photographer and later became an audio-visual correspondent. Finally and after working for overseas media concerns, he set up his own organization called 'Asian News International' (ANI).

Today, ANI is one of India's leading TV news sources not just for news, but for a host of other programming. Every time you watch a live news item on any news channel, you are bound to spot a microphone belonging to ANI.

The very first function that Prem covered was at the Constitution Club, which, at the time used to be on Curzon Road, now called Kasturba Gandhi Marg. This club provided an informal meeting point for the members of the Indian constituent assembly. (In 1965, it relocated to Vithalbhai Patel House, where it continues to be housed today, while the Kasturba Gandhi location saw the construction of six blocks of apartments, initially for delegates of an UNCTAD conference. Since then, the apartments have housed various government officials). After Prem had shot his pictures, Madan Nayar, one of our college mates and I, called on each of those in the photographs, in a bid to sell them at the fabulous price of Rupees 5 per picture. The two of us were helping our friend.

Our friendly relationship continues till date and we three are the best of friends. Prem is the Chairman of Asian News International today. He was also a representative of the international news agency Visnews, which had millions of readers around the world. Madan, on the other hand, retired from ITC and worked with me in SITA for some time too.

And Kebabs......

Do you remember that story of how I loved eating on board a train as a child? I must expand on it at this point.

When I was Chairman of U.P. Tourism, I had to visit Lucknow frequently. Apart from others, I was very friendly with the Gupta family who run the Clarks Group of Hotels. Often, I would have dinner there, as their restaurant was very famous. One evening, I complained to the chef that the *kebabs* were not good. Very quietly and discreetly, he told me that since Lucknow was famous for its *kebabs*, I should try some of the best the city has to offer. He pointed me to Imtiaz, a famous *kababchi* (a maker of *kebabs*). I was told that Imtiaz had a small, streetside shop, very close to the hotel, and that I must visit it. I did and was amazed at how good Imtiaz's *kebabs* tasted. Subsequently and whenever I returned from Lucknow to Delhi by night train, I would pick up Imtiaz's *kebabs* and *rumali roti* and enjoy those—just like I used to relish my mother's *paranthas* in my childhood!—on the train back home.

When the ITC group was opening the Maurya Hotel in New Delhi, its Chairman, Mr. Ajit Haksar, told me that he was looking for a great chef to make *kebabs* at one of his restaurants. I mentioned Imtiaz. He was hired and immediately became famous at the Maurya.

When we met again two to three months later, Haksar thanked me profusely for introducing the chef to him. From a small, street-side *kababchi*, Imtiaz has today become the internationally-renowned Master Chef Imtiaz Quraishi and a very highly-paid one at that. It's a tribute not only to Imtiaz, but also to that great administrator and business leader, Ajit Haksar, who stopped at nothing but the best for his Maurya Hotel.

Incidentally, when I enquired from Haksar over drinks whether it is true that Imtiaz gets a very high salary, he said, "Of course, yes, in fact more than some of the department heads."

His philosophy was to pay a good chef so much that neither would he quit, nor could anyone else afford him.

When I became the President of the Rotary Club of mid-town Delhi, I held my installation function at the Maurya. Many members of my club remember that dinner to date.

Imtiaz was the chef, of course, and boy, what a dinner it was!

Tourism and Racism

The first and the only time I encountered racial discrimination was in the United States.

I was visiting Memphis, to meet my very good friend Willa Sue Love, who had travelled to India six times. Willa belonged to a rich cotton-farming family, held large investments in the cotton industry and was a prominent citizen of Memphis.

Tan Chee Chye, SITA's Manager from Singapore, Hiroko Fukuyama from Japan and I were on a promotional trip in Memphis. Willa Sue Love very generously invited all of us for lunch at her favourite club in Memphis, of which she was a prominent member.

Whether you believe it or not, we were denied entry. The reason? I was considered 'non-white, *i.e.* I was 'black', and 'blacks' were not allowed in the club. Willa was furious, but it did not help. She apologized profusely but I kept telling her that it was no fault of hers and that things like this happen sometimes. I also told her that I did not consider it as an insult to be black.

Willa, however, whose friendship my family and I have cherished for a long time, was not one who was going to forget this incident.

Three years later, she invited Aruna and me to Memphis on the occasion of her grand-daughter being crowned 'Cotton Queen of Memphis'. We gladly accepted her invitation and spent a few days with her. During that visit, she made it a point to take us back to the same club for lunch. We were accompanied not only by the Cotton Queen, *i.e.* her granddaughter, but by Willa too. But this time, Willa was the president of the club. Nobody stopped us.

Willa then hired a boat for a river cruise and invited over 100 guests, including the entire managing committee of the club to celebrate the crowning of her granddaughter as 'Cotton Queen of Memphis'. And to drive her point home, can you guess whom she invited to crown her granddaughter? Me.

What a grand display of old friendship and fierce loyalty! Aruna and I were the 'Guests of Honour' with the members of the club's managing committee, who had but a few years ago denied me entrance, now present as mere bystanders.

But Willa was not done. While thanking the guests, she narrated the whole story. The applause was thunderous, but I could see a few southern grins on the faces of those present.

The Cotton Queen of Memphis being crowned by a non-white for the first time! That was Willa, proving her point in her own sweet way to make up for the insult I had suffered.

15 | Hobbies, Food and Extra-Curricular Pleasures

How serious should one's life be? I often wonder. It's a tricky question. In our pursuit of professional success, we sometimes tend to forget other aspects of our life. While work is a wonderful and essential accessory and obviously the mainstay of life, I believe it's equally important to be content and happy in one's leisure time.

Let's be honest. Can one's life be truthfully called complete without some diversions or hobbies? I don't think so. *I feel hobbies and diversions aren't just important, they're essential in life. They are the fuel on which we survive.* I believe that all young people must have a constructive hobby or two, because when one grows old, hobbies and friends are what will sustain them. Otherwise, time hangs on one's hands and that isn't a pleasant thing. Believe me, I know what I'm talking about and can personally vouch for this. My fairly busy schedule notwithstanding, I now find that time often hangs on my hands, because I never developed a hobby in the real sense. It is one of the few things I regret.

I regret that I didn't do more serious reading, or follow up on my interest in photography. When I was young, I was trying to prove the point that though I had a poor academic record, I would succeed in life. In doing so, time just flew. My desire to 'reach' and stay on the 'top' of my profession was so strong that I never had the time for what I then considered to be expensive pursuits—hobbies. So all other 'trivial' pastimes went flying out of the window. It's really a pity. A person is not a complete human being unless he or she has a hobby. A hobby reflects the inner self of an individual, his creativity, interests and values, etc.

About the only two hobbies I now try to pursue, albeit in small doses, are listening to Urdu *ghazals* and watching plays.

I do like travelling and during my career, have probably traversed nearly a million miles—mostly on work—by air. I have visited around fifty countries. And yet, I have not really seen most of these places nor enjoyed them in the true sense, with very few exceptions. All the travel was mostly related to work, so there simply wasn't any time to lounge about and soak up the local atmosphere.

To an extent, this is something that I'm now able to catch up on and it is turning out to be pleasant, though expensive.

Travelling now has become much more relaxing and vacations have become a vocation. Aruna and I have begun to enjoy cruises. We loved our cruise around the coasts of South America. We were in Chile when the disastrous earthquake hit that country. Unfortunately and due to my sudden illness in London just a week before our departure, we could not take a Danube cruise we had planned in September 2011. But we made up for it in June 2013. We have sailed down the Nile on board an Oberoi boat and cruised the Caribbean with Neeraj, Kavi and Shreya.

For our fiftieth wedding anniversary, Aruna and I returned to what has remained our favorite hotel in Bombay, today Mumbai—The Taj Mahal Hotel.

There is a reason. It was where we had stayed during our honeymoon, in a beautiful suite facing the Gateway of India. And it is where we enjoyed Currimbhoy Salad and Bombay Duck several times.

There is a funny story linked to the Taj. Once, Aruna and I had checked into the Air India-owned Centaur instead. On our first evening, we went down for cocktails. When we returned to our rooms, we found all our belongings missing from our closets. Even our luggage had been removed. We went back to the front desk to report a robbery.

The General Manager came up and joined his staff, all wearing broad smiles. "No Sir," he laughed, "Mr. Ajit Kerkar of the Taj Mahal took your belongings. He insisted that you cannot stay anywhere other than in his hotel!"

We have usually stayed at the Taj. There was a particular suite that I liked. If I was travelling to Bombay, I would always request that suite. Even if it had been booked, the Taj would somehow ensure I get it.

So, when we arrived at the Taj to celebrate our 50th anniversary, one of the first things we did is to ask for a Currimbhoy Salad and Bombay Duck. But those items had been off the menu for years. The ever-obliging kitchen and the restaurant staff launched a massive search in the archives of the hotel. Eventually, they managed to find a recipe and served a Currimbhoy Salad to us. But somehow, it didn't taste the same.

Still, we did have a magical experience. After all, we got the exact same suite we had stayed in during our honeymoon—in the old wing and facing the Gateway of India.

It remains to be seen how many more adventures my health will permit. I am willing and ready.

I don't know if indulgence in politics can be called a hobby, but as I have outlined, I was extremely interested in student politics. Like most Indians, I do discuss politics a lot, indeed it seems to be our national hobby today. But I don't take a personal or active part. Like several of my countrymen, I too, am an armchair politician who can discuss current affairs passionately but does little to improve matters himself. It is, at best, a peripheral interest. Indeed, this has been the case right since 1953 when I left university and gave up active politics. Nevertheless, I consider myself a responsible citizen.

Golf! Teeing Off!

Does one have to talk much about golf? Not really. It is a sub-culture in itself. Those who love the game, literally live by it.

I joined the Delhi Golf Club primarily because it was considered fashionable and sociable to do so. But in later years, I had to give up golf, because I developed a serious tennis—or call it golf—elbow.

I do feel that if I had continued to play, I would have been a healthier person. Many years later, I proudly witnessed my grand-daughter, Shreya Ghei, become the Ladies' Open Champion. She also captained India at the Asian Games Golf Tournament held in China in 2010.

Food!

When Confucius said 'food is the first love', he might just have had people like me in mind. My past record, my girth and my more than 50-year-old affliction with diabetes, speak for themselves.

Let me put this plainly—I love food, of any kind. But I must confess that my favorite is Indian, followed by Italian and then Chinese cuisine.

Most Punjabis are 'foodies' and I have been one of no mean proportions. Food wasn't just important to me, it was almost a passion. I became a sort of ready-reckoner on the availability of diverse food items in Delhi. I used to venture out a lot in quest of good food. My list of delicacies was endless. There were so many different temptations pulling me in different directions.

Those were the days of relatively few restaurants. Davicos (later called Standard Restaurant above Regal Theatre) and Wengers were beyond one's budget. Occasionally one could afford Laxmi at Chandni Chowk, or United Coffee House at C.P.

It is only after 1947 that Delhi saw the growth of restaurants. Today, Delhi boasts of fine-dining from all over the world.

Therefore, my forays way back then were limited to sweets shops, *dhabas*, or small establishments that offered mostly one or two dishes. The one restaurant whose food I enjoyed the most was Gaylord, I tried almost all their main dishes. What a shame it closed down!

My knowledge of cuisine was vast. Talk about any tasty preparation and I'd know a thing or two about it and who makes it the best.

I could tell you about the best *Ma ki Dal* and *Paranthas* in Murthal, near Sonepat; I could expound on the kebabs in Meerut, hold forth on *Kesar da Dhaba* in Ambala (and of course, the *Bharawn da Dhaba* in Amritsar), I could wax eloquent about Gyani's in Kasauli, the Chicken Stroganoff at the then popular Volga, the lamb chops at Embassy, the *Chana Bhaturas* at Kwality; I could sing paeans to the famous *lassi* whipped up by Mithan Halwai at Kashmiri Gate—whose *rabri* came all the way from Mathura; I could rave about the chicken patties at Gaylord; the *shammi kebabs* at Wengers; the *chaat* on Shah Jahan Road; I could describe in evocative detail the offerings of *Paranthe Wali Gali*, the *jalebis* at Dariba; the *Dahi Pakori* on the steps of the Central Bank in Chandni Chowk, the *seekh kebabs* of Jama Masjid, the *kulchas* from Paharganj; the *biryani* from Matka Pir; the mutton stew from Karim's in Jama Masjid—oh yes, I could go on and on.

Any chef worth his name will endorse the eating of sweets after a meal. I agree wholeheartedly. I had a sweet tooth, sorry a sweet denture! New York cheesecake was one of my favourite desserts. So were pancakes and waffles—generously soaked in syrup—for breakfast. And as for Indian sweets, they're all welcome.

These were just a few of the irresistible snacks and meal items that were dear to my heart, or should I say, stomach. Today all of them have disappeared from my diet chart and been replaced by tablets and insulin shots. But alas! I do cheat! (About three times a day!)

Being fond of food, I suppose it was befitting that some of my friends and acquaintances made me discover some of the finer points of different cuisines. My good friends, Krishan Malik, formerly with

The Times of India and my lawyer, the late Satya Dev Sharma were two individuals who taught me about the nuances of non-vegetarian and vegetarian food respectively. In the 'foodie' department, both Krishan and Satya Dev were my partners-in-crime.

Everyone has his own concept of what good food is. Today, it has expanded to include international cuisine. Health foods have become a fad.

But at this age and thanks to my wife's strict control, I am told that good food is healthy food. I agree whole-heartedly. (But I still cheat, whenever I get an opportunity).

The Coffee Club

To describe my Coffee Club days, I must take you back to my youth and my first 'encounter' with coffee.

It was 1945 and I had just completed my matriculation. My friend Bhagirath Bhalla told me about the India Coffee House, where a new beverage, 'coffee', was being promoted. One evening, we decided to try it out and made our way to the coffee house, which was located on Queensway, today's Janpath.

In those early days, the India Coffee House nurtured a tradition— it offered complimentary cashew nuts along with a cup of coffee. On the first visit, we relished the nuts. But after literally just one sip, we found the coffee totally unpalatable. It was a small adventure that had gone awry. Feeling a bit sorry for ourselves and keen to save our money—which in this case happened to be eight *annas*, that is, half a rupee in today's terms for the price of two cups— we decided to 'cop out'. On the pretext of visiting the toilet, we slipped out without paying. Quite proud of our escape, we ran away, tickled at the fact that we had saved our money and avoided that awful brew.

When I was studying for my Master's from 1949–1953—my 'gradual graduation' as I told you, my association with coffee started again. This time, at the University Coffee House. More than coffee, the main attraction was girls.

There were many good waiters around. But the one I recall most fondly is Tahir, a true host who often helped us out by giving us additional coffee for a small personal consideration. Give Tahir a rupee and he would get extra refills faithfully. If you didn't have money, he would give you personal credit. And if you wanted a message delivered to a lady, he would do it for the small tip of one rupee.

Later in life, in 1953 to be precise and when I joined Mercury Travels, the India Coffee House on Janpath became my regular haunt. I started to meet up with a few friends at 11 a.m., which meant slipping out of the office. At the bustling Coffee house, I befriended a host of personalities including eminent statesmen, journalists and artists like I.K. Gujral, Inder Malhotra, K.B. Kachru of the Statesman, Krishan Malik of the Times of India, Jatin Das, a freelance painter and Prem Prakash, photo-journalist and founder of ANI. Prem Prakash, who, as I mentioned earlier, is today my longest-standing 'coffee-mate' and personal friend.

Both at the university coffee house and at the one on Janpath, the chief and only topic of discussion was politics, politics and more politics. Of course, that focus shifted a bit during our days at university to 'girls'. Full justice was done to both subjects, and they were discussed and analyzed a hundred times over.

I was introduced to my current 'Coffee Club' in 1961–62. Its original members included Mohinder Puri, R.K. Narpat Singh, Kishan Bans Bahadur, Brij Bans Bahadur and Som Sikand, the oldest in age but the youngest at heart.

After a disagreement with his brother, Brij Bans, Kishan Bans Bahadur left the club. Ken Syal, Som Sikand and yours truly, continued. For a brief period, Satya Dev was our new inductee. Then came two new members: Prem Prakash, a friend from college days and D.V. Kapur, Director, Reliance Industries. As always, we were very well looked after by the waiters at all the establishments we frequented.

Originally, we used to meet at Alps, one of the most upscale restaurants of that era. It was owned by Tej Pal Singh and his brother and located on Janpath. Later, the same venue became the Lufthansa office. When Alps closed, we shifted to Laguna, owned by the Khanna family who operated the Claridges Hotel in Delhi. But since we didn't find Laguna hospitable enough, we moved to Gaylord, another famous eatery owned by Peshori Lamba and Iqbal Ghai, where, incidentally, the coffee was well complemented by chicken patties. When parking near Gaylord became a problem, we shifted yet again: this time, to the Imperial Hotel, where my SITA office was located in those days.

Imperial Coffee Club—Myself, Kishan Bans Bahadur,
Som Sikand, R.K. Narpat Singh, Brij Bans Bahadur

Out of the original members of our 'Coffee Club', there are only two of us left today. At times, there is nothing new to discuss. We repeat ourselves. D.V. Kapur has stopped joining us. I suspect it is because I could not endorse his political opinion.

Still and till date, our discussions at our 'Coffee Club' center around political news and events, though we occasionally dabble in business headlines too. There's no dearth of spirit and our discussions are quite animated, to say the least. But we never fight. I think it's fair to say that one of the reasons for our strong and continued friendship is the fact that we're all pursuing different professions, and have no mutual business dealings whatsoever. On several occasions, our wives, too, have expressed a keen desire to join us for a cup of coffee. But they have always been politely and diplomatically refused. Any female intrusion, except in the realm of imagination, isn't permitted.

The Coffee Club remains an intrinsic part of my life and missing out on that particular cup of coffee is almost unthinkable for me. During my professional years, I rarely made an appointment that clashed with it. Over the years, several Secretaries and Director-Generals Tourism, who became friendly and knew of our Coffee Club, would never ask for a meeting that clashed with our sacrosanct institution.

So steadfast have we all been, that our 'Club' is even mentioned in the Imperial Hotel's book on its own history.

I have also been fond of theatre. It's unfortunate that unlike in London or New York, no city in India, except, to some extent Mumbai, has a strong tradition of theatre.

Delhi is particularly impoverished in this respect. Other than the occasional play put up by the National School of Drama, there are only one or two good theatre repertories. Tom Alter is probably the most regularly-seen stage actor. The worst thing about these shows is that they never start on time. In fact, they don't start till the audience, in sheer desperation, starts clapping.

My other love is to listen to *ghazals* whenever possible. My friend from my travel days, Mrs. Indira Verma, is trying hard to re-induct me into the *ghazal* circles of Delhi. I hope it reawakens the passion for a hobby in me. As I said earlier, that is what is most needed when one grows old.

A good, enjoyable hobby is a must. One should try to develop one as early as possible and then nurture it.

16 Lighter Moments— Laughter: The Best Medicine

Doctor Diet, Doctor Quiet and Doctor Merriment—this was the prescription given to me by a senior physician. And I must say, it makes sense.

Doctor Diet I cannot talk about, because I deal with him regularly, almost three times a day. At each meal, I am reminded of my food habits—not so much the quantity, but the quality. Calories are counted. The only sensible control I observe is over alcohol. But I do follow my wife, Aruna's advice to not snack in between meals. Of course I break that rule sometimes, explaining that I am doing so only to 'change my taste'. My food habits show all over me and more so, on my weighing-scale. The needle keeps moving up, no matter what I do.

As far as Dr. Quiet is concerned, I am a more serious adherent to his rules. Firstly, I sleep—thank God—for a minimum of eight to nine hours every night. And since I cannot sleep as soundly as in a school or college class anymore, I regularly take a nap in the car. The movement of a car reminds me of my cradle. I can sleep really well in cars, on planes—almost anywhere in motion.

As for Dr. Merriment, I am almost a devotee.

If laughter is the best medicine, lighter moments must surely be a doctor's prescription for good health and spirits. During the course of my life there have been lighter moments galore, and it is with a sense of pleasure that I recall some, though not necessarily in the order in which they occurred.

One incident that comes to mind is when PATA Life Members met in India. Being part of this prestigious fraternity, naturally I had a personal interest in their India visit and overall welfare. You will remember the time we took some of our good friends to Rajasthan on a trip. There, we decided to indulge in some unusual and harmless fun. We first managed to pull off an imaginary 'break-down' of our bus, on the lonely road to Samode, formerly a small, princely state in Rajasthan, some kilometers off the main Delhi-Jaipur Highway. Then, we stage-managed a hold-up by 'highway dacoits', carrying *lathis* (sticks), toy pistols and one toy '12-bore double barrel' gun.

Needless to say, the 'highwaymen' were all SITA staff, dressed in *lungis* and pyjamas.

Each 'hostage', that is each member of the group, had to pay up a hundred U.S. dollars. They were all shell-shocked. I pretended to be very concerned, but encouraged them to cough up to save our lives. I also handed over a few hundred rupees myself. The gangsters threatened a few ladies and snatched some chains and pendants.

There was more organized 'drama' waiting at the Samode Palace. When we entered, there was total darkness. I ensured that every-one believed we had come to the wrong hotel. The staff first refused to open the massive gates of the old palace that was now a hotel. Suddenly, the lights came on. Fireworks exploded and everyone was heartily welcomed. And of course, everyone's looted money and jewellery was returned.

Without boasting, I can say that all my friends remember that trip with great fondness. In fact this was the beginning of what we later called the 'Dreams Trip'.

Another light-hearted incident of note in my professional life is the circumstance in which the decision on duty-free shopping at Indian airports was finalized. I was strongly in favour of having duty-free shopping introduced at Indian airports.

One evening, we had a small gathering at my home which included the Chairman, Central Board of Excise & Taxation, G.S. Sawhney and the Joint Secretary, Ministry of Economic Affairs, P.K. Kaul, who later became Cabinet Secretary and also served as India's Ambassador in Washington, D.C.

Sawhney was adamantly against the introduction of duty-free shopping at Indian airports and refused to budge from his position. He believed it would lead to smuggling. Kaul and I, on the other hand, believed that it would be more convenient for Indians returning home to do their shopping of imported goods particularly liquor, upon arrival. Later that evening, we were all to attend a Ravi Shankar concert at Modern School. Tickets had been hard to obtain but we had them.

Seeing Sawhney's obstinacy over duty-free shops, Kaul and I forcefully declared that there would be no concert until Sawhney agreed to allow the duty-free scheme to go ahead. It was blackmail, plain and simple, but it worked. Sawhney agreed and, the rest as they say, is history. We have duty-free shopping at most of our international airports today. The traveller is happy and the country saves foreign exchange.

When in Rome, Do as the Romans Do

Well, I suppose I didn't.

On one of my trips to the city, I took a taxi to get to my destination without knowing that it was located—literrally—opposite my hotel. The ride took only some minutes and I was there. When I asked the driver what I owed him, he said 'nothing', as he didn't take money from 'fools'. I couldn't help thinking this was very unusual coming from a taxi driver and that too an Italian. My later experiences with Italians were not so pleasant. In fact, most of them were downright irresponsible, if not, cheats.

The passion for coffee prevailed throughout those years.

Once during a TAAI Convention in Cochin, I happened to be chairing a session. One of the panelists was the venerable S.K. Kooka, popularly known as Bobby Kooka, the then Commercial Director, virtually the No. 2 of Air-India and one of JRD Tata's favourites.

At that time, the main issue confronting the industry was agents' commissions from airlines. The agents wanted more than 9%, Air-India and other airlines wanted to pay less. It had become a contentious issue. At the panel discussion, Mr. Kooka had referred to travel agents as the 'apple of my eye' and the 'cream in my coffee'.

However, when we had breakfast together that morning, I noticed that Bobby Kooka took his coffee without milk or sugar. During the summing up of my next presentation at the convention and on a lighter note, I remarked that Bobby thought of us travel agents as the sugar and cream in his coffee, but took neither in his cup of the beverage himself.

My witty remark drew its share of applause but Bobby was furious with me. No one had ever scored a point against him. So much for 'milk and honey' and 'black' and 'white' coffee.

Remember the adage that 'one's mouth can land one in trouble'? Well, that's what happened to me another time.

In New York City in 1953, I just happened to refer to an industry colleague as a 'gay person', meaning, of course, that he had a happy disposition and nature. I'd meant it as a compliment. In India, one used the word often without anyone taking offence. At that time, I didn't know the western connotation of the word 'gay'. You can imagine my embarrassment when it was pointed out to me.

All Dressed Up, and Everywhere to Go!

That's what my very first train-ride from Los Angeles to Palm Springs in December 1955 was about. Dengler, the owner of SITA, had a nearly 100-acre ranch in Palm Springs, which was also the SITA headquarters. I was nattily turned out in a tweed suit in anticipation of meeting the Denglers. I thought it would be the appropriate way to meet the top boss's wife and was keen to make an impression. Imagine my surprise when I saw Mrs. Dengler with bare feet and in shorts! It was hot, desert country and everyone was dressed casually. And there I was in my tweed suit.

Then, there were the Days of the Creased Suits...

During our earlier travel days, we travelled with a very meagre foreign exchange allowance of about 20 to 25 dollars a night. Vasant Kotak, a good family friend and Director, TCI, advised me to save foreign exchange by not getting my suits ironed in the hotel but hanging them on the clothesline in the bathroom and running the hot water in the tub instead. The steam, he said, would take out most of the creases. On one such occasion, the clothesline broke and my suits got thoroughly drenched. I had to spend a 'fortune' out of my foreign exchange allowance, to have the suits dry-cleaned. Needless to say, this is one trick I never tried again.

O Romeo, Romeo! Wherefore Art Thou Romeo?

This brings to mind another incident involving my friend, Vasant Kotak. Vasant was a flamboyant and colourful character. He was fond of music, played the *sitar* and had a slick way with women. While travelling overseas, he would take off his wedding ring. At one of the ASTA conferences, he made a beeline for two pretty women. Later, he invited me to join in. Acting on a mischievous impulse, I yanked my wedding ring off my finger, went up to Vasant and offered it to him, as though it were his—all this right in front of the ladies. Boy, was he upset that his evening had been ruined!

God is Everywhere. Even on Commercial Flights...

His (late) Highness of Bharatpur, a princely state of Rajasthan, was a friend and client. He wanted to carry along with him a statue of Lord Govardhan (Lord Krishna) while travelling around the world on PanAm. Nothing unusual about that—lots of people carry statues of gods and deities along with them. But this was a different ball game altogether because His Highness wanted the statue placed on the vacant seat next to him, and didn't want to pay for the seat.

We had a 'situation' on our hands. I discussed this rather delicate issue with PanAm's regional director, Jerry Gerald and finally struck a 'deal'. The deal was that the airline would provide the second seat free of cost and in return, would have the right to use four photos of His Highness and the statue in their magazine, 'Clipper News'. It was a barter of the most unusual kind but a barter, nevertheless. Lord Govardhan travelled worldwide, and everyone shared His 'blessings', both the Maharaja and PanAm were happy and I got the praise.

Kissa Yatra ka!

Rai Bahadur Gujar Mal Modi, Chairman of the Modi Group, wanted to travel abroad with his wife. This was to be their first overseas trip and he had two requests. Desiring a grand 'send-off', he wanted a band to come right up to the plane itself. After considerable lobbying, we managed to get a band allowed past the immigration counter and right up to the last barrier. His second request was that his hotels in America should allow his wife to prepare '*shudh*' vegetarian food. Not an easy task to accomplish, especially when it came to the Waldorf Astoria in New York. First, they refused. Finally, with the help of our connection through SITA, New York and Mrs. Modi's persuasion, we managed to 'break the ice' and I was told that Mrs. Modi did, indeed, cook at the Waldorf Astoria.

Saheliyon ki Bari

It was a case of woman power at its best. During the time of S.N. Chib, Director-General Tourism, the Department of Tourism was staffed mostly by ladies. Highly educated, sophisticated and from respectable families, they were recruited because they were endowed with a degree of *finesse* and were eminently suited for handling tourists.

I was a frequent visitor to their office during that period. Most of them combined personal charm and *elan* with professionalism in tourism marketing. Some like Vibha Pandhi, Asha Malhotra, Hira Chandrana, Kanta Thakur, Vatsala Pai and Veena Sanyal became good personal friends. Only Anjali Mehta, the senior-most, stayed aloof. Those days, the department was housed in the Taj Hutments across the road from the Imperial Hotel. The first room was the office of the Director-General, Mr. Som Nath Chib; the next was that of Gopi Kadappa, his deputy. Then followed a row of rooms, occupied, at some time or another, by the ladies. I used to find any excuse to visit the ladies and they were all very helpful and friendly. Some became good family friends. Mohinder Sethi, Kudesia and Gopi Kadappa were my gentleman-friends. Unfortunately, Mohinder and Gopi never got along well. Gopi was a little scheming but overall, the whole crowd was straight-forward and open-minded. The lady officers, with the exception of Mehta, were all very friendly.

Pranksters (One is never too old for fun)

There was always time for fun. At the Manila PATA Conference, I recall a major prank, of which I was the chief instigator. The gentlemen at the receiving end were Mr. Sundra, Chairman ITDC; Mr. Ramanathan, Chairman, Airport Authority of India; and Mr. Jagdish Parekh, Managing Director of Lee & Muirhead. With the help of the local Manager of Air India, I and some 'accomplices' stage-managed 'telex messages' to all three of them. The messages were as follows.

The one to Sundra informed him that from the position of Chairman, ITDC, he had been transferred to that of Chairman,

Coal India and was to return immediately to India to relinquish his old post and take up his new one.

The one to Ramanathan told him that upon his return, he was to take over as chairman, ITDC, in place of Mr. Sundra.

And the one to Parekh said that he had been appointed as a Visiting Professor to the Management School in Hawaii. He was thrilled.

We had opened a can of worms. What followed was a cross-section of emotions.

Sundra was outraged, Ramanathan was delighted, and Parekh was happy. Sundra and Ramanathan immediately contacted Air India to fly back home. One to stop his transfer and the other, to assume his 'new' office. At a function hosted by the Indian delegation that evening, Sundra was absent while Ramanathan and Parekh were literally on Cloud Nine. When the truth was revealed later, Sundra and Ramanathan were both very upset with me. Professionally, both were important to me. But both were perfect gentlemen, so we ended up enjoying the April Fool's day prank together and they were nice enough not to hold it against me. As for Parekh? Well, he just smiled it away.

Good Horse Sense!

During my first overseas trip as a student in 1951, I happened to dine with a young Frenchwoman in Paris.

This was no ordinary occasion. I was in Paris, a 20-year-old, enjoying the company of a charming lady. So this warranted a little bit of showing off.

I was asked about my dietary preferences. But without knowing even the basics of French cuisine and because I didn't want to sound old-fashioned, I promptly declared that I would go for the specialty of the house, but that it should not be beef.

The waiter named a dish in French. I could not understand a word but repeated that as long as it was not beef, it was fine. My lady companion also ordered the same. In due course of time, the waiter appeared at our table. Ceremoniously placing two silver tureens before us, he said: "*Bon Appetit*, *Madame* and *Monsieur*, enjoy your meal!"

I stared at a large chunk of meat. Fearing it may be beef steak, I looked at him questioningly.

"Sir it's not beef," he assured me. "It's horse meat, the delicacy of the house!"

Those were the years after World War II. There was a shortage of meat. In fact and in countries like Germany, there was very little variety of food available.

I don't think I can quite explain exactly what went through my mind at that moment. And as to how I tackled, yes tackled, but didn't eat the 'delicacy' that was horse meat? I leave that to your imagination.

Conned in Tokyo!

This incident took place in Tokyo several years ago and involves me and S.K. Misra, then Secretary Tourism, holding the extra charge of Chairman, ITDC, whom I sometimes affectionately refer to as 'SK'. (Many of his friends call him 'Chappie', but I am uncomfortable with that. To me, he is Mr. Misra). We were in Tokyo and walking to our hotel "The Imperial" at around 10 pm, after attending a reception at the Indian Tourist Office, which was then located in Ginza. Suddenly, we were accosted by a well-dressed Japanese man who, surprisingly, addressed us in broken Hindi. We got talking. He told us that he had worked at the Ashok Hotel for several months to negotiate the opening of a Japanese restaurant. Soon, he invited us to his nearby restaurant for a drink. We were taken in by his friendliness. The two of us, veterans of international tours and the seasoned and confident travellers that we both were, accepted his hospitality.

A few minutes after sitting down, he invited three girls to join us, introducing them as his friends. He offered us Scotch and the ladies ordered champagne. I had a suspicion that it was only lemonade. But it didn't bother us either way because we assumed he was the host.

After about twenty minutes, he excused himself to attend to some business and promised to be back very soon. We and the ladies had one more round of drinks. Forty-five minutes later, our 'host' was yet to return. We began to get nervous.

We wanted to leave. But the restaurant's manager, the 'real one', demanded that we pay the bill, not only for our drinks but also the champagne and—for the ladies' company. We said that we were guests of the owner, who had just left. The manager told us that he had never seen that man before.

So here we were, the 'Secretary Tourism' and 'Chairman' of SITA, two veterans, who had fallen for one of the oldest tricks in the trade.

Those were the days of foreign exchange shortage. Between the two of us we did not have the money to clear the bill. Those were also the days when Indians had no credit cards, certainly not legal ones. Finally and leaving behind SK in the bar—literally, as a hostage, I walked to the Imperial Hotel, picked up some money and came back. Somehow, we pooled our resources to escape the clutches of the unscrupulously friendly Japanese.

For years, we never told this story to anybody, so ashamed were we to have fallen for a trick. But now it can be told.

Just a Bottle of Wine

This incident takes the cake, as far as my frugal habits are concerned.

The day I signed the agreement to sell SITA, Hans Lersch, Chairman of Kuoni Switzerland and Ranjit Malkani, Chairman, SOTC, said we should celebrate the occasion. As we were the recipients of the sale money, I was the host. There were about seven or eight of us including Arjun, Neeraj, our consultant Vikas Vig and a few others. We were dining at the Club at the Taj, Bombay.

I am no *connoisseur* of wines, but Hans being Swiss, loved good wine with his food. As we are old friends, I asked him to select the wine, and he did so, ordering two bottles. Even a non-wine drinker like myself, enjoyed that particular wine. While the dinner was on, I went to the men's room and on the way, asked the steward to show me the wine card, so that I could note down the name of the wine for future use.

When I looked at it, I noticed that the price of that particular wine was Rupees 20,000/- plus taxes. I literally hit the roof.

When I came back to the table I whispered to my son, Arjun, "Sonny, I am not signing the bill for the wine, it goes against my grain." He laughed and whispered back, "Dad, you have just received a cheque for a handsome amount and you can surely afford to entertain us with this wine." I said, "No Arjun, you have to sign for these two bottles. You can put the charge on my room but I will not sign the bill for such an expensive item." And sure enough, I did not sign this bill as an official expense, but paid for it myself. To this day, I will not spend such huge amounts merely for my drinking pleasure.

The Infamous Martinique

In 1955, I underwent training in New York with SITA, USA along with two other gentlemen from London and Tokyo. We were put up at the Hotel Martinique, very close to Macy's Store. The room rate was U.S. $ 4.75 per night. We used to leave the hotel early in the morning for office and would return very late in the evening.

Those were the days of hardships. I used to buy myself breakfast at an automated restaurant called 'Horn & Hardet' for 25 cents on most mornings. It included a small glass of juice, pre-cooked eggs, two toasts and a cup of coffee or tea. Yes, 25 cents. I wanted to save money.

Further and to save the bus fare of 15 cents, I would walk 20 blocks each day from the hotel to office and back. Those were the days when every penny counted (and they still do).

When we got back to the Martinique, we would always discern a lot of noise and female voices in the corridors.

After a few weeks, all three of us discovered that the hotel was quite famous—or infamous—for providing short-term rentals for 'ladies of the night' and their customers. We were embarrassed. Here we were, three young people who had come all this way for training. We wanted to work hard and get our jobs. We could do without this distraction. We spoke to the Manager and told him that we were going to move to another hotel, as his was very noisy. But during our conversation, he discerned that we were actually going to be in New York for at least a few months. He did not want to lose three customers who were paying a regular room rent and were going to be staying long. So he first changed our rooms to what was considered a quieter floor. Next, he offered us complimentary continental breakfast with juice, coffee, bread & butter, rolls and jam, but no eggs. We jumped at the offer. At least I did, to save those 25 cents.

After a month's stay, the Manager decided to be even nicer to us and he said he would offer us a free full breakfast on Saturdays and Sundays. What a luxury that was! We could have either two eggs or pancakes or additionally a waffle, during those weekend breakfasts. It was sheer joy. Suddenly, it was no longer a problem to ignore those noisy ladies. But the story, of that visit to New York, does not end here.

Can I Drink the Water?

The trip to New York in 1953 was my first one to that city. On the very last day, I decided to spend one night at the 'Waldorf Astoria' the famous luxury hotel in New York. I wanted to experience that luxury, not knowing whether I would ever come back to New York or not. I checked in for one night at the fabulous rate of

US $ 15 per night. It was expensive but then, so what? I thought I had arrived in life. Ever since then, it has remained my favourite hotel. The last time Aruna and I stayed there was in May 2015, when we were visiting the US to attend the graduation ceremony of our granddaughter Shreya, who studied at Yale.

Back in 1953, I also had this urge to act like American tourists do in India. After checking in, I asked the receptionist rather loftily (remember, this was well before the days of bottled water): "Tell me, is the tap water here safe to drink?" The gentleman at the reception stared at me. He had obviously never been asked that question before. Somewhat irritably, he said, "Of course, Sir". I laughed gleefully within myself, because that was the one question an American visitor to India would always ask a guide or a hotel receptionist. When you're young, it's great to get even.

While on the subject of hygiene and hotels, the following memory comes alive.

The Hotel Classification Committee

The Second Hotel Classification Committee was chaired by Mr. S.D. Khanna, the Deputy Director-General, Tourism. I was a member. The first committee had been headed by Mr. Kadapa, as Number Two in the Tourist Department.

Even inferior hotels were claiming to carry four or five stars. Consequently, the main purpose of the Committee was to standardize the criteria for star classification in order to prevent such misrepresentation.

It was equally the intention of Mr. Chib, the Director-General Tourism, to set benchmarks of bare minimum requirements for a starred hotel and thereby give all establishments an opportunity to match international standards.

The Committee decided to be rather flexible and even accept improvements that were on the drawing board and to be completed in the next few months. The members included *inter alia*:

Mr. S.D. Khanna, Chairman, Ms. Thangam Philip, Principal, College of Catering, Bombay and myself as the representative of the Travel Agents Association of India. Our inspections of hotels were replete with some very hilarious incidents. I won't name the hotels, but you must get a taste.

While visiting the kitchen of a hotel in one city, I asked the dish-washer whether his establishment used hot water to clean dishes. He assured me they did. It was confirmed by the manager, who was accompanying our team. Now, the catch was that as per hotel standards, the temperature of the water is supposed to be around 40–45 degrees Celsius. We asked the manager to wash a dish in hot water of that temperature.

He could not. The reason was that the dishwashers had no gloves to wear as protection against water that hot. "Please don't bluff us, we are not fools," we told the manager. Our message to the managers was to be upfront and honest with us, and that we would be willing to accept their statement if they made the necessary changes. Very soon, word spread that this was one of the points that we were checking.

At the next hotel in the same city, we posed the same question. Sure enough, the manager said "yes"—but didn't rest at that. He whipped out a pair of gloves. But they were brand-new and even had the original dusting powder on them. A short distance away, we could see the empty box in which they had come, in a waste paper basket. The manager had tried to outsmart us but failed.

One of the conditions for a '5-Star' hotel was, that there should be a shop in the hotel arcade that stocks daily needs like toothpaste and shaving cream along with souvenirs. A well-known hotel belong-ing to a well-known chain had opened a shop in a hotel under inspection.

One of our members went up to the shop manager and innocently asked what their approximate daily sales were. He was given some figures. On buying some items, he was given a receipt. It bore the number 0001. That was the first sale made at that shop!

At another hotel, we found new furniture being installed, just as we arrived. There were several such incidents. But there is one that is particularly worthy of narration.

A Shared Experience

One of the distinguished members of the committee was Miss Thangam Philip, then the Principal of the College of Catering in Mumbai. A respected personality, Thangam was my contemporary at Delhi University. While I was in Hindu College, she was in Lady Irwin. We became good friends and I have the highest respect for Thangam Philip's integrity and professionalism. Some years after our Classification Committee days, there was a function held at the Taj Mahal Hotel, Mumbai to felicitate her. It was being presided over by Mr. Abid Hussain, ICS. I was also invited to speak and offer my best wishes.

In my course of my laudatory speech, I remarked: "My friends, I will tell you a secret. Thangam is one lady with whom I have been in more hotel rooms than with my own wife." There was laughter all around. It was a fact, that as members of the Classification Committee, we had truly visited more hotel rooms together than I had ever done with my wife Aruna. Thangam was a very sporting person and laughed along with everyone else.

Whenever she met me after that and irrespective of the company around, Thangam would always turn around and say, "Inder, when are we next going to a hotel room?"

Bless Thangam for that sparkling sense of humour!

Get the Photo Right

Yet another incident I recall as one of life's lighter moments, is related to my dear friend Mohinder Sethi. Mohinder was a Kesdhari Sikh gentleman with long hair, who had served as Director, India Tourism Office in Colombo, Tokyo and Sydney before becoming Deputy Director-General, Tourism.

With Mohinder Sethi

During his posting in Tokyo, he had his hair cut and his beard trimmed. Unfortunately, his mother died while he was in Tokyo and he had to rush back to India for the final rites. However, Mohinder had failed to change his passport photograph. Consequently, he arrived at Palam Airport with a passport photograph showing him as a Sikh gentleman although he now had short hair, was clean-shaven and—turbanless. Even though he was holding an official passport, the Haryanvi Immigration Officer would not permit him to enter the country because his passport photograph did not resemble him. Mohinder produced several identity cards. All showed him as a turban-wearing Sikh. But the more heatedly Mohinder argued, the tougher was the stance of the immigration officer. In those days, one had the 'influence' enough to enter the Customs and Immigration enclosure. Since I was standing just a few feet behind the Immigration counter, I went across to enquire what the problem was.

Pointing to me, Mohinder told the officer that here was Mr. Sharma of SITA Travel, who would gladly confirm that he is

Mohinder Sethi, Director of the India Tourism Office in Tokyo. The officer recognized me. But on the spur of the moment, I became mischievous. I told the officer that I hadn't a clue as to 'who this gentleman was'.

Suddenly, all hell was let loose. The officer grabbed Mohinder by the hand. Using the choicest of Haryanvi abuses in a loud voice, he tried to drag him to the cabin of a senior official. It was quite a scene. Here was India's 'Director Tourism', Tokyo, a Senior Class I Gazetted officer bearing an official passport, being dragged to a police cabin.

I rushed up and told the senior officer that I was only joking and that he was, indeed, Mohinder Sethi. After some persuasion, the immigration officer calmed down, Mohinder was released and allowed to leave the airport.

But when we got into the car, I was at the receiving end. Mohinder was raving mad and gave it to me for causing all that embarrassment. But the sport and friend that he was, he soon forgave me. Mohinder died early and his wife Surjeet (Jitty, as all call her) settled in Australia with her two daughters, Tutu & Ninu. They are our very good friends and in fact, we are almost like one family.

17 | The Family Man: Home, Hearth and My Dearhearts

You don't choose your family.
They are God's gift to you, as you are to them.
—Desmond Tutu

They say that the richest man in the world is the one who has the love of his family and friends. By that yardstick, I dare say I am a very rich man, a multi-millionaire.

A million emotions are rushing through me as I write this. But I will contain myself. Let it suffice to say that it is with a deep sense of pride and gratitude that I will talk about my family.

My family has been wonderful, understanding and most importantly, indulgent all along. They tolerate me with a smile. I wouldn't be overstating the point if I said they have also taught me a lot.

First, there were my parents: intuitive, supportive and most importantly, forgiving. Being the first-born and the only son, they indulged, guided and supported me, and lead me along the right path. They demanded no earthly or monetary returns from me. They wanted me to be a good human being.

If I could afford to be an honest businessman in my later years, it is because my wife Aruna, unlike many other wives, was not demanding. She was not besotted by jewellery or other expensive items. She was and is, a simple, dedicated doctor, wife, mother and grandmother.

I am equally fortunate to have two very loving, intelligent and devoted children. My first-born daughter Neeraj, and my son Arjun.

With Neeraj on Her
Birthday, 1969

My Son Arjun at 4.
My Favourite Picture

My daughter Neeraj had taken a B.Com. (Hons) degree and wanted to qualify as a chartered accountant. She did her articles with Mohinder Puri & Co., a company founded by my very dear friend, guide and philosopher, Mohinder Puri. Mohinder and I were at University at the same time and our build was similar. Often Mohinder, the gentleman, was blamed for the mischief that I wrought. By the time I started my business, he was a well-established and reputed Chartered Accountant heading 'Mohinder Puri & Co.', popularly known as MPCO.

Mohinder was very fond of Neeraj, not only as a friend's daughter, but as a very conscientious learner. Mohinder assigned her to several difficult positions so that she could be a versatile all-rounder. By the time SITA began to grow, I needed someone to help me out with the financial planning of our company. Finance management was never my strong point. I was more of a PR and Marketing man. Once Neeraj was experienced enough,

I requested Mohinder to let her join my company. Neeraj was somewhat hesitant, so Mohinder and I decided that he would literally fire her from MPCO and thus create a situation for her to join SITA Travels. This is how Neeraj came to SITA in 1985. To start with, she had to work under Mr. B.R. Kapoor who was the Financial Advisor, but later, she took on full responsibility for Accounts. For several years, she also looked after SITA's branches across the country and later developed SITA's outbound business. She is a perfect business leader. She was the first lady President of TAAI. She was also the first lady member of the Rotary Club of Delhi Midtown.

In 1999/2000, my son Arjun came up with a great idea of creating a special tour on which high-priced, invited guests would usher in the new year and century in luxury tents on a hillock close to the Amer Fort in Jaipur. A unique marketing idea at that time and unparalleled in its bold thinking. Selected customers, high pricing and a luxury product. Riding on elephants, camels, sipping cocktails with the Maharaja of Jaipur, dinner at his illuminated residential palace, special silver *thalis* (plates) and flowing champagne: luxury in true Maharaja style. The camp was a great success and became a talking point within the industry. His Highness Jai Singh of Jaipur personally received the guests and they dined with him in traditional fashion—an eleven-course dinner with music and Rajasthani folk dancers in attendance. Tourists came to the party on elephant-back. And there was a polo match with players riding elephants. In fact, Jai Singh threw open his palace—but not his purse! to treat these guests. Oh boy, what delectable ambience! And it was my son Arjun, who did it all and did so in style.

Like many other people, I realise and deeply appreciate the true value and worth of a family. It is one's foundations and I pray it remains so. *Amen, Ameen, Ashirwad!*

But and as is the case with all human beings, my family life, too, has been a mixed bag of happiness, worries, hassles and problems though fortunately, it mostly revolved around happiness.

I am a touchy and sentimental "fool" by nature. Consequentially, little things and gestures would either please, or annoy me. As you can imagine, this caused a few piquant 'situations' along the way.

The one thing I can't complain of is having led a boring life. My life has been a bagful of events.

My school days were not so spectacular, but there are still some wonderful memories.

My daily routine was uneventful and rather dull. Walking to M.B. School (Municipal Board School) at Reading Road, New Delhi, near Birla Mandir. Teacher Pyarelal, taking us through mathematics. Panditjee, who taught Hindi and Sanskrit and had convinced my father that I should study Hindi, instead of Urdu, since I was a Brahmin. This had resulted in an early and gruelling change in language in Class 6. Today, I know both languages but have no proficiency in either. Though I read both and without taking away from either of them, I still enjoy Urdu poetry and *ghazals* more than Hindi *kavitas*. My Head-Master Mr. Bhatnagar, used to wear a suit, come rain or shine, all through the year. He was a very stern man, who always carried a small cane, hidden in his coat-sleeves.

My college life was a different story altogether. It was vibrant, action-packed, contained a fair bit of romancing and also—I am afraid—a lot of wasted time by indulging in politics, instead of pursuing my studies.

I 'graduated gradually'. Indulge me if I have repeated this through these memoirs.

But I do so for the benefit of the younger generation who may be reading this and to reinforce certain messages.

If I hadn't wasted two years, I would have completed my Master's at the age of 19. Instead, I did so at 21. At that time I didn't realize it—and neither will you, young readers, till you are my age, because as you grow older, time becomes much more valuable. Now, I am convinced I wasted time. But there was a positive flipside.

My dabbling in student politics sharpened my personality. It gave me self-confidence and taught me a thing or two about dealing with people. And I do believe it helped me in my professional life too. My carefree attitude and vagabond image didn't go down well at all with my father and cost me the chance of getting a good job through his contacts. Who knows where I may have ended up, had that not been the case!

I won't harp too much on the academic munificence bestowed on me by my college—Hindu College. But it gave me a great 'gift' in the form of my meeting Aruna and my growing friendship with the wonderful lady, who was later to be my wife. I also developed a strong and long friendship with Prem Prakash, a leading journalist and charming individual, Madan Nayar who retired from ITC, Mr. Krishan Malik, formerly of The Times of India, and many others.

As I often say, the College may have failed to fully educate me, but it certainly succeeded in giving me the love of my life, Aruna.

In 1947, Aruna's parents had migrated from Lahore to Delhi with her and her two younger brothers, Vinod and Suman. Her father, Dr. Ram Labhaya, had been a professor of ophthalmology at Grant Medical College.

When she first set eyes on me, she was young and impressionable. As she later confessed to me, it was my skill at public speaking and debating that had drawn her to me. (Between you and me and quite frankly, I probably had no other sterling qualities).

Aruna's mother, Shakuntala Labhaya, was a Master's in Economics from the famous Kinnaird College for Women, Lahore. She was a bundle of energy with a strong will, likes and dislikes. Aruna's parents always wanted an IAS officer as a son-in-law. Those days, someone working in a private firm was looked down upon. I was certainly not their first choice, but Aruna's insistence prevailed.

Now back to Aruna, the shy and simple girl that she still is.

Guys, there's a lesson to be learnt here. Don't hesitate to say things boldly to a woman, if you fancy her. Your glib talking might just do the trick and fetch you well-deserved rewards. At least try.

As a student, I didn't exactly have money spilling out of my pockets. For the first year, my daily allowance was four *annas* (25 paise) a day. Not very generous, but it was sufficient for me to buy two *bermis* (puris) and a small *kullar (*earthen pot) of *lassi* for lunch, from the then famous Mithan Halwai at Kashmere Gate.

Later, my allowance was increased to Rupees 15/-. So by then, I could afford a visit to Carlton Cafe, once or twice a month. My version of luxury translated as an occasional cup of tea at the Cafe (sometimes even entertaining Aruna and sitting for hours in the cabin, gossiping and holding hands). There in the romantic ambience of a cosy kiosk, I went about the serious business of wooing Aruna.

After finishing her pre-medical, she joined Lady Hardinge College, where I continued to woo her.

We had two favourite meeting places, our own little hideouts. When I had the money to spend, I would lay it on—with a *samosa* and a *gulab jamun* at her College Gate on Panchkuian Road. When she was treating, it was usually an ice-cream at the college's other gate towards the Madras Hotel end. It was made by Kwality and the vendor was a Sikh gentleman, who gave liberal credit to students.

Now this may pale in comparison to some of the wooing done today, but believe me, it was momentous enough for the two of us at that time.

The Artful Dodger that I was, I'd occasionally take her out for a spin around the city, on the pretext of teaching her how to drive. It was our version of a romantic outing. I had the use of the car, as my father was transferred to Karnal. As incharge of the National Dairy Research Institute (NDRI) in Karnal, he had both a staff car and a one-horse carriage that carried two passengers and one *sayees* (a man who takes care of the horses and stands at the back).

After two years in Lady Hardinge, Aruna went to Dibrugarh, where her father was the Principal of Assam Medical College. At the time, I had a strong feeling that she was shifted to Dibrugarh so that she could be kept in 'safe custody', away from what her family considered my 'bad influence'.

During this period of separation, we both became prolific letter-writers. I could receive my mail freely, but she used to get hers via the local post office. It was quite an effort for her to find an excuse to go out for a walk to get the letter, then read it and finally hide it.

Finally, the time came for us to get down to the nitty-gritty and talk of marriage.

Initially, both our families played spoilsport and objected to the alliance outright. Aruna's parents wanted a suitable match for her, preferably an IAS officer, while my family wanted a Brahmin girl. Both families were aiming for a conventional, arranged marriage for their offspring.

A tricky situation developed, not very uncommon in India. Finally, we each piled on pressure and put our foot down within our respective families.

I distinctly remember those days. My father went back to his village to get his elder brother's permission for his son to marry a non-Brahmin girl. Fortunately, it was given. Similarly, my mother had to get permission from her elder brothers.

Aruna's parents, on their part, finally agreed when I got a job with SITA in New York, even though the truth is that they never considered travel agency work to be a respectable profession.

In a way, that was one of the first major hurdles I overcame in my personal life.

Finally, after a period of trial and tribulation and all this drama behind us, wedding bells chimed! We got married on December 7, 1957.

Newly-Weds, Aruna and I

By that time, my father had retired, and Aruna's father was working as a WHO expert in Sri Lanka. Our wedding was simple and in the Hindu tradition.

I have no hesitation in declaring that being married to Aruna is, and always has been a very pleasant experience and something for me to cherish.

Like all, or at least most marriages and for several years, our lives were replete with pleasurable moments, some 'ups and downs', some irritants, occasional disagreements. But throughout these decades, our union has been basically one of constant affection, trust, respect and love.

Aruna & I Dancing Together,
made for each other

Celebrating our First New Year
after our Marriage

Aruna & I—Sutluj River,
Himachal, 1968

Aruna and I in Venice
during our early travels

To be perfectly frank, Aruna had to bear with many of my idiosyncrasies, while she herself has always been very supportive and accommodating towards me. She led a comparatively simple life. She is a highly-qualified professional in her own right.

Though she has retired from the CGHS as a medical officer, she has, for many years, been admirably immersed in social work as part of the Delhi Commonwealth Women's Association charity projects. Twice a week and along with another colleague, Aruna works from a medical van parked on the streets of Dakshin Puri. She works in all weather conditions, surrounded by over a hundred poor patients, with pigs and dogs running around, and no decent toilet facilities. On two other days, she works at the Association-managed charitable dispensary in Zamrudpur.

My Aruna is a simple person of no guiles. While working as a full-time doctor, she also fulfilled her duties as the wife of a busy travel agent who had a very vigorous and often demanding social life. She has also been a very good mother, raising our two wonderful children, Neeraj and Arjun.

Such was Aruna's devotion both to her profession and to mother-hood, that because our first child Neeraj, was born while Aruna was still completing her internship, she resumed her duties after merely seven days. But as a doting mother, she would still come back home twice a day to feed Neeraj. And she managed all this in a calm, cheerful and loving manner.

For a long time, Aruna kept her cards close to her heart. Though not totally at ease with the vast and varied travails she encountered because of being married to me, Aruna maintained a stoic silence all these years and remained silently supportive.

It is only recently that she spoke frankly about the discomfort, concern and the bit of jealousy she had felt during the earlier days, when she, as a simple girl, saw me mingling freely with lots of foreign and Indian ladies, merrily dancing away at social functions. All these years! And she had never breathed a word of

Daddy, Mama, Usha and Self

Self, Aruna, Guruji

those apprehensions to me! She had never conveyed to me that some aspects of my behaviour had angered and upset her!

Now of course, she's fully aware of the larger picture and understands why a travel agent, a marketing person and the head of a service organization had to lead a seemingly colorful and extroverted life that included being friendly to all, even other ladies.

I deeply appreciate my Aruna—her magnanimous and understanding nature and the fact that she never mentioned these things all these years, merely to be supportive.

Like all human beings, I too felt, over these years, that Aruna lacked some qualities. The fact that on the surface, she seemed to take little interest in my profession and could thus, never be a good counsel or support to me. I can't say how much more I could have achieved in life if she had been those things, but it's hypothetical now and hardly matters any more. To her credit, I must say that, at least, she never interfered.

Aruna has been deeply engrossed with the medical profession and lately, with her devotion to Guruji. She was never an outgoing person and to people who don't know her, she may have seemingly 'failed' to broaden her horizon with worldly knowledge. Indeed, her outward calmness often gives the impression that she is disinterested in worldly affairs. But Aruna has always been a simple, doting wife, a loving mother and now, an adoring grandmother. Aruna's two younger brothers, Vinod and Suman, both lawyers, decided to settle in America.

My core family was a small one too. I had two sisters. One died when she was less than a year old, while my other sister, Usha, ten years younger to me, is my loving and doting kid sister. While we have deep affection for each other, we were never really companions owing to the vast difference in our ages. I can't remember ever having quarreled with Usha.

Like a good sister, she often covered up for my mischief during my college years. But when she was growing up I was already too busy with my profession.

After getting married, she moved to Calcutta, where her husband Ram C. Lakhanpal, a chartered accountant by profession, was the manager of Titagarh Paper Mills, Kankinara, near Calcutta (now Kolkata). Usha would visit Delhi during her children's school

Celebrating the New Year with Aruna, Usha and Ramji

Self, Shreya, Avantika & Ankita

Ramji, Usha, Poonam, Ranjit, Myself, Aruna, Neeraj & Kavi

Lakhanpal Family—Usha, Ranjit, Gauri, Myself, Shivan & Aruna

Myself with Avantika, Ankita, Ankur and Poonam Khanna

vacations and stay with us for just two weeks, far too short a period. Ramji, my brother-in-law, was a very simple gentleman. He retired as Director of Bird & Company. When the family moved to Delhi after his retirement, he found that he could not adjust to Delhi life. Ramji was not an outgoing man, preferring to mostly stay at home. He was a very organized, meticulous person.

Usha and Ram have two children, a daughter, Poonam, and son, Ranjit. Poonam graduated in Delhi. She did her Company Secretaryship and stayed with us during those three years. She was such a well-behaved child that I don't recollect when either Aruna or I, had to ever pull her up. Poonam is now married to Ankur Khanna, also a chartered accountant, who worked with ITC, KLM and is now with ICCI. They have twin daughters, Avantika and Ankita, who study at NYU in New York. They have mostly lived abroad—in Ghana, Saudi Arabia, China, Singapore and are now in Dubai.

Usha's son, Ranjit, is a bright young finance professional who did his schooling at Doon School, graduated from Hamilton College and did his Master's at Columbia, an American university. He spent most of his adult life away from the family, but is a devoted son, cheerful nephew and responsible husband. He has a subtle sense of humour. He works for Credit Suisse in Singapore as their Managing Director. He is married to Gauri Sikri, a very bright, self-confident girl who loves her work. They have a ten-year-old son Shivan, who's a very bright kid.

Incidentally, I was instrumental in bringing these two young people together. During one of my visits to Hong Kong where Ranjit was then working with Credit Suisse, he accompanied me to a party hosted by Gauri's mother, his future mother-in-law, Veena Sikri, the then Indian High Commissioner to Hong Kong. She has held several very high positions in the Ministry of External Affairs.

Mrs. Sikri was a member of IFS. The Sikris are a very delightful couple: simple, intelligent with no pretensions about their high position. That's how the liaison between young Ranjit and Gauri began.

> *"It is a wise father that knows his own child."*
>
> —**William Shakespeare,**
> **'The Merchant of Venice'**

All parents should strive to know their own children. We are blessed with two.

Neeraj, my elder one, was born on 11th March 1961, when I was 30 years old and while Aruna was still completing her internship.

Neeraj was a studious and diligent child, though not a topper. In fact, she had problems settling down in her first school, Carmel Convent. Young Neeraj was anti-establishment and that, too, in a convent school, so we constantly received complaints. Finally, we had to pull her out of that institution. Much later in life, we realized that she had a somewhat tomboyish personality. Later, she joined Modern School, New Delhi. It had a far more liberal approach to education and Neeraj took to it straightaway. After completing her B.Com., Neeraj qualified as a Chartered Accountant. She did her articleship from Mohinder Puri & Company. She had developed a friendship with her future husband, Kavi, during her schooling days. Initially and though Aruna knew, I was in the dark about this friendship. So much for my being a perceptive, 'worldly-wise' parent!

Finally when Kavi had qualified as a CA, Neeraj approached Aruna and for the first time, mentioned and expressed her desire to marry Kavi.

She was hesitant to speak to me, as she felt that I might refuse because Kavi wasn't a Brahmin. She had obviously misread my somewhat mildly-religious bent of mind.

Of course, I hadn't forgotten the fact that I had faced a similar problem when I wanted to marry Aruna. She is not a Brahmin either.

We met Kavi, who had also just qualified as a Chartered Accountant. When we encountered this young man, a pleasant individual with a lot of practical wisdom and common sense, we happily gave our consent.

Kavi has his own firm. He is a practicing Chartered Accountant and his firm also does some factoring business. Additionally it now represents some National Tourist Boards. Kavi's father, Mr. Purshotam Ghei, was Director of Marketing, Bharat Petroleum at the time, though he had originally worked for Burmah Shell. Purshotamji impressed me with his character. He was a gentleman *par excellence*. I'd like to mention an incident that illustrated his high character.

At Neeraj's wedding, we gave Kavi's parents a few envelopes as *sagan* (gift) for their relatives, as per normal custom. Publicly, Purshotamji accepted the envelopes, but later insisted on returning them. Till this day, I have those envelopes with the exact sums of money lying with me, and one day I will donate them to charity.

Though fond of his drinks, Purshotamji was a very understanding person and delightful company. So is Kavi's mother, Sushma Ghei. She's a soft-spoken, mild-mannered and wonderful mother-in-law to Neeraj. Lately, she has been joining Aruna in going to Guruji's temple. She's one of the new devotees that Guruji talked about. What superb luck for us and our daughter to have such in-laws!

In keeping with her general nature and character, Neeraj's life panned out in an organized fashion. She qualified as a CA and then worked with Mohinder Puri's firm to gain practical experience. In 1985, she joined SITA as my executive assistant. Slowly but steadily, she settled down in the company and started coordinating and looking after the various domestic branches, and later the outbound division, which had grown gradually under the leadership of Kedar Kapoor.

Kedar and his wife Janak had already been my colleagues in Mercury Travels in the mid 50s. Kedar was responsible for opening and supervising our various branches. Neeraj took over the Outbound Division upon Kedar's death in 1989. By the time SITA was sold in 2001, we were the definitive leaders in the Inbound segment and almost at the top in the Outbound segment too, which had flourished and grown well under Neeraj's leadership.

The 'SITA Travel Academy' was my daughter Neeraj's brainwave. It was first an in-house training school and later became an IATA-recognized industry training school. Subsequently, it grew further, taking on the avatar of the Kuoni Travel Academy.

Neeraj was very diligent and extremely cost-conscious—in fact overly so—and her chartered accountant-mindset made her look for and ferret out, mistakes and shortcomings everywhere. I think she would make an excellent finance minister.

When I took a backseat in TAAI, she became very active, rose to become the youngest TAAI President ever and remains the only lady to hold this prestigious position so far.

Neeraj is meticulous but often fastidious. And that quest for perfection can, on occasion, slow down progress. But she is always sure of her arguments and reasoning. She is a hard task-master, but generous at heart.

Her husband Kavi is a delightful son-in-law, who makes one feel very comfortable with his relaxed, carefree attitude. He is a self-made man who set up India's first 'factoring house'. He has also been bitten by the travel bug and has developed one of India's first and best-known destination management & marketing companies, TRAC Representations India (Pvt) Ltd.

Kavi is a 'happy-go-lucky' person, a very understanding father and husband. Unfortunately, the building that housed his New Delhi office caught fire—not once, but twice. The last blaze in November 2012 was a total disaster, as his entire office was razed to ground and nothing could be retrieved. He shifted his Delhi operations to another building and established an office in Dubai. Kavi is now in his fifth year of operations in Dubai and runs his businesses there, in addition to those in India, very successfully.

Holding My Grand Daughter, Shreya

Neeraj and Kavi's greatest joy and asset is Shreya, their delightful daughter, our first grandchild and an exceptional young lady.

On the day Shreya was born, it was raining very heavily. I was pacing up and down outside the delivery room in the hospital, anxiously awaiting the birth of our first grandchild. Kavi and Arjun were in another room, enjoying themselves. After the delivery, the nurse came to show me the new-born baby. In my excitement, I just snatched the baby from the nurse and ran upstairs to Kavi and

Playing with My Second Grandchild, Baby Amaraah

Arjun. It was a very stupid thing to have done. In the first place, I should not have grabbed the baby. By doing so, I exposed her to germs. Secondly and by rushing upstairs to Kavi and Arjun with the new-born in my arms, I overlooked the fact that I could have slipped, anything could have happened. But such was my excitement! The birth of our little granddaughter filled us with so much joy. She was almost named Megha, because the day of her birth was cloudy and there was heavy rain but later, formalized as Shreya. I announced her birth to my friends by writing this letter which brought a lot of cheer to all of us.

27, Sunder Nagar,
New Delhi 110 003
July 26, 1993

We have the good news. We are grandparents. Our daughter, Neeraj and son-in-law, Kavi gave us the gift of a baby girl on Tuesday 6th July at 0837 hrs. The baby may be named "Megha" (The Clouds—*this being the monsoon season and it has been raining almost daily*).

We cannot decide whom she resembles, but she is a sweet darling. Weighing 3.4 kg at birth, she promises to be a tall girl.

Unlike other visitors to our shore, she had a quick and a pleasant surgical entry to this world.

Immigration Officer, Dr. Mangla Telang and the Customs Officer, Dr. Deepak Yadav were faster and more polite than their counterparts at Palam or JFK. She neither had any excess baggage nor any dutiable article and just made one loud declaration and crawled through the green channel. And who else but the oldest Transfer Assistant of SITA was the first one to receive her.

Finally we have got a pleasant hobby—BABYSITTING.

Yours sincerely,

Aruna & Inder Sharma

Shreya continues to be a source of great joy for Aruna and me even now. On some of her birthdays, I tried to dress up and play different roles. Once, I was a chef, on another occasion a snake-charmer and yet another time, a Scottish bagpiper. On her 13th birthday, I even became a bard. It was the one and only time in my life that I wrote a poem, dedicated to the little one. Here it is:

> *There was nothing vague*
> *The sky was full of Megh*
> > *All over Delhi were rains*
> > *Neeraj was in pains*
> *Dadi was shopping*
> *Nani was hopping*
> > *Dadu was laughing*
> > *Nanu was waiting*
> *Papa was enjoying*
> *Mamu was toying*
> > *God sent us a gift*
> > *Our spirits got a lift*
> *A girl was born*
> *I blew my horn*
> > *She was cuddly*
> > *Certainly not ugly*
> *She was a cutie*
> *A definite beauty*
> > *God is Saakshi*
> > *She is a Laxmi*
> *She has no hairs*
> *I ran up the stairs*
> > *Cuddling her in my lap*
> > *I lost my cap*
> *Nurse was shouting*
> *Nanu was laughing*

The month was July
We all became high
Sixth was the date
If you miss I will hate
Megha was the name
Golf became her game
As there were no holders
She travelled on my shoulders
She gave no kiss
So I always miss
Shreya is she now
I don't know how
Today she is thirteen
And now a teen
She is now a Miss
So I must get a kiss
God has blessed her
That is why we love her.

You don't have to guess too hard to know how much she means to Aruna and me. She's been consistently in the top three in her class, often standing first. She did the family proud by wearing national colours and representing India at the Asian Games Ladies Open Golf tournament before she was 18, beating her paternal grandfather, Purshotam Ghei, to a similar achievement by two years (In 1951 and at the very Asian Games—a Nehruvian vision, the 18-year-old athlete and sprinter, Purshotam, had carried the torch in the National Stadium).

Shreya went on to win the Women's National Championship in 2010. She shared yet another honour once bestowed on her grandfather, Purshotam Ghei—the Rudra Award, which is the highest distinction awarded to a student of Modern School. During her childhood, Shreya dabbled in several hobby-building and extra-curricular activities. Her parents tried to get her interested in classical dance, Indian music, tennis and riding. But Shreya soon found her real passion and—a champion golfer was born.

Shreya values the importance of time. Between her studies and golf, she found ample time for her late pet Buddy, a beautiful pug who was succeeded by Rio, a naughty Spitz. Shreya is the 'apple of my eye' and now, my second grand daughter, Amaraah, is fast catching up with her.

Thank you God, for your generosity in giving me both my grandchildren. But back to my own children again.

Our second child, Arjun, was born on 15th December, 1965. He grew up in a protected environment. He also attended Modern School and was above average in studies.

Unfortunately, I was so overworked and obsessed with developing SITA, that to my regret, I neglected seeking closer contact with my children during their formative years, especially with Arjun. Fortunately, no real harm was done, as both my children showed great maturity and adapted well to their circumstances under Aruna's guidance.

Arjun has always acted 'out-of-the-box', but in a good sense. He wasn't a rebel, but unknown to me, he always felt that I showered more attention on Neeraj. Perhaps because traditional Indian male thinking dictates that girls and boys can't be treated equally, since girls get married and are likely to move away from the family's professional interests. No matter how liberal and even-handed one tries to be, Indian society conditions one to place greater hopes and expectations in a son. But to me, both Neeraj and Arjun have always been equally qualified to take on the challenges of family businesses.

Much later in life, I realised that Arjun had initially even resented the fact that he started at the bottom of the ladder and as a mere trainee at SITA. Later on, of course he realized the value of having done so.

On my part, I was trying to emulate Henry Ford, who decided to teach his son the ropes of the business by starting him off at the shop-floor level. So also, Arjun was sent to Madras for training at the junior-most level, because I wanted him to learn the entire business framework, step by step.

He resented this for several years. But today, Arjun realizes the pricelessness of such a move, and I dare say it has contributed towards his excellent professional outlook.

Arjun Sharma is a full-blooded business executive and has built and catapulted his new company, 'Le Passage to India' to the top echelons of inbound tour operators. He and his company have won many awards. Arjun is also a very active and excellent marketing person who constantly comes up with new ideas and irresistible travel initiatives. He has grown into a very dashing, enterprising and knowledgeable individual. He has groomed himself through sheer hard work, acquiring knowledge and broad-basing his concepts all the while. Arjun Sharma has today emerged a superb business leader and is a personality to be reckoned with, in the inbound travel industry. As head of Le Passage to India, he has achieved all this in his own right. LPTI has, in a short span of 10 years, become India's number one inbound tour operator, winning national and international recognition. He has served as Chairman of WTTC India, as Senior Vice President of IATO and as Vice-Chairman of the PATA India Chapter. He has addressed several national and international seminars. He is an active member of the Young Presidents' Organization.

On the personal level, Arjun is likeable and personable, capable of thinking and doing multiple things at the same time. His versatility surprises and impresses me. He likes to call himself a 'team player', but in my opinion, he's more of a 'team leader' and an excellent one. He builds a team, guides it well and is determined to succeed. That is his real strength.

When it comes to business, he has a somewhat overbearing and dominating personality, but that doesn't take anything away from his leadership qualities. He's a natural leader, armed with a passion to do different things successfully at the same time.

I may have been a cautious, penny-pinching person, but not so Arjun, who is flamboyance personified. He is also an extremely generous, liberal and large-hearted friend and a philanthropist, who is passionately involved in the education of street children.

One of his peripheral hobbies is investment, for which he's done comprehensive research in the Indian share market, to his and the family's advantage. He's an entrepreneur of the highest order. He's a keen art collector and has a very fine collection of paintings by a variety of Indian and foreign artists.

He and his wife Jyotsana tend to and feed, several hundred stray dogs every day.

Arjun has been threatening to retire at an early age and devote himself to charitable work. Well, good luck to him too.

Incidentally, all these youngsters wanting to retire at fifty does make me reflect on the fact that at fifty, I was working my backside off and still building up SITA. The thought of retirement at that age was perhaps the farthest thing possible from my mind. But that was *my* life. Each to his own, as I say.

Arjun's marriage to Jyotsana took place on January 21st, 2007. Within a very short period of time, Jyotsana endeared herself to both Aruna and me. Jyotsana was a fashion model and a professional in her own right. She is independent and busy raising their first child, Amaraah, who was born on January 6th, 2009.

My second grand-daughter Amaraah's entry into this world was relatively uneventful. It was a normal delivery and Jyotsana took it in her stride. Amaraah is a sensitive child, playful, loving and caring. And like with Shreya, I couldn't wait for her to grow up a little, to be able to carry her on my shoulders to a travel conference. Of course, my opportunity came some years later.

Today, the little one is a bundle of energy, very active and intelligent for her age. She is learning to ski—surprisingly—on

Dubai's indoor ski slopes. She also learned the sport in Europe and won the first prize in a contest. God bless her. I am sure she will be a quick learner and grow up as a 'doer'. In August 2016 and just after I had partially recovered from an illness, I was told that her room had been redone beautifully. Amaraah took Aruna to see it. But when I asked her to show it to me too, she shook her head firmly, wagging a remonstrative finger. "No *Dadu*," she said. "There are too many steps to climb." Here was my little eight-year-old granddaughter Amaraah, so concerned and conscious of my inability to negotiate stairs. How wonderful!

Baby Amaraah with Dadu

Whenever I wonder what my life span will be, I know that I have relatively little time left for our dear Amaraah. But I pray that before I 'kick the bucket', Amaraah will be old enough to remember her *dadu*.

Both my grand daughters are very dear to me and a source of great happiness. *I hope they will think of their grandparents in much the same way, when the leaves of the book are turned and we move on. God bless both our grand-daughters.*

18 | Guruji

JAI GURUJI
OM NAMO SHIVAI SHIV JI SADA SAHAI
OM NAMO SHIVAI GURUJI SADA SAHAI

Guruji

When it comes to religion, I'm a bit different from the norm. I was born a Hindu. I am proud to be one. But I am equally proud to be an individual who respects other people's religions. I respect all religions. However, I don't appreciate their teachings or actions when these are forced upon others. Peacefully expanding the message of one's religion is acceptable, but not by lure, or force or allurement.

So what can I call myself? An atheist? A moderately religious person? Or, one who couldn't care either way?

I am certainly not an atheist, I do care for Divinity, I believe in a divine force. So that leaves me with only one choice: that I am religious. But what if God bears a hundred different names? So be it. As long as He is Divine, I know Him only as God. Religion is strictly a personal choice and personal belief. It should not be imposed on others either by pressure or coercion or allurement. Preach your religion, but practice it peacefully.

My mother was a religious person. She wanted her children to worship God and be religious too. But who was her God? For her, God manifested Himself in many forms—be it as Krishna, Ram, Ganesh, Shiva, Laxmi, Saraswati or any other. She mostly worshipped Lord Krishna and so did my father. My mother would say, these are representations of the various virtues or forces that we respect. God is one. You can call HIM by any name. You can worship HIM in a temple, gurudwara, mosque, church or synagogue. HE is omnipresent.

One day I asked her: "Mama, you worship God. So can you show me God? Do you know anyone who has seen God?" She answered with silence.

Like ladies in every true Punjabi household, my mother used to churn *dahi* (yoghurt) in a big metallic vessel every day. On one such occasion and about halfway through her churning, she called me and pointed to both the *lassi* (buttermilk) and the butter she had extracted from the curd.

"Son, do you see the butter?"

I nodded, curious to know why she asked.

"It came by churning the curd and from the *lassi*," she said.

I nodded again.

"Now do you see any butter in the pot full of *lassi*?" she asked next.

I shrugged and shook my head. No, I do not.

"That is the thing, my son", she said gently, "There is butter in that *lassi* too. But you have to churn it to see it. In the same way, God is in all of us. But we have to churn our conscience to see Him."

I have never forgotten those words.

The problem is that all of us want to see God, without bothering to do some churning within ourselves. Ever since I heard her explanation, I do believe there is someone, somewhere. Call HIM Bhagwan, Allah, God, anything you like. But HE is there.

I respect my background. I was raised in Hindu traditions, but they weren't very ritualistic. My parents were Brahmins and so am I, for all practical purposes. My father worshipped Lord Krishna in his own privacy but was not an overly religious person. My mother also worshipped Lord Krishna but was more religious, used to read the Bhagvad Gita, listen to religious discourses and practice a few rituals. She came from an orthodox Brahmin family but adjusted to my father's beliefs and lifestyle. She would occasionally visit Haridwar and take a dip in the Ganges. She would regularly visit both Birla Temple and Hanuman Temple in New Delhi.

I grew up in that environment. But it is only later in life that I formed a somewhat regular habit of visiting temples and also started doing my morning *Pooja*, for a few minutes. The fact is, that while I was sailing in turbulent waters that were far removed from the known family traditions of worshipping Lord Krishna and Hanumanji, my body and soul were not totally connected to divinity.

In 2000, my nephew Balbir Punj, a BJP leader and Member, Rajya Sabha, one day mentioned a 'Guruji'. According to Balbir, this Guruji was a source of enlightenment. One who did not ask for anything, didn't preach and only gave *darshans* and blessings. There were just a few rituals to be observed. The *Gurbani* and other religious hymns are played at all times. Then, tea is offered as *prasad*, and one was expected to drink it. Thirdly, the partaking of *langar,* where one sat down—sometimes with three other totally unknown devotees—and shared the *langar* from the same common plate meant for four people, was a must.

One never sang any *bhajans*, never asked any questions, one just silently sought Guruji's blessings. This description, though lofty enough, didn't impress me. Balbir continued to insist that I should visit Guruji at least once. But I was not convinced.

Then suddenly, an opportunity emerged.

My good friend and relative, Prem Sharma, invited Guruji to his home, probably to express his gratitude for becoming the Director of the CBI. I went alone because at that time, Aruna, who comes from an Arya Samaj family and does not believe in such ritualistic expressions, was away from Delhi (Today, Aruna is a faithful devotee of Guruji, but more on that later).

At Prem's place, there was a gathering of some 250 eminent and prominent government officials and others. The *Gurbani* was being played. After waiting for about half-an-hour, Guruji emerged from the house. With HIS shaven head and dressed in gaudy robes, HE was a striking personality. Wearing a broad smile, HE sat down on a very ornate, high chair. I was shocked and taken aback by HIS attire. I saw distinguished civil servants and their wives paying obeisance to Guruji, several ladies pressing HIS feet. We all stood in a line to pay our respects.

Prem introduced me as Inder Sharma, a cousin. HE smiled. And that was the end of my brief meeting with Guruji.

I was not impressed at all. In fact, I was somewhat disappointed that there was no discourse, no preaching, no advice or anything even remotely spiritual; only the ornate setting and what I then thought of as blind faith.

I left the gathering without partaking of the *langar*, or even the tea *prasad*.

I was, to put it mildly, disturbed to see such a gaudily-dressed gentleman being worshipped in such a fashion. I left without so much as saying goodbye to my friends.

Later, I mentioned this incident to Balbir. But he persisted. Then one day, he drew my attention to the fact that Arun Shourie's wife, Anita, had been cured by Guruji's blessings. I was aware that she couldn't walk properly and was unstable on her feet. I was also aware that lately, I had seen her walking a little bit. I knew Arun Shourie only slightly, but Balbir asked me to go and see him and check about Guruji.

I have the highest regards for Arun Shourie's integrity and intellectual honesty. So Aruna and I decided to visit them one late afternoon. Hesitatingly, I enquired from Arun Shourie as to how his wife was cured. I asked if they'd gone to the United States or any other foreign country, for medical help. Unhesitatingly, Shourie told me it was all due to Guruji's blessings. My curiosity was aroused. I requested him to take us along, when he visited Guruji next. He said he was going right after our meeting and would be happy if we came along.

Those days, Guruji used to receive devotees at the residence of a devotee, Sudhajee at Empire Estate on MG Road. HE gave darshans on four days a week—Thursday, Friday, Saturday and Sunday. On arriving, we saw about 60 people sitting and listening to *Gurbani*.

Shourie bowed to Guruji. I was surprised, because Shourie was showing the same devotion as I had seen in other people at Prem Sharma's residence. He touched HIS feet, and bowed down with folded hands right on his knees. I was behind him and Shourie only said, "Guruji, this is my friend". He had not completed his sentence when Guruji responded in a way that totally shook me. "Yes, I know he is Inder Sharma," HE said. "He was the owner of SITA, he came to Prem Sharma's home and left without having *Langar*."

I was taken aback to say the least, as I had never mentioned this to anyone. Was this, indeed, divine power? Or black magic?

I sat down amongst the people. The gathering soon swelled to about 80 devotees. We listened to the *Gurbani*. There was no preaching, no reading of scriptures and no questions asked. Some people, mostly ladies, continued to press Guruji's feet and occa-sionally talked to HIM in quiet whispers. This looked very odd to me. Yet again, I saw very senior bureaucrats, army officers, businessmen and politicians, all touching Guruji's feet to seek HIS blessings. We had our *chai* (tea) as *prasad.* I had my *langar,* sharing the same *thali* (plate) with three total strangers, which was difficult to start with, but one took it in one's stride as *prasad.*

We left at about 11.00 p.m., once again bowing to Guruji who sat in HIS ornate chair, bedecked in shining, flowing robes. That had been my first, real introduction to Guruji.

By the end of the evening, something, had touched my mind, though not my brain as yet. My visits continued and a new chapter started in my life. Was it a religion, was it ritualism, was it a cult, was it a movement, or was it a fad? What was I getting into?

There were certain indescribable forces which were attracting me towards Guruji. I couldn't pinpoint these yet, but I continued my visits.

There were certain norms to be followed; leave one's shoes outside, walk in a line, bow to Guruji, sit down wherever there was space, take the tea *prasad*, meditate by concentrating on divinity or, on Guruji. I tried concentrating on Guruji. There was no preaching, only devotional songs.

You shared the *langar,* you took Guruji's permission and you left.

If HE occasionally asked you to stay back, you did so in the company of a few people, and were offered tea or occasionally *halwa,* prepared by devotees. Or, if you were lucky enough, as we became after some time, you were taken for a cup of coffee late at night to one of the city's five-star hotels. When you entered Guruji's room, there was but one message: "Leave your 'ifs' and 'buts' outside, along with your shoes. Surrender to Guruji in totality and HE will take care of you."

This was difficult for me to understand then and sometimes, even today. Aruna, too, has completely surrendered to Guruji, like several thousand other devotees have. Today and over weekends, several thousands flock to Guruji's *Bade Mandir* (Big Temple) in Chattarpur, all seeking HIS blessings. No preaching, only religious music over tape. No rituals, only a simple *prasad* of two *chapattis*, a *dal*, a vegetable and a sweet, all as HIS blessings.

Our chapter with Guruji will actually never be completed, since HE is our LIFE now.

For both Aruna and me and as with other devotees, there are some 'logical' reasons too, the proof offered by certain events that happened to us.

The sharing of thoughts through community-song, is called *satsang*. We participate in those, seeking Guruji's blessings. Irrespective of one's age or position, everybody who comes, addresses others as Uncle or Aunty. We know several people who attend the *satsangs*, though we hardly remember their names. They are only uncles and aunties, fellow-devotees of Guruji.

Let me now relate and share with you only some of the 'graces' or blessings, that we received from Guruji, and with which we continue to be bestowed, time and again.

Our first realization or, revelation, happened in the winter of 2002.

I fell sick and was admitted to Ashlok Hospital. I was running a high fever, had breathing difficulties and a cough, to start with. The doctors diagnosed it as congestion of the lungs. Nothing serious, and yet and for over four weeks, my temperature remained consistently high and I continued to have problems breathing. I began to lose weight. Various tests were conducted but nothing revealed the cause of my illness.

To verify the blood tests, Dr. Alok Chopra even forwarded my samples to different labs for second and third opinions. But the results were the same. There was nothing wrong and no infection was detected. Yet, I had a high fever and was losing weight. Gradually, I reached a stage when I could hardly swallow. By then, I was only on liquids and an intravenous drip.

I was then subjected to some nuclear diagnostic tests at Ganga Ram Hospital. Nothing was discovered. And yet, the fever persisted.

In her despair, Aruna would visit Guruji four days a week at the Empire Estate, where HE was staying. One day, HE called her on HIS own and enquired the reason for her concern. Aruna explained my condition. Guruji asked someone at the *sangat* to bring 10 green chillies. HE gave them to Aruna along with a *prasad* consisting of two *chapatis* and a handful of vegetables. Even though HE was told that I was unable to eat solids, HE said that the *chapatis* must be fed to me, as these are HIS *prasad*.

It was midnight when Aruna reached the nursing home. She tied the green chillies on my ten fingers and asked me to eat the *prasad*. I was flabbergasted as I could hardly swallow, but I made the effort. I took almost half-an-hour to eat those two *chapatis*, but I could eat them and I did.

This was repeated the next night. My doctors were surprised. Today, both Drs Alok and Ashwini Chopra are followers of Guruji themselves, as are doctors of many other leading institutions.

On the third morning, my temperature came down to normal. After two more days, Guruji asked Aruna to shift me from the nursing home to Sita Ram Bhartia Hospital. We took an appointment with the medical consultant and took my records with us. This was my first visit to this particular doctor. To my utter disgust, he only glanced at my records and neither used his stethoscope, nor did he check my blood pressure. Other than asking a few questions, he did little else.

I was extremely weak and on a wheelchair. Still, the doctor told me that I was perfectly alright and I need not use the wheelchair. In fact and against my protestations, he instructed his orderly to remove it and told me to walk back.

I did, though, haltingly. Aruna attributed it to Guruji's miracle. I was still somewhat skeptical and attributed it to sheer coincidence. My wavering doubts about Guruji's divinity remained. But I soon recovered. Later on I asked the doctor whether he knew Guruji. He said he had never heard of HIM.

Subsequently, several incidents occurred, but I kept attributing them to coincidence or chance, rather than to Guruji's blessings. Yet, we continued to join the *sangats* and enjoy those periods of absolute calm, replete with blissful and happy feelings. That phase would last from a minute to maybe an hour, or longer. Every incident I heard of, I would partially attribute to Guruji's divinity and partially to coincidence. This period of wavering between confidence and doubt, continued for some time. Guruji neither preached, nor asked for any donation. All HE wanted you to do was to surrender to HIM—to leave all your problems at HIS feet, for HIM to solve for you.

Then one day, I mentioned to Guruji that I would not be coming over the weekend, as I was going to my village where I wanted to reconstruct the family temple dedicated to Mata Rani, our family deity.

HE promptly said: "Inder, *Mandirs* and *Gurudwaras* are in one's heart. Many build these, but you can worship God without them. Remember your elders had also built a dispensary there. Why don't you restart that?" It was a fact. My father had built a dispensary which was being run and managed by his elder brother. After their deaths, it had remained unutilized. The building was razed and

Sign Board-dedication of Ambulance and Laparoscopy Machine to GKD

the land sold by a relative. For various reasons, I had never gone back to my village after my father's death and literally hated it.

So how did Guruji know about facts which even my own children were not aware of? I was startled. The next day, I embarked on my journey.

Non-believers would call it coincidence, but we then experienced a miracle. When we approached the farmer to whom the land had been sold, he told us that in the official records and even 25 years after the sale, the land was still in our family's name, as he had not registered the land in his name but was only holding the sale letter in his possession.

I paid him the price he asked, he returned the sale letter and reverted the land to us. My faith in Guruji and HIS divinity began to take on a new dimension. Was it coincidence? Or was it Guruji's divine power?

I know now. It was Guruji's blessing. We rebuilt the dispensary and dedicated it to Guruji. Today, we manage it and provide medicines and consultation at a highly subsidized cost of Rupees 5.00 for five days of medicines. Recently, Aruna donated an air-conditioned ambulance to the dispensary's supervisory hospital in Dhariwal. Almost 1000 patients from the village and the areas around use the dispensary, on an average of 50–100 patients visit it every day.

Another instance of Guruji's blessings is related to Select CITYWALK.

In 2002, my daughter Neeraj and son Arjun brought to me a proposal to join hands with ICICI investments and build a shopping mall of an over 1 million square-foot area in Saket in New Delhi. Originally, ICICI Investments were the major share-holders and our partners, at Select CITYWALK, Yograj Arora's family were financial partners with minority shares. In 2001, I had sold SITA and we had spare funds. We were willing to venture out and try a new business and were looking for new investments.

The young lady from ICICI investments either charmed us or manipulated the negotiations in such a fashion that we were convinced, particularly my son Arjun, to pay the initial cost of purchasing the land at the drop of the hammer, when DDA auctioned it. We thus invested approximately 25% of the estimated price.

Once we were committed and had deposited the initial fund— with ICICI paying nothing, we were relieved.

The time to pay the last installment was 9th March 2004 which, too, passed and the very final extension that DDA gave us, was for June 6th, 2004. But that year and during our negotiations with ICICI, we were presented with terms and conditions of their investments whereby we would have been holding the baby and they would have taken the cake, the lion's share of profits. In a nutshell, the proposition had become totally unprofitable, impractical and impossible for us. There we were, having paid a sizable chunk and left holding the baby.

We had three choices. We could accept the totally disadvantageous terms of ICICI. Or, lose the initial deposit. Or, go for it by ourselves.

While all this was going on, my visits to Guruji continued. But I never mentioned our conundrum to HIM. I said not a word, and, as in the past, never asked HIM for a favour. As always, HE granted them on HIS own.

My emotions were probably very apparent, because one night, Guruji called me.

"Why do you look so worried, what is your problem?" HE asked.

"It is nothing, Guruji, nothing. But it seems that one day, I may have to steal and sell your *juttis* (sandals)", I joked. It was a typical Punjabi phrase about how a person who is down-and-out, starts stealing other people's shoes.

The next time I visited HIM and as I was taking permission to leave, Guruji smiled broadly. "You can take my *juttis*," HE said, gently.

I was ecstatic. I brought back HIS slippers and kept them in my *puja* (prayer) room. (Aruna and I worship these to date). In reality of course, I continued to worry about real issues, about how on earth Guruji's slippers were going to get me the balance of 75%.

The next evening, the same sequence took place again. This time, HE asked me on HIS own why I was still anxious. "It is nothing, Guruji," I said, trying to make light of my worries again. "Except that one day I may have to sell your *juttis*."

HE laughed heartily and asked Aruna and me to bring 43 old five-paise coins, which had a hole in the centre. I had no idea where to get those, as such coins had been out of circulation for a long time. I began to make frantic enquiries. Finally, somebody disclosed to me that such coins were still available in Chandni Chowk and at the Tibetan Market on Janpath.

The next day and armed with 43 coins with holes in the centre, I went back to the *sangat*. Guruji took them in HIS hands, murmured some divine message or blessings or a *mantra*, and gave them back to me, saying I should put two coins into running water every day for 21 days. On the 22nd day, I was to immerse the last one in a river along with 5 kg of *chana* (black gram).

I took the coins back, saying nothing except "thank you".

From the very next day onwards, Aruna started throwing two coins in the river Yamuna. After two to three days, it dawned on me that the immersion of the 43rd coin on the 22nd day would coincide with June 6th, 2004, and therewith the expiry of the deadline for paying the remaining amount to DDA. I felt or, realized that there was a message therein. I renewed my efforts with greater vigour.

Meanwhile, the entire team was frantically looking for sources to raise money, and none were materializing.

- We had never borrowed money in all the years of SITA's inception and expansion. Therefore, we had no credit rating and we had no track record in setting up a mall.
- We had no business plan, except for the one prepared by the ICICI team, the correctness of which we could not verify.
- We had no political connections worth their name.

In this mood of desperation, I rang Deepak Parekh, then Chairman HDFC, with whom I had developed a formal acquaintance when I was on the Board of Directors of Air-India.

"Deepakji, I wish to come and meet you in Bombay," I told him. "I have a plan for a shopping mall and I need money." I mentioned to him I had no collaterals, no experience and no reliable business plan. He laughed and said, "Inder, I am leaving tonight for New York and won't be back for several weeks. However, out of the total amount, I will be happy to sanction you a third. Contact my office in Delhi and they will do the needful." Bless Deepak Parekh for his confidence in me. We felt encouraged, we had crossed the first hurdle. But we still needed twice as much as Deepak Parekh had sanctioned.

The next day, a dear friend of mine, Kaku Khanna, informed me that he would be happy to introduce me to the then Managing Director of the State Bank of India, Mr. Bhattacharya. He said, "I will only introduce you but I will make no recommendations." We tried Mr. Bhattacharya's number. But discovered that he was in New York and would not be back for another week.

Time was running out. Then suddenly and within about 20 minutes of that unsuccessful attempt to reach the State Bank Director, my friend Kaku received a call. It was Mr. Bhattacharya. He said he was returning to Delhi the next day, as the Finance Minister had asked him to and, that he could give us half-an-hour for a meeting and a presentation.

On that day, it was my son Arjun who was in hospital. So my daughter Neeraj and I went to see Mr. Bhattacharya at the State Bank's guest house in New Delhi. Since we had been given only half-an-hour to discuss the project, I outlined four things very briefly.

- Firstly, that we have no experience or clue of shopping malls, that we had never run this kind of business, that we were only good in the travel trade.
- Secondly, that the business plan I was presenting had been prepared by ICICI and I could not vouch for its correctness.
- Thirdly, that we had no collaterals to offer, except our good intentions and the project.
- Fourthly, that as far as the shopping retail area was concerned, we would not be selling it, like all the other malls in India had been doing so far, but would license/lease the area to good customers and nurture a profit-sharing relationship with them.

"We will maintain and manage the mall ourselves, and it's our desire to create a unique experience in the retail industry just as we did with SITA in the travel business," I concluded.

Mr. Bhattacharya was somewhat taken aback by this honest admission. He asked his team, whether they thought this new philosophy for a shopping mall would do well or not. Since I had not interacted with that team, I knew nobody on it. I had no political connections and I had enjoyed no prior business relation-ship with SBI. Yet and within half-an-hour, Mr. Bhattacharya and his team told me that they would sanction the lion's share of the remaining amount. Within three days, I had the funds sanctioned. Now, every bank was willing to lend me the relatively small, remaining balance.

The entire loan application was processed in the shortest possible time without any political pressure or even relationships. With nothing, except Guruji's divine blessings.

We got the loan and paid the entire remaining amount at the due time.

I immersed the 43rd coin in the river. And the next day, I returned to Guruji's *sangat*.

As usual, I bowed down and touched HIS feet and HE blessed me. Then and in *shuddh* Punjabi, HE said: *"Aakhir tera kaam ho gaya naa, tainu mil gaye paise. DDA de paise tu dae dittae naa, jaa hun teri mall chalae hi chalae."* (After all, your work has been done, you have got the money. You have paid DDA, now your Mall will be a roaring success).

I had never told HIM the reason behind my anxiety. I had never given HIM any figures. I had not told HIM of any deadlines. Yet and with HIS Divinity and grace, I had come out of the biggest crisis of my life.

That is Guruji. Those, who have complete faith in HIM get HIS blessings. After that, several incidents concerning my problems, or my children's problems kept cropping up. That is life. But without ever mentioning these to Guruji, these problems were solved, time and again. And the minute they were, HE would allude to them and would usually say, "Ok, so this, that or another problem of yours is now solved."

We were attracted to Guruji like metal to a magnet and we worship HIM as the ultimate divine Guru, an incarnation of Shivji.

Members of the *sangat* would often share their experiences: Some were simple, others inexplicable and yet others were nothing short of miracles. People from all walks of life flocked to HIM. By themselves and not by pressure or inducement. There were students, professors, doctors, businessmen both rich and poor, highly-educated intellectuals, religious leaders, journalists, army personnel including some generals, and politicians of course, both budding & practicing. We saw people like Ms Mehbooba Mufti, Mr. Pranab Mukherjee, Mr. L.K. Advani, Mr. Arun Nehru, Mr. Atal Bihari Vajpayee, to name just a few, at Guruji's *sangat*. In fact, it was a diverse cross-section of humanity that came to worship Guruji and seek his blessings. Some known medical practitioners and armed forces officers were always present in large numbers. And all those who surrendered selflessly, were always fortunate to receive HIS blessings.

In the early hours of May 31ˢᵗ, 2007 and when Aruna and I were vacationing in Kasauli, we received stunning news. Guruji had decided to change his *Chola* from his human form. HE had left all of us for HIS divine dwelling.

We were shell-shocked. We rushed to Chandigarh to catch the Jet Airways flight to Delhi. When we reached the airline counter, we were told that the flight was full and that all passengers had checked in. Even as we were deciding on the logistics of driving back to Delhi, the Jet counter staff came up to us. They told us that a couple had just cancelled their seats upon hearing of an accident in their family. Fortunately, they had no check-in luggage and neither did we. Thus, we got the last two seats and managed to reach the temple, where Guruji's earthly body was placed, for devotees to pay their last homage. We did so, humbly and crying like children.

Thousands had gathered and the funeral pyre was lit by Guruji's father, to renderings of the Guru Granth Sahib and the Bhagvad Gita.

The Divine was merging with Divinity....

The earthly presence of Guruji continues even today. Every day, several thousand devotees gather at the Shiv Temple beyond Chattarpur to pay their homage to Guruji and seek HIS blessings. Miracles, if you call them that, are still happening to people, they are still experiencing HIS blessings. Today, there are several thousand more devotees then before. On HIS birthday or death anniversary, several thousands gather both in Delhi and at HIS village Dogri, near Jalandhar. Several devotees hold *sangats* at their residences. HIS followers are now in the millions and all over the world.

Guruji truly lives on in the hearts of millions and HE always blesses the true devotee.

Who was our Guruji? His Story

Guruji was born to a Sikh family in Dogri, a village in Jalandhar District in Punjab. HIS mother died early but when we met HIM, HIS father Bapaji, a simple Punjabi farmer, was still living in the village. We are told that Guruji, even during HIS childhood, would spend hours on HIS own, immersed in prayer. HE had HIS schooling in the village and ended up taking Masters' degrees in both Economics and English.

HIS first known and acknowledged presence as a spiritual leader can be traced back to the days when HE lived in Jalandhar. The house where HE lived has now been turned into Guruji's mandir. *Langar* is still served every evening to those members of the *sangat* who visit it.

Later on, Guruji shifted to Delhi. In the beginning, HE lived in a devotee's house. That is when people started visiting HIM. Later, HE shifted to another devotee's home in Empire Estate on M.G. Road. That is where we first met Guruji. HE was a very handsome man, a powerful personality who was always smiling and whose kind demeanour held a unique attraction.

In the evenings, HE would often appear to be in a pensive mood, as though HE was thinking about something very deeply. HE wore fancy gowns when HE gave *darshan*, but was otherwise dressed mostly in bush-shirts and pants. Guruji was a simple man, a frugal eater and a very generous person. People did drop money in the donation box, but that was at the *Bade Mandir*. All contributions were voluntary. HE never sought donations. At the daily *sangat*, devotees were served tea and *langar*. Guruji lead a normal life. HE took HIS *sangat* occasionally for coffee around midnight at one of the five-star hotels, be it Maurya or Taj. They all knew HIM and would immediately set up a table for HIS party. HE normally drank cold coffee.

It is appropriate and fitting that I close this book, the memoirs of my long life, with an invocation to the Divinity we were so blessed to meet on earth. It is befitting of the humility and gentleness of our Guruji, that I leave you here with an invocation to the Divinity who gave us focus, center, purpose and devoutness to God. We call HIM Shivjee or *Guru Hamare*, but HE was right here on Earth.

All doors opened for us and we are eternally grateful. But the one that Guruji opened, let in a light that still glows brightly in our hearts and will continue to illuminate us at all times...

OM NAMO SHIVAYA SHIVJEE SADA SAHAY
OM OM OM
OM NAMO SHIVAYA GURUJI SADA SAHAY
JAI GURUJI

Tributes

Tribute to My Dear Husband

by Dr. (Mrs.) Aruna Sharma

It was during my college days that I first met this remarkable young man named Inder Sharma, at my friend Nirmal's house. As I learnt later, it was love at first sight for him. Almost in *filmi* style, he started following me and tracking my movements in every way. He would even wait each day at the bus stop and board the same DTC bus that I took to college.

Inder & Myself

I noticed and was aware of him. I was impressed by his debating skills and his being an eloquent and good speaker. Somewhere, his good-mannered nature and his perseverance paid off and—I took a liking to him too.

We were young and I was naive and we started discovering life and love together: through the 'our' time at the Hauz Khas *bauri*, tea at Carlton Cafe and—long drives in his father's car.

My father had a transferable job and I moved to Assam Medical College. This left him very disturbed and me filled with longing. We kept in touch through letters and sometimes, phone calls. Our love for each other was all-consuming.

During our courtship of 6 to 7 years, we encountered our share of disapproval and resistance from both sets of parents. From Inder's, on account of my not being a Brahmin—and him needing approval from the elders in their village. And from mine, because Inder was not a 'professional' nor well-settled.

Thankfully for us, our love finally won and we received their consent for matrimony.

My parents had groomed me to stand on my own feet. I was a 'simpleton', with no knowledge of the nuances and ways of the well-heeled and fashionable world. I would never know what to wear and it was always Inder who would decide my attire, be it the *saree* or the jewellery, always keeping in mind the given occasion. He personally groomed me—not only in my dress sense, but also in other aspects of life.

When I look back today, I cherish every moment of our togetherness on the journey of life. He was more than caring and when he was on his travels, he would never forget to call to check on me each day. Sometimes I wonder—and it amazes me—how one can love and care so much.

We shared over 65 years together. We walked in step with each other. And yet, not a single incident comes to mind when he either scolded me or raised his voice. He could go to any length for my happiness and always gave me the comfort and reassurance of being by my side, come what may.

For him, I was truly his life partner and he would insist that I always accompany him for any function, be it a professional, family or social occasion. We would be out partying together, virtually every night of the week and it became known in all circles that Inder will always be accompanied by his wife. He would proudly tell all "that he never steps out without his doctor".

My Inder showed me the world. What I am today is all his labour of love, time and education.

I cannot tell you how much I miss his presence. It is those sweet memories that keep me going.

I thank Guruji for blessing my darling Inder with an additional ten years and me—another decade of beautiful memories with him.

JAI GURUJI

ARUNA

Tribute to Dad

by Arjun Sharma

I thank GURUJI and the Universe that I was born to a most amazing and legendary father, Inder Sharma.

For Dad, SITA World Travel was his first-born. For us, the closest identification with him as kids and his role in the industry was an aeroplane. Whenever we saw one flying in the sky, we would say, "Look! That's Dad going somewhere!"

While I was growing up, he never encouraged

Dad & Me

me to visit the office. But the few times I did, it was to collect stamps from his secretary and office colleagues. He encouraged me to build a collection of stickers of all the airlines he had flown on. As my collection swelled, I would urge him to fly the airlines which were missing from my album.

Dad left schooling issues to Mom, as he was busy building SITA. I was never a great student and probably, the black sheep in the family when it came to academics. But it was always reassuring to hear Dad say that he, too, "graduated gradually". It was always a wonder for the family that he had friends of all ages who claimed they were with Dad in college. It was only later that I realized he had spent many years graduating from college.

It was during my years in high school, that I first started getting a sense of working in the tourism industry. I was very enamoured by Dad's travel, and entertainment of foreign tourists and visitors in our home. As a child, I would sometimes sneak into his office. If I tried to sit in his chair, I would be shooed away by Mrs. Butalia. You will have to earn the right to sit on this chair first—by studying and working hard, she would scold.

As my high school years drew to an end, he urged me to start attending the office for a few hours every day—not with him, but as a management trainee at the floor level. On April 1, 1984 and straight after my 12th Board exams, came my first initiation into the world of tourism. I began to attend office part-time. As a trainee, I would be doing the most basic, ground-up jobs. Those included writing hundreds of tickets, picking up clients from airport, writing books of accounts, etc.

I soon began to enjoy learning about travel and tourism so much, that even Dad was a bit upset: at my spending so much time in the office and not concentrating on my college education. However and many years later, he told me that he was secretly very happy to see I had imbibed his passion for tourism and that I had spent so many hours at the grass-roots level of the profession. I realize now that doing that has given me greater insights into the industry, even beyond my father's expectations. Strangely and though I wish he had, he never pushed me to get an international education.

In the late 1980s and just after I had joined SITA, I remember going to Dad with a plan to build a hotel on the Delhi-Jaipur Highway. It began with a plan for only a restaurant complex with a few rooms, but had expanded into a full-blown resort.

Dad had always encouraged me to think out-of-the-box. So on that occasion too, he said: "Whatever land you buy should not cost us more than 25 lacs." Consequently, we acquired 12 acres for 2 lacs each. When I asked him for more money to buy some adjoining land too, he said: "Son, don't be greedy, this is enough."

What an amazing lesson for a 20-something-year-old kid it was. Along with him, I soon became very actively involved in building The Heritage Village Manesar, a premium resort on the Delhi/Jaipur highway. Dad was very clear he wanted Rajasthani *Haveli* architecture; and much before it became fashionable to talk of green buildings, he was very clear he wanted a very eco-friendly resort. His brief to the architect was to use Laurie Baker brick architecture. Among the many green initiatives he had suggested and which were implemented in the project, that was a particularly revolutionary idea. I can safely say that Dad's vision of the resort in Manesar put that sleepy Haryana village on the global map. Several years later and seeing the activity we had managed to create at the resort, the government of Haryana decided to set up an industrial township.

Some years later, I approached Dad again, this time about building a hotel in Goa. Once again, he encouraged me to acquire the land and do it. This time, he let me develop the concept and build the hotel all on my own. To be vested with that kind of faith from one's father was overwhelming. When I explained to him that I wanted to build a new concept, an 'All-Inclusive Hotel', he took only 30 minutes to understand my pitch. He then gave me the go-ahead to implement what would be a first-of-its-kind establishment in India. The early stages were difficult. High interest rates (20%) took away all our profits. In spite of that, he never discouraged me from persisting with my dream.

Years passed. Dad finally moved me under his own right-hand man, Mr. Ghulam Naqshband, who headed SITA's Inbound Division. My elation was short-lived as, to my horror, I could not have asked for a tougher boss. But that is exactly what Dad wanted for me: a baptism by fire. I worked closely with Mr. Naqshband over the course of my career at SITA. By the late 1990s, I was more or less heading the Inbound Division of SITA along with Mr. Naqshband and together, we produced overwhelming profits for the organisation.

I particularly recall one conversation Dad and I had, on the consolidation that was happening in the World of Tourism. We spoke especially of our key European markets, where vertical integration was underway and would soon threaten small players. It was probably this conversation that led to the sale of SITA on 23rd March, 2000. Even though I was surprised that he would contemplate selling SITA, his ability to make that decision with clear-sighted business acumen amazed me. Yes, for Dad, it was an emotion-charged, tough business decision and Neeraj and I fully endorsed it.

I realize today it could not have been easy for him. Indeed, pundits of the industry today, laud him for his timing, because just as he had predicted, the tourism industry has changed immensely since then.

There were more surprises. One of the most amazing things he did in his deal with Kuoni was—to give Neeraj and me 'as dowry' to them. He did this because he wanted his children to work in the multinational environment of a professional company and away from the family business. It was an invaluable experience; one, that immensely helped me round my personality and understand new business concepts which were alien to a family business. When Kuoni asked us to leave the organization in 2002, he was very upset. I still recall his bear-hug when I went to see him thereafter. Personally, it had been a huge setback for me. But all Dad said was this: "Son, when one door closes, many others open." Those words were so true. In fact if I ever write my autobiography, it shall be titled, "Thank God I was fired!"

After SITA, Dad created the new brand, Select Group. We went to him with the proposal for Select CITYWALK in 2003. He was in Manesar, recovering from a chest infection. Once again, he did not as much as blink, and encouraged us whole-heartedly. He simply placed his trust in our ability to take big and measured risks and pull off a huge project. He staked his entire wealth and—the rest is history.

The shopping centre business was alien to us. Yet, he had the courage to step out of his comfort zone and invest in a new venture in his mid-70s. Initially, the project ran into difficulties. But thanks to Guruji and Dad, it saw the light of day. Select CITYWALK's success is a combination of Guruji's blessings and Dad's crisis management.

As I look back on my formative years on this planet, I can completely attribute my growth as an individual and as a human being to my upbringing as his son. He never said no to me for anything. On hindsight, I wish he had, because some of my decisions and actions probably bothered and hurt him for which, I am truly repentant. Yet, he never discouraged or persuaded me against taking them. Once again, Dad was my Rock of Gibraltar. He stood by me and placed his faith in me.

Today, I sit on his chair and at his desk: the same that he had acquired in 1953, when he started his first business. When I run my hands over this desk, I can sense his humbleness, his hard work, his commitment to people and his ability to look at the big picture. He was always the "Go-To" person whenever there was a crisis. In a crisis, he had an amazing sense of calmness and clear thinking and could break an issue down logically.

When I invested in Le Passage to India Travels & Tours Pvt. Ltd. in 2005, he was very happy to see that I was still maintaining a strong foothold in the tourism business and keeping the Sharma flag flying in tourism. When LPTI won the First Prize at the National Tourism Awards in 2007, there was a very proud father in Vigyan Bhavan that day. Incidentally, SITA came second that year. I walked up to him and gave him the award. "I am so proud that the Number 1 and Number 2 companies have my DNA", he said.

We have won many 1st prizes since then. Dad made it a point to come and see me receive the National Award from presidents and ministers. In 2013, I decided to sell my majority share to my partners, TUI Travels. He was a bit apprehensive. But when I told him I wanted to spend more time with the family and concentrate more on the Mall business, he understood and immediately advised me to go ahead. For him, his family was supreme and came first. He had seen me work very hard since my early years and at that moment, he intuitively understood my needs.

Given the earlier turbulence of my personal life, my wife Jyotsana and our adorable daughter Amaraah were the bright spots for my Dad. He welcomed Jyotsana into the family and was always happy when she spent time chatting with him. Jyotsana's huge animal welfare work puzzled him a lot but nevertheless, he was always supportive of all she did. Once, when some "not-so-*sunder*" residents of Sunder Nagar complained to him about dogs, he shooed them away.

Amaraah was the twinkle of Dad's eyes. He loved her like crazy and would wait for her to come and kiss and hug him. On her first birthday, he came dressed as Santa Claus, much to the delight of all the kids. He encouraged her to ski and like Shreya does, he also wanted to see Amaraah play golf. There was not a day or moment that he would not inquire about her. For Amaraah, her Dadu was a big, cuddly teddy bear and the most amazing and loving grandfather.

That Dad was a legend in the travel and tourism industry is an understatement. Even over the last 20 years when he was not so involved in tourism, his vision for this industry and his views on which direction it needs to take, were highly contemporary and accurately forecasted the needs of the industry. His speeches of yesteryears are still contemporaneous and insightful.

He taught me a lot of lessons in his simple but eloquent ways. Some of his quotes stay with me in every business decision I take. He would say: "Son, profit is your birthright if you work hard, but profiteering is not." He would also say, "Son, the top line is vanity, profit is policy, but cash flow is a reality." For someone who claimed he was not adept at accounts, his wisdom about cash flow could not be more accurate.

Dad has left huge shoes to step into. For Neeraj and me, Dad has, in fact, left a huge legacy at work. It was his dream and deepest desire that the two of us work together and build an even bigger enterprise. I, for one, shall humbly try to imbibe his values and life-lessons in my personal and professional life and am constantly working to expand the business, without compromising on his ethics, values and traditions.

To my father, I have this to say: Dad, if I can be a small percentage of the man you were, I will feel blessed and honoured. Neeraj and I seek your blessings and good wishes in our future endeavours. We hope to continue your legacy and make you proud. Thank you for bringing me into this world and making me what I am today. I am blessed to have been your son.

JAI GURUJI
ARJUN

Tribute to a Loving Father

"Feeling I could fly on your tall shoulders"

by Neeraj Ghei

My darling Popsicle,

On the path of life that you strode down with such confidence and courage, you gave me rich reason to try and fit my small feet into your giant footsteps.

In one way or another, you silently touched and enriched so many lives.

You, the man who started his career by receiving tourists at the airport, took your last flight to Haridwar to reunite with your

Dad & Me

Maker. And how our roles were reversed. As children, we sat on your lap. During that last flight, you sat on ours. I wanted to hang on to you forever.

I am truly at a loss for words because it's tough to talk of you in the past tense. You were, are and will not be just my father. You will always remain my Hero with a capital "H". I have worshipped you all my life and we truly shared a very special relationship that went beyond any ordinary one between a father and his children.

Mentor, friend, guide, teacher, inspirer: you simply meant the world to me.

Dad, when I was growing up, you taught me so many important life-lessons in your own subtle style, leaving me with many precious memories that I hold close to my heart.

I remember...

- holding your hand and taking my own first, tentative steps.
- sitting on your tall shoulders, feeling on top of the world and looking down with no fear of falling. High up there, feeling safe and secure.
- looking at planes and—every fat man—and murmuring, 'papa'.

I well recall the planning that you undertook for my birthday parties: the magic shows, the puppetry, the bear and monkey dances. I remember your teasing every morning just as I drank milk (which I hated), that you had read in the paper of so many children choking on *malai* (cream) stuck in their throats.

I couldn't wait to receive your postcards from your travels. I know now that it was your way of showing me the world in a kaleidoscope, through the eyes of a father to his daughter. It was the best bonding any daughter could have had.

We took sixteen summer holidays at Shimla's Wildflower Hall. It was always Cottage No. 1. We had our *chaiwala*, our daily dose of *pakoras* and *jalebis*, our walks along the *pakdandis* of the Mashobra Hills. How can I forget you sending your driver to Shimla or Sanjauli just because your little girl would throw a fuss and refuse to eat without '*dahi*'?

How we travelled!

Our trips to Kashmir, the houseboat stays, the *shikara* rides, our sojourns at the Highland Park in Gulmarg and the trips to Pahalgam and the Bobby cottage. Our picnics to Sohna and Sultanpur soon became regular winter get-togethers.

And how we enjoyed your foodie events!

The *chaat* parties you threw by the Claridges poolside, your barbeque lunches (where everyone thought you had done the grilling!) your 'cooking' mutton curries for us—yes, when the whole household had to help in putting together the ingredients so that you could—direct the operation, stir the curry a few times and—take the entire credit!

I remember our trips to CP and Central Court Hotel to eat hot dogs, to Standard restaurant for its Softy ice-cream, followed by more of the same at India Gate during a leisurely stroll on a summer evening. And the fun times on the lawn eating mangoes in the rain, picking them out of a bucket filled with water.

I miss our great *Holi* celebrations. I miss us sleeping on the lawn on *charpais* on a hot summer night.

I miss those carefree days with you, Dad....

I remember tagging along to those great TAAI conventions which became my playground for learning, imbibing the ways of the industry. (When I later became its President, it was a proud moment for you, though to me, it seemed almost natural to follow your footsteps.)

I remember the evening before you were to drop me to the boarding school, Tara Hall in Shimla: you got cold feet, held me tight and told mom you could not bear to send me away.

That was followed by nightmarish Carmel Convent which I hated attending. (I thought you were sending me away to school to spend more time with the new arrival in the family, my brother Arjun!)

I shudder to think of how lousy a student I was at that school, and how often you (and mom) were summoned to listen to an endless litany of complaints about how anti-establishment I was.

And yet, you never reprimanded, scolded or punished me. Instead, you silently changed my environment; the best thing to happen to me.

When I would just about scrape through Hindi exams, I remember you confessing that you could not write Hindi. To cheer me up, you showed me a letter you wrote to your mother which began with *"Mari Pyari Mama"*!

And how well I recall our first overseas trip together when I turned 18!

None of my school friends believed that I, your daughter, had never travelled abroad till then! But that's the thing, Dad. Your silent, unspoken actions taught me to value the little things of life.

I remember you teaching me how to drive on the India Gate lawns. I was a good student—I learned in a day. But you then told me that I could take the car out on my own, only when I had proved to you that I could change the tyre all by myself too!

You taught me so much self-reliance when I was young. You consented to let me study at faraway Delhi University if I agreed to commute by bus. Whereas, if I joined LSR nearby, I would be allowed to use the car. But I am, after all, your daughter. How could I choose the easy way out?

Mom told me later that on my first day, you followed my bus to the university and saw me stumble out of it, hurting my knees. Mom says you cried but—you never told me that, just in case I succumbed to the softer option of the other college nearby.

Thank you Dad, for giving me such a strong base in life. It has held—and will always hold—me in good stead.

I remember being flummoxed when I met your own 'college friends', who, at times, looked a generation apart from you. Jokingly, you explained that to us, by saying it was only because you had "graduated gradually".

How can I ever forget how you always encouraged me in my professional pursuits, like when I chose CA over medicine? (Despite Mr. Mohinder Puri - MP - telling me to study anything but CA, since he felt it was a profession unfit for women).

I remember worrying of failure while studying it. But you kept reminding me cheerfully, that like you, I too, could 'graduate gradually'.

I remember senior Mr. Puri pulling you up for making me travel by bus to work in his firm and how—discreetly and supposedly unlinked to that chastening—you allowed me to buy a 1961 Fiat.

Then, how can I forget your ganging up with MP to 'sack' me so that I could join SITA? You must have known that unless you did so, I wouldn't have come! (Just saying, Dad, no regrets...)

Dad, you always let me make my choices. You gave me my space, you offered suggestions and opinions while accepting me as I am and letting me make my own decisions. You encouraged me to stand on my own. You supported my endeavours while allowing me the freedom to experience the world myself. You encouraged me to dream and set my sights on the sky but—with my feet on the ground.

You would keep telling me how important it was to be self-reliant and say "Make sure you don't have to depend on any man… be it your father, brother or husband."

You were a great inspiration and my best source for values.

As the years went by, I realised, Dad, that you were a much greater human being than I ever thought.

Then came the Big Day.

I remember telling you, "Dad, I am in love, he is not a Brahmin boy but I want to marry him."

Your first reaction was: "I didn't realise that you were old enough for us to start thinking of your marriage!" (I was 25 then, Dad). "Thank God you found your own. Now you can't blame me if you made the wrong choice," you said with a chuckle.

I remember feeling torn between the two of you when you asked me to organise for Kavi to meet you at home or in the office, while Kavi insisted on not meeting the "Lion in his Den", but only on neutral territory. You compromised. When the two of you met at *Machan,* all by yourselves, I was chewing my nails and had butterflies in my tummy. Your approval of our relationship meant so much to us.

I remember you telling the orthodox members of the family with great pride, that it was an arranged marriage and justifying your lie later on by saying, "I told them no lie! After all, I *am* making all the arrangements for the wedding, aren't I?"

I remember you most carefully guarding the keys to our hotel room and not letting any of my wild friends ruin it on our wedding night.

In later years, you reminded me time and again, how truly lucky I was. "Your marriage would not have lasted with anyone else," you would say.

In more recent years and when I told you that I was torn between you and Kavi, who had moved to Dubai some years ago, you were firm. "Go be with him," you said. "He needs you."

Your joy at Shreya's birth was unparalleled. You wrote a memorable, loving, humorous letter to announce her arrival.

You carried her on your shoulders at so many TAAI Conventions and designed amusing cakes for her birthday parties. Her golf and academic achievements became a source of strength for you when, in mid-2014, you fell ill seriously and were so weak and unable to walk.

But you healed yourself against all odds as you were determined to walk again, in time for her graduation from Yale. With great pride, you insisted on a celebratory cruise in the Caribbean, for the family to celebrate the momentous event. Those amazing memories are etched in our hearts forever.

You really wanted to live to plan Shreya's wedding and see her getting married in style. That was not to be. But I promise to try and ensure she holds a reception at the Imperial, just as you always wanted.

Dad, you had a great sense of humour, perfect comic timing and a hilarious way with words. The spontaneity of your responses, reactions and wisecracks would bring a smile to one and all.

You were childlike in many ways and your creative sense of celebration was so unique and personal.

You dressed up two large dolls in Modern School uniforms for our 25ᵗʰ wedding anniversary. You would enthrall Shreya and her friends on her birthday by dressing as Santa, or a chef, or a Scottish bagpiper in a kilt. And you sportingly cut the 'boob' cake that Kavi had designed for your birthday, without using a knife and—at the appropriate place.

One of the best summaries of your truly exemplary life came from your granddaughter Shreya, when she was 17. She said she had learned from you that "the higher one goes in life and the bigger one becomes, the more humble, down-to-earth and humane one must be."

My professional journey with you was exhilarating. I learned bottom upwards. I learned that God was in the detail and I was tutored in the values of diligence, single-minded focus, fair play and team-play. I was taught to instil integrity, compliance, transparency and humility in all that I did, irrespective of the results.

You gave Arjun and me the responsibility, the platform and much of the credit both at SITA and Select CITYWALK. Nothing would have been possible but for your direction and the DOORS that YOU OPENED. Your name and SITA's reputation together were the best business card one could ever hold. And your humility was such, that you never took credit for the achievements, always giving it to the teams.

At SITA, your strategy of first taking on the competition in areas where they were weak and then challenging them on their turf, paid rich dividends. I feel blessed that I had a role to play in helping SITA expand its domestic network of offices and making it a household name across the country. Even today, one meets people who think SITA is still your company.

And I well remember my moment of the greatest joy: sharing the EON Fusion Award 1999 with you.

Your mantras—"The Customer is King" and, "Treat each one the way you would want to be treated", were infused into all our dealings at SITA and CITYWALK.

When people said *"Tussi toh builder ban gaye!"* (you've become a builder!) your response, that you were merely bringing the customer-centric focus of the travel industry to a brick-and mortar business, was so true!

For you, Select CITYWALK had to mean something for everyone. It had to touch lives, enrich and leave lasting impressions on those who visited, shopped, worked there or, were connected with it in any way. Your eye for detail never ceased to amaze me; how you would pick that one, most pertinent issue, that none of us had thought of. It was always a subtle reminder, that we still had a lot to learn.

Your intuitive grasp of the nuances of a business you began to learn in your mid-70's, stunned me. Your observations and suggestions—be it when you reviewed its construction, approvals, funding, or leasing, and that too, over the shortest period of 30 months—were always so ahead of times that I would be simply awestruck.

It seems like we were divinely blessed and HE, was rewarding your *Karma* and your eternal wish, to "die with your boots on"!

You instilled in us the confidence that we were the best and had to strive tirelessly to stay ahead.

Dad, at SITA, you were its only owner. Yet, you established a fine foundation for working in partnerships. Despite being overwhelming majority stakeholders in CITYWALK, you would always say that one should never let one's partners sense that and that one must, instead, respect them as equals and work to achieve consensus. You lived by that philosophy.

Your belief in giving back to community and society strengthened, when your tryst with Guruji began. And while you continued to support many charitable initiatives in tourism, your personal homage in restarting your ancestral dispensary, after Guruji showed you the way, acquired many new dimensions.

At CITYWALK too, you told us to take our CSR obligations seriously. You dedicated the *Jamunwala bagh* (a project in partnership with the Government) to the residents of the Khirki village on my birthday, 11th March 2017, with great delight. It was the last public function of CITYWALK you attended.

The memories are many and the pages too few.

So for all the times I left it unsaid, this comes with thanks for all that you have been to me. For the understanding, the caring and the love you've shown in so many ways.

This tribute comes with gratitude to you for all the learning, the values you instilled and the enormous legacy you have left us.

You once told me: "I shall grow old but never lose life's zest, because the road's last turn will be the best."

Your road, Dad, has reunited you with your Maker and your *Guruji*. HE gave you a new lease of life when HE gave you HIS divine *prasad* and said..."*Ja ji le, tenu dus saal dite.*" (Go live, I give you ten years).

Just a few months ago, Mom and I noted that this was the tenth year.

You have also reunited with many of your much-loved and closest friends: Mohinder Puri, Mohinder Sethi, Vibha Pandhi, Ken Syal, Sati Uncle, Vasant Kotak and many many more.

So, Dad, quickly set up your Coffee Club again up there in your divine abode. Restart those conversations about women and politics. Make sure you get your Famous Grouse and your favourite *meetha*. Mom can't stop you now.

Until we meet again, my popsicle, I send you loads and loads of love and gratitude. We will soon raise a toast to the best husband, father, son, brother, friend, employer and business associate and—celebrate the wonderful life you lived.

JAI GURUJI

With love and only love

NEERAJ (Daddy's girl)

PS: As we release this book on Mom's birthday, we do so with joy, pride, love and with a promise to uphold your values and lessons in life. We vow to walk through the DOORS that YOU OPENED and down the paths that you chose. This book will serve as an inspiration to many. To me, you will always, always be my hero and live in my heart for ever and ever.

JAI GURUJI

NEERAJ

I shall grow old but never loose life's zest because
the road's last turn will be the best

Tribute in Verse

By Kavi Ghei

How do you capture the life of a man who touched each of our own lives, in words? One who guided us through the maze of life, was there for us whenever we needed him and even when we didn't?

My tribute aims to capture the many facets and colours that marked his life: a good son, a reliable brother, a loving husband, a respected businessman, a great father, a doting grandfather and a trusted friend.

Your Will is Your Desire

You are what your deep driving desire is,

As you desire ......
So is your will,

As you will, ...
So is your deed,

"Mr Paaji & Me"
(what I affectionately
called him)

As is your deed, ...
So is your destiny,

And as is your destiny, ...
So is created our legacy!

Early

A thirsty spirit saw
The visible as a mirage
And the unseen as an oasis.

(Khalil Gibran)

The early years we were not there ......
To see you blossom and the ......
Loss is ours.

Yet we believe we know how you grew ......

For a bit of you, is in each of us,
and as we pass through a phase,
yesterday, so did you.

Probably,
We experienced as you did ......
Did we see you blossom?
...... May be not.

But every pleasant experience for us,
...... Wishes it was an emotion you saw,
then too.

The Two of You

I searched
and searched
the world around
and this
one thing
alone I found......
of all the gifts from God above,
the greatest gift to man is
love.

(E. Moore)

You ensured that seeing both of you together ......
was the complete picture.

The calm and contentment ......
did not let us look elsewhere or beyond ......

Both of you together were the horizon ......
and as far as our vision could see.

Both of you provided the other strength
and complemented each other ......

One's weaknesses ......
were the other's strengths.

Picture perfect, ...
the two, together
Alas, incomplete ...... Apart.

Your Kingdom

Your peace is in our well-being.
Your pain is in our discomfort.
Your resolve is in our desire.
Your action is our upliftment.

You do not question our motives.
You do not scuttle our thoughts.
You do not judge us.
You forgive our indiscretions.

You gave us an understanding of relationships
that each of us be able to emulate when we play the same role.
Irrespective of your beliefs,
you stood with us and you stand by us.
You comfort us by just being there.
Your presence is our strength.

We only pray that may each member of the family,
in some small way,
give back to you
what you have given to them.

Your Friends

Blessed are those ......
Who can give without
remembering ......
And ......
Take without forgetting ......
There lies the strength in you.

Professional

Thou givest us everything at the price of an effort.

Starting with nothing in your armour
without a background,
or money, nothing other than your vision and
determination and perseverance.

You embarked to create your dreams of a better tomorrow for
yourself and your industry.

What do we say about this saga,
which has become an epic?

Who are we to judge history once it has been created?

Only let us savour and acknowledge that God was kind
to let us view
it from so near.

Just You

I have no yesterdays,
Time took them away
Tomorrow may not be
but I have today.

I feel no emotion,
I feel no remorse
I only feel an inner satisfaction, an inner peace
I am safe on life's course,
I am being watched,
I have no fear
For I have lived fully with
all that was dear.

We always knew you would grow old ......
But never lose life's zest ......
for you always knew that ......
the road's last turn would be ......
the Best!

An encore! ......
A hurray ...... And how!!

Wherever you may be ......
you leave behind your legacy for all to see ......
A bit of you is in me!

JAI GURUJI!
KAVI

Tribute to Nana

By Shreya Ghei

Nanu dressed as a chef, with me on my birthday

Y ou were a man with a great sense of humour, warmth and wit. You will be missed. From the very young age I was, when you carried me around on your shoulders, right up to the time you came for my college graduation in 2015, you were always full of life and energy. There was never a dull moment that I can recall. You always had so much to do and so many people to meet. You lived life to the fullest.

I was constantly amazed by your knack for remembering stories from your childhood and early career, in such great detail. This book has been a revelation in itself. You have given us all such a close peek into your life: interesting twists and turns, ups-and-downs, pride, love and - vulnerability. The anecdotes of the lifelong friendships you formed and the numerous experiences you had during your travels around the world, are a testament to the fulfilling life you led. With so many valuable lessons throughout the book, both personal and professional, I am sure readers will love it just as much as I did.

I will remember and cherish your constant banter, jokes and humour at the most unexpected and inappropriate moments. Those qualities stand out in your writing as well ! The time you dressed up as a chef for my 14th birthday and then, as a Scottish bagpiper on my 15th, you never failed to make those around you laugh.

Reading this book reveals a very different side of you. The explorer, the hard worker, the leader, the one who stumbled but - got back up and knocked hard enough, till all those doors opened...

Nana, thank you for leaving behind a treasure-trove of memories, valuable lessons, wisdom and witty banter.

I am proud to be called your granddaughter. You have left behind a great legacy and I hope I can emulate even a few lessons that you've left for me in your book!

JAI GURUJI !

Love,

SHREYA

Nana & Me on My Graduation Celebratory Cruise

Tribute to Papa

By Jyotsana Sharma

Papa as I called him, was the quintessential gentleman of a bygone era. He lived his life with grace, honesty, humility and self-discipline in all facets of life. He was a good listener and could be approached for anything at any time. We would often confide in each other, about one's innermost feelings. I too, shared a special bond with him. I always sought his mature, sane advice. And he would whisper it to me: in gentle words and with a kind, paternal smile in his eyes.

Papa & Me

We had brazen, verbal honesty and our craving and drooling for Delhi's street food in common. Sometimes, we would even sneak a bite or two behind Mom's back. The doctors had forbidden him such food indulgences, but surely not drooling!

We often sat alone, with just ourselves for company. At those times, he would often travel back in time down his unique life-journey, enthralling me with his experiences and anecdotes, perhaps even encouraging me to chase and fulfil my dreams and visions and be a "stronger woman".

In the ten years that GURUJI gifted to him, I started looking upon him as my second father, as I had lost my own at a very young age. But our bond had already grown stronger in 2016, when he became increasingly confined to the house, with occasional visits to the hospital. I put aside most of my own interests to be able to be beside him. I do regret not having spent more time with him in the initial years. A fast-paced social life, the arrival of my dear daughter Amaraah, marital duties and - my animal outreach initiatives took up all my time and attention. I so dearly wish he could have been with us for many more years, to guide our child—his doting granddaughter, Amaraah.

He was a devoted and loving grandpa. Amaraah and he would often sit together and he would tell her stories about his own life with both humour and knowledge. He would often wonder how much my daughter would remember of those times when he is gone. But I know now just how much I had underestimated their strong bond and her deep, cosmic connection with her *daddu*.

On Republic Day 2018, I asked Amaraah to hoist the National Flag at our Manesar resort in place of her demised *daddu*. With tears welling up in her large, beautiful eyes, she turned to me and said: "Mama, I miss my *daddu* very much. So from now on, I do not want to call our resort Heritage Village Resorts and Spa. It will be "SITA" for me, because my *daddu* loved that name very much."

Such was his charisma that the doyen who established SITA Travels in India, has left his legacy imprinted forever in his granddaughter's heart. As I hugged my Amaraah, our tears flowed freely for our beloved Papa and *daddu*. But despite the sadness, my soul was content. For I know that Papa's spirit will forever dwell in and guide, not only me, but his granddaughter Amaraah too.

May Guruji bless his soul, he will forever have a place, deep in my heart!

JAI GURUJI !

JYOTSANA

Tribute to Daddu

By Amaraah Sharma

My Daddu,

I am the luckiest girl to have had the sweetest and cutest *daddu*. My *daddu* would always play with me and teach me tricks like wiggling his ears and sticking out his tongue. I tried to copy him, but was not able to do it.

Whenever I hugged my *Daddi*, he would say: *Daddu* is "J"!

I will always remember my *Daddu* in my heart and he is everything to me. His favourite colour was

Daddu **& Me**

maroon. He would always ask me what I want. And then he would say to me: let's go for a walk, hand-in-hand, without telling mama or papa. He used to take me to eat ice-cream.

My *daddu* is with Guruji!

JAI GURUJI !

AMARAAH

Select CITYWALK—An Iconic Retail Destination is Born

by Neeraj Ghei and Arjun Sharma

The journey of Select CITYWALK began when Dad was in the middle of well-earned retirement, after selling our travel company, SITA World Travel. In early 2003, Mr. Yog Raj Arora (Yogiji, as he is fondly called)—a learned Real Estate, Tax and Valuation Consultant for the Select Group, approached our family with a proposal for a DDA property in Saket, South Delhi. As Dad would often say, it was a high catchment area due to go under the hammer. *"I was not at all familiar with the retail landscape, and had no idea, whatsoever, what this would involve."*

Whenever he recalled the moment of collaboration with Yogiji, he would remember that he had articulated his biggest fear at the time by saying: "my kids may just blow up hard-earned life earnings."

Yogiji, on his part, recalls that momentous meeting with Dad, in the following way.

"Our chairman, Mr. Inder Sharmaji was my mentor, my guide and my guardian, as he filled the vacuum created by my father's rather early demise. I never expected that what started as a simple, "professional-client relationship" would leave me so enriched. During my consultancy days with Select Group, I had very little interaction with Chairman Sir. But, he reposed so much trust in me that he accepted my proposal for the bid for the DDA and took me, therewith, as if I were his own son. I became part and parcel of the shopping centre venture. He gave

me so much love, affection and guidance and always treated me as the eldest among the three of us. His strong commitment towards the moral obligations of a commercial organisation taught me so much that I hadn't learnt during my 37 years of CA practice. At Select Infrastructure Private Ltd and under his direction and guidance, we fulfil our obligations towards corporate governance, patriotism and Corporate Social Responsibility. Further, it is due to his sensitivity towards the nation and society that we help various NGOs and celebrate national holidays in the shopping centre. We have inherited a legacy of honesty, strong moral character and commitment to social causes and in that legacy, he shall always be with us in spirit, to guide and inspire us for all times to come."　　　　　　　*—Yog Raj Arora*

The situation was tough. Among others, two big real estate groups— MGF and DLF—were also taking part in the bidding. We outbid them at the auction which took place in November 2003 and paid 25% of the bid amount. After that, only three months were left to make full payments. But during those three months, there wasn't much progress and that was when the alarm bells started ringing. If we couldn't fulfil their agreements and meet the dates, we would be in a bind, losing our entire down payment. The final, extended deadline, 6th June, 2004, was fast approaching.

That was the time when Dad took the reins of the funding requirement in his hands. When the bank flatly refused to help, we felt like we were standing on the edge of a cliff. This could have been the worst decision, and prove our critics right. But as they say, God is great. Armed with nothing but good intentions and Dad's excellent work reputation, everything fell in place. *Call it karma if you will*, but this experience also made us realise that 'building and selling' was not the ideal way to go about this mammoth project. The rest is history. The financial world reacted positively to the plan and banks said, *"Thank God; you're doing this! We have been waiting for years for someone to come up with this model."*

The team that put Select CITYWALK together didn't approach it like they knew everything about everything. We were open to learn, to benchmark practices and to use the best methods to put things into place. And thus began the journey of Select CITYWALK under the supreme guidance of Dad, who strongly believed that all hard work comes with divine intervention. As much as you put in, there is something above all of it that blesses and drives your efforts. *Our Guruji's blessings.*

The Making of Select CITYWALK

We started work in February 2005 and opened the centre in October 2007 with an occupancy of 60 percent by brands: an unprecedented feat that not many seasoned developers can boast of. We worked under immense pressure but with dedicated coordination and team spirit. Every step had to be stronger than the previous one. The neighbouring big developers had already sold all their spaces. But the moment they realised the promise our model held, they started buying back those spaces. But by then, the journey of Select CITYWALK had already begun.

The shopping centre would merge the aesthetics of the conventional "high street" market places that the capital was traditionally used to, with the technical know-how, comforts and utilitarian features of an internationally-placed shopping centre. The uniqueness of the shopping centre would be the "Retail Lease Only Turnover Based Plan" with a strong focus on service.

It couldn't have been done any other way. Other project developers had minimal control over tenancy i.e., over whom to lease the space to. In contrast, this 'by invitation only', revenue-sharing model realised Dad's dream of showing equal responsibility towards both retailers and shoppers. This made Select CITYWALK the forerunner in the lease model and as pioneering developers of a concept completely alien to India, we proved to be trendsetters.

It goes like this: one buys experience, the other buys space, and Select CITYWALK provides for both.

As the Select CITYWALK team was put together based upon individual qualities, domain knowledge and specialisations, each person's shortcomings were complemented by the other's strengths. The ensuing division of responsibilities propelled us, the three directors, to develop our own important roles in the process. Each one of us did his/her best to be progressive and experimental, in spite of holding diverse viewpoints. Yogiji, the spine of the company, oversaw construction, security, engineering, operations, and other such mission-critical areas. As for the two of us: Neeraj became the 'go-to person', the trouble-shooter who smoothed over everything, from day-to-day businesses to financial matters and bank dealings. Arjun became the brand head, drawing upon his vast marketing experience in the travel industry and joined forces with a team of marketing analysts to create an indefatigable marketing aura. We were assisted by a very able core team that included Pranay Sinha, Shilpa Malik, Shashi Sharma, S. Srinivas, G.K. Sharma, DNS Bisht, Sanjeev Manchanda and Yogeshwar Sharma. Dad strongly believed in the inclusion of an Advisory Board and of independent directors to the Board. This would ensure not only a fresh and new perspective but also unbiased advice and direction to achieve our goals. And so from time to time, he inducted luminaries such as (Late) PK Kaul; Former Cabinet Secretary and Chairman SEBI, SK Misra; Former Principal Secretary to PM and former secretary at the ministries of Tourism, Civil Aviation & Agriculture; Ashwani Kumar; Senior Advocate & ASG, PR Khanna, Chartered Accountant and Former director of UTI Asset Management Limited, SBI & DCM Shriram Ltd., (Late) Ravi Kathpalia, Former Controller General of Accounts, India and Finance Secretary, Nripjit Chawla; Management consultant IIM, Calcutta & formerly with ITC Hotels and MAX India Limited, PD Narang, Associate Member of the Institute of Cost &

Works Accountants of India and Piyush Mankad; Former Finance Secretary & Controller of Capital Issues, Ministry of Finance.

Landscape and Walkthrough

When work first began on the shopping centre, the three of us (Yogiji, Arjun & Neeraj) realised that Delhi Development Authority's vision didn't quite match ours. What ensued was a long back-and-forth on DDA's plans versus Select CITYWALK's plans. As Select CITYWALK worked with its own young design architects from DP Architects Singapore and Design Forum International (then called TCS), we realised we would have to work very hard to get all the alterations we wanted.

The design envisaged by DDA was like that of any other market such as South Extension. They visualised this to be another market place, with back-lanes fitted with ACs, etc. Further, it allowed one mandatory basement parking and made the second one optional. When we decided to go with the Lease Model scheme, we realized that the longevity of the project could only be achieved with a proper long-term plan and investments. The flaw in the philosophy of a 'sell model' is that developers don't think long term. Here, we believe that by holding assets for a long period of time, the construction stage must also be planned for a long term. You can't take any shortcuts, so this was the trigger for the Select CITYWALK team to plan parking on three levels and, an open-air plaza, as a community space that would make the shopping centre relevant for the neighbourhood shopper.

The original plans had also envisioned the front open-air plaza (now called *Saanskriti*) to be the ground level parking, while the shopping centre itself would be two rows of shops, with their backs to each other. Simply put, it would be a slightly larger Khan Market or South Extension (two highly successful high-street formats in New Delhi which primarily cater to High Net-worth Individuals or HNIs).

The other major change took place around the proposed hotel towers. Centred around the iconic Dome in the middle, double towers were originally planned on either side of the hotel. We prognosed the waste of infrastructure (like double elevators), space and energy that this would entail. Despite the higher costs that enforcing and strengthening the upper levels of the building would involve, the team was determined to rework the Select CITYWALK design. Apart from these changes, the Select CITYWALK team stood by every other requirement of the original government design, like keeping the exterior facade homogenous both structurally and aesthetically (by using the same pink bala flower stone in the whole complex).

To ensure that no shop would have a disadvantage or advantage over another, a customer circulation plan was evolved in such a way that the two large anchors, Pantaloons (now H&M) and Arcelia (now Zara), were as important as the mini-anchors, Esprit (now Pantaloons), Gourmet Food Bazar (now Modern Bazar) and Mango. The Atrium itself is a focal point of Select CITYWALK and one of the most expensive promotional platforms in retail today. It has played host to countless events, seen the launch of innumerable brands and entertained umpteen patrons.

The Select CITYWALK team realised how essential the open-air landscaped plaza, *Saanskriti* would be for the aesthetics and overall experience of the shopping centre. This gave birth to yet another novel feature of Select CITYWALK, never seen before in retail. *This landscaped plaza* is today an open urban space, synonymous with cultural events, art shows, promotions and celebrations. And then came October 2007, the moment that witnessed the birth of Select CITYWALK, now poised to revolutionise the Indian retail market, with the simplest, yet most meticulously thought-out module.

Today, Select CITYWALK is often regarded as the benchmark for modern retailing in Delhi and the NCR region. With more than 192 internationally-acclaimed brands, serviced apartments, cinemas, a health club, destination restaurants, cafes, bistros and more, Select CITYWALK is one of the most checked-in destinations for South Delhi's affluent consumer population today. Many leading international and domestic brands consider the centre with the highest sales and revenue per square foot, an ideal launch pad. The shopping centre recently completed a decade of a successful and revolutionary journey and celebrated its tenth anniversary with happy shoppers.

The services offered at Select CITYWALK are carefully planned to cater to the needs of diverse shoppers. Besides privileged parking for pregnant ladies, wheelchair services for senior citizens and the differently-abled, help desks and other innovative services like the REWARDS programme, Select CITYWALK is the first shopping centre to offer free home delivery service to enhance the experience of shoppers.

In 2017, Select CITYWALK, joined hands with the South Delhi Municipal Corporation to make a contribution to the Prime Minister's widely-acclaimed "Swachh Bharat Abhiyaan". A firm believer of "charity begins at home", the centre took responsibility for neglected land which was a dumping ground, opposite the shopping centre and converted it into the beautiful Jamun Wala Park. The 95,000 square feet of area has been provided STP-treated water for horticulture and landscaping, disabled-friendly ramps, energy-saving LED lights, surveillance and security systems. The park also consists of an open gymnasium, badminton court, a kids' play area, space for yoga and meditation and a joggers' trail. This perfect example of beneficial transformation is now open and the facilities can be enjoyed by the entire community.

The Lieutenant-Governor of Delhi, Shri Anil Baijal, termed the park the *"best example of coordinated efforts among agencies in Delhi"* and lauded Select CITYWALK, the SDMC commissioner, Dr. Puneet Goel, civic bodies like DDA, PWD and Delhi Police for achieving the milestone in less than eight weeks. Mr. Inder Sharma, Chairman, Select CITYWALK said, *"It is a proud moment for us; to have successfully executed this public-private partnership to create this beautiful park in place of a junkyard and endow it with facilities for kids and adults. A lot of hard work went into this transformation and we're happy to have made this small yet significant contribution to society."*

We Conclude with the Apt Words of CEO and Executive Director Mr. Yogeshwar Sharma

"Whatever I have learned from our beloved Chairman has moulded me into the person I am today. He always said that listening, feedback and interaction are critical to run a business successfully. Once, there was contradictory feedback and suggestions from consumers which were beyond our power. At that time, our Chairman said something that stayed with me. "We cannot be everything to everybody," he advised. "Take feedback constructively and see what best fits your company's ability to deliver. Feedback is good, but too many opinions will only confuse." He also believed that the "back of the house should be as spick-and-span as the front of it—if not better." At Select CITYWALK, a lot of emphasis is laid on this philosophy. At Select CITYWALK, all vendors are paid as per our commitment. This too, is a lesson passed on by the Chairman. "Don't keep anybody's due money, don't be unreasonable with any stake-holder and fulfil the obligations made," he would say. "Respect even verbal commitments made by your colleagues. No one should have to follow up for monies due to them."

Chairman had another exemplary quality. If he had promised his presence at an event or accepted an invitation, he would make sure to reach ahead of time.

He was a man of few words. He would never make people wait and never give them the feeling that they were unimportant.

And the one thing I follow religiously is to make notes. A short pencil is better than a long memory, he would say. I am grateful for all he taught me and proud to abide by it to date."

END

Receiving the Padma Shri Award in 1990 from President Venkatraman

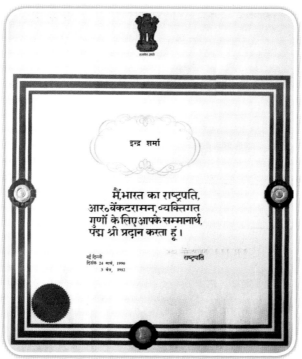

The Padma Shri Award Given to Me by President Venkatraman

Aruna & Myself with Margaret Thatcher at PATA Conference

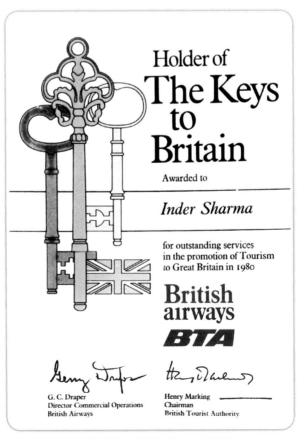

Holder of
The Keys to Britain

Awarded to

Inder Sharma

for outstanding services
in the promotion of Tourism
to Great Britain in 1980

British airways

BTA

G. C. Draper
Director Commercial Operations
British Airways

Henry Marking
Chairman
British Tourist Authority

Award Holder of The Keys to Britain

Mr. P.K. Kaul, President, Delhi Chapter
Giving Me PHD Chamber Life Time Achievement Award

Getting the Life Time Achievement Award
from Governor Jagmohan at ASSOCHAM Meeting

Receiving Life Time Achievement Award
from FICCI for Outstanding Contribution
to the Tourism Industry

Myself Receiving FICCI Award

Myself Receiving Old Students Association 'Hindu College Distinguished Alumni Award' for Outstanding Service to the Country and Distinguished Record of Public Service
L to R: Mrs. Sheila Dixit, Mr. Lalit Bhasin & Justice Kaul

Myself at PATA 1998 Receiving Chairman's Award

Myself & Aruna after Receiving Chairman's Award at PATA Manila

Myself, Jon Hutchison and Arjun at 22nd Som Nath Chib Memorial Lecture

Myself Addressing 27th Annual Convention TAAI—The Travel Agents Association of India

Myself and Aruna at WATA General Assembly December 1989

Myself with Dr. Karan Singh

Dr. Karan Singh and Myself
at a Travel Function

Dr. Karan Singh & Myself at PATA WWF Bagh Mitra Awards Function—
the Last One Attended

Back Row Mrs. Sundra, Front Row—
Myself, Mogens Jensen, Mrs Yasho
Rajya Lakshmi & Dr. Karan Singh
at PATA Opening Session

Australian Football Team came to India—
Myself with Mama & Dr. Karan Singh

Hans Learch and Me at Taj Mahal Hotel Delhi, 24th March, 2000

The Evening at Taj Man Singh after Signing the
Sale Agreement with Kuoni, March 24th, 2000

SITA Top Management, March 2000, at Sale of SITA

Mama's Boy & Dad's Girl—Myself, Neeraj and Aruna, Arjun

Arjun, Neeraj, Aruna & Myself

Arjun, Aruna, Myself & Neeraj, August 2017—Our Last Photo Together

Arjun, Myself & Aruna in February 2017—My Last Birthday in Office

Arjun, Aruna, Myself, Kavi & Neeraj

Myself, Aruna with Poonam, Ranjit, Usha, Neeraj, Jyotsana and Ankur

Sharma & Punj Family

Aruna & Me in a South Indian Temple

Kavi & Neeraj

Arjun & Jyotsana

Aruna, Shreya & Myself

My Granddaughter
Shreya Ghei—
Lady Golfer

My Granddaughter
Shreya Ghei Winner of
93rd All India Ladies
Open Golf Championship

Kavi, Ulrike, Myself, Shreya, Aruna, Suman at Shreya's Graduation at Yale

My Granddaughter Amaraah
with My Walking Stick

My Granddaughter Amaraah—
Ski Champion of the Family

Amaraah, Myself, Arjun, Aruna, Jyotsana

I have Passed on My Crowning
Glory to Amaraah

Enjoying with My Princess Amaraah
(Both with a missing tooth)

Saptrishi's College—
Suri, Myself, Lalit Gujral,
Mehra, Raj Kumar

Myself, Sati with Kavi in Our Later Years

After Mock Wedding Myself & Aruna, Millie & Tan Chee Chye,
Gloria & Hal Henderson, Sue & John Rowe

Mr. S.K. Misra, Myself & Aruna

Guruji

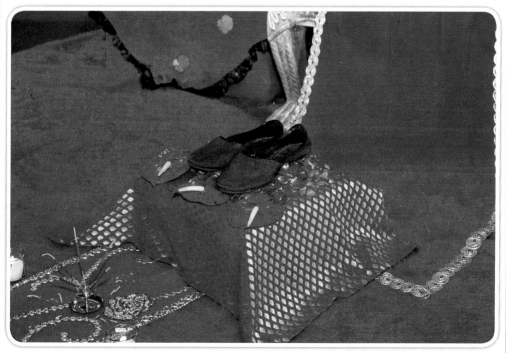

GURUJI'S Jutti's Given to Me as a Blessing

Guruji, Aruna & Myself

Aruna, Myself & Usha Praying to Our Guruji

Sharma Family Offering Aarti to Guruji

Jyotsana, Arjun, Amaraah,
Myself and Aruna at Guruji's Satsang

Aruna, Myself, Neeraj & Kavi at Guruji's Satsang

Guruji Ki Dispensary with
Photo of Guruji

Ambulance Donated by Aruna to the Salvation
Army Macrobert Hospital, Dhariwal

Myself, Aruna, Usha, Neeraj with Doctors and Staff at Lalowal

SIPL Team—Arjun, Yogeshwar, Myself, Neeraj & Yogiji

Laying Wreath at Amar Jawan Jyoti, India Gate on Kargil Diwas, 26th July 2016

Arjun, Yogiji, Neeraj & Myself after Laying the Wreath at
Amar Jawan Jyoti, India Gate, July 2016

Our Team of Select CITYWALK at India Gate after Laying the Wreath in July 2016

With Lt. Governor Mr Anil Baijal at Jamun Wala Park Dedication to
Public Ceremony on 11th March 2017 (My last public function)

At the Jamun Wala Park Function on 11th March 2017 (My last public function)

L'IMPERIAL NEW DELHI

Le Imperial Coffee Club Coverage—English Version

Among the important people who made the Imperial their meeting venue during the last fifty years, is a group of businessmen and entrepreneurs from Delhi. At the hotel they are known as the "Coffee Club". They arrive punctually, every afternoon, and sit down at a table in the verandah of the 1901. Among them: Inder Sharma, (former head of SITA World Travel), B.B. Bahadur, K.K. Syal, Satya Dev Sharma, an important member of the Indian student movement, who went on to write "In the shadow of the Kremlin", K.B. Bahadur, Prem Parkash and Som Sikand (ltr).

Today, the Imperial has become a symbol of modern India where opportunities abound. As in the past, the founders and CEO's of big multinational companies like Google, Boeing, Flextronics, Exxon or Intel use it as their base to pursue their Indian ambitions and their investment projects worth several billion dollars.

Heads of state from all over the world come to the Imperial. His Royal Majesty, the Prince Alwaleed Bin Talal Bin Abdulaziz Alsaud, nephew of the late King Fahd of Saudi Arabia and the richest Arab in the world, came here. The Canadian Prime Minister, Paul Martin made his way to the Presidential suite. The Italian president, Carlo Azeglio Campi verified that the spaghetti in the San Gimignano restaurant was cooked just right! Boutros Boutros Ghali, former Secretary General of the United Nations stayed here, as did Luca Cordero di Montzemolo, CEO of FIAT and Ferrari. Jerry Hall, Dan Aykroyd and Their Majesties, Padmini Devi of Jaipur and Maharani Scindia of Gwalior attended a presentation on an exhibition of the miniatures of Kishangarh in the Royal Ballroom.